SCOTTISH PROVERBS

SCOTTISH PROVERBS

Compiled and edited by

Colin Walker

Birlinn

This new edition published in 2000 by
Birlinn Limited
8 Canongate Venture
5 New Street
Edinburgh
EH8 8BH

www.birlinn.co.uk

ISBN 1 84158 057 0

British Library Cataloguing-in-Publication Data
A catalogue record for this book is available
from the British Library

Designed and typeset by
Edderston Book Design, Peebles
Printed and bound by
Omnia Books Limited, Glasgow

CONTENTS

Introduction vii

Acknowledgements. xvi

Proverbs in:

A 1
B 29
C 45
D 52
E 59
F 66
G 75
H 84
I 126
J 162
K 163
L 167
M 182
N 194
O 204
P 208
Q 213
R 214
S 218
T 234
U 282
V 283
W 284
Y 302
Z 328

Bibliography 329

Glossary 330

INTRODUCTION

The word 'proverb' traces its origins to the Latin '*proverbium*', which meant literally a 'set of words put forth' – that is, 'commonly uttered'. It is a compound formed from the prefix *pro* – 'forth', and *verbum* – 'word'.[1]

However, the definition of a proverb is no simple matter and has occupied scholars from Ancient Greece until the present day. Generally it is accepted that a proverb is a short, pithy traditional saying, which contains some widely accepted knowledge, or which offers advice or presents a moral. The celebrated Spanish writer Cervantes said that a proverb is 'a short sentence drawn from long experience'. Lord John Russell defined the proverb as 'the wisdom of many and the wit of one', whilst according to Lord Bacon 'The genius, wit, and spirit of a nation are discovered in their proverbs'. This volume also contains many phrases and sayings which are not strictly proverbs as we use the term today, although we may still think of them as such. This situation arises because, prior to the eighteenth century, it was common for the term to also include metaphors, similes, and descriptive epithets. I have included these 'rogue' phrases or sayings, as much for the continuance of the tradition established by previous collectors, as from the difficulty of finding any easy rule by which to distinguish them. The essence of a proverb lies in it being a 'traditional saying', i.e. something which has commonly passed from one generation to another by word of mouth. Hence it would not seem appropriate to reject any of these 'rogue' sayings as their usage embraces much that is essential to the true proverb. As David Murison writes in *Scots Saws*[2] –

> a proverb is essentially a social phenomenon . . . handed down by word of mouth from one generation to the next.

In his book *On the Lessons in Proverbs*[3] (1852), Richard Chevenix Trenchard argues that there is one quality of the proverb which is the most essential of all:

> . . . popularity, acceptance and adoption on the part of the people. Without this popularity, without these suffrages and this consent of the many, no saying, a proverb, however fulfilling all other its conditions, can yet be esteemed as such.

---

1. John Ayto, *Dictionary of Word Origins* (Bloomsbury 1990).
2. David Murison, *Scots Saws: From the folk-wisdom of Scotland* (Mercat Press 1981).
3. R. C. Trench, *On the Lessons in Proverbs* (3rd Revised Edition, London 1854), being the substance of lectures delivered to Young Men's Societies at Portsmouth and elsewhere.

What then is the importance of proverbs to Scottish culture and heritage? Proverbs provide us not only with the wisdom gathered by our forebears but also with a unique insight into the way of life or social mores of past generations. Many of the proverbs contained in this book date from a pre-industrial Scotland, when the majority of people still lived off the land or sea, and contain the rich vocabulary associated with these disappearing or extinct lifestyles. A strong impression is created of a society in which hard work was necessary merely to subsist, and the Scottish work ethic is well to the fore in many of the sayings. Many of the proverbs are based upon giving advice on how to steer a steady path through life whilst avoiding the pitfalls. According to Murison:

> A repertoire of proverbs embodies the group morality of a somewhat worldly sort based on the main idea of making life's journey with the maximum avoidance of trouble, and of keeping going without running imprudent risks.

Although we would no longer consider them to be 'politically correct', there are a considerable number of proverbs relating to marriage guidance, or giving advice to men on how to deal with women. From these sayings we can trace the changes which have taken place in our society. As the poet William Motherwell put it, in his eloquent introduction to Henderson's book of *Scottish Proverbs* in 1832:

> The study of proverbs may be more instructive and comprehensive than the most elaborated scheme of philosophy; and in relation to changes in the manners of people, their customs, and various minute incidents connected either with places or persons, they often preserve particulars which contempory history has failed to record.

Hence, for any true student of Scottish culture, there are two reasons for studying proverbs: (1) their intrinsic worth, and (2) their associations with the history and wisdom of past generations of the race. Andrew Cheviot illustrates the historical importance of proverbs in the preface to his collection of 1896,[4] when he relates the following tale –

> The well known, and frequently quoted proverb, 'The mair mischief the better sport' is given in most of the previous collections, but there is a story connected with it which is related in none of them. On the day appointed for the execution of Lord Lovat, of the '45, when the guards entered his cell to conduct him to the place of execution, they informed his Lordship, that the platforms erected to give the public a

---

4. Andrew Cheviot (Rev. J. H. Watson), *Proverbs, Proverbial Expressions and Popular Rhymes of Scotland* (1896).

good view of the gruesome procession to Tower Hill had collapsed, causing the death of several persons. 'Weel, weel,' grimly replied the doomed nobleman, 'the mair mischief the better sport.' Now such a striking historical incident gives an interest to this proverb apart from, and superior to its intrinsic value, because instead of being regarded merely as an abstract saying it becomes associated in our minds with the striking personality of one of the most remarkable characters of Scottish history.

In many ways, a book of proverbs can be said to contain the philosophy of the people, or a nation's distilled wisdom. The latter phrase would seem particularly appropriate when one counts the number of Scottish proverbs relating to drink! It is also interesting to see which subjects do not receive the amount of coverage one might expect. Motherwell noted the following:

> We have nothing almost of politics, and as little directly, unless a satirical hit, of religion. Perhaps both the one and the other may have been considered too much out of the way of folk who found themselves busied, and more profitably occupied with their own callings than with matters which they could not well understand or easily control.

Perhaps the strongest thread running through most of the proverbs contained in this book relates to the Scottish nation's pawky sense of humour.

For a language such as Scots, with its rich oral tradition, it is essential that we conserve the proverbs of the past. Proverbs are an essential part of our living culture and heritage, and should be valued as such. In his book *A Complete Collection of Scottish Proverbs* (1721) James Kelly bears testimony to the widespread use of proverbs at that time. He says that 'there were current in society upwards of 3,000 proverbs, exclusively Scottish'. He adds:

> The Scots are wonderfully given to this way of speaking and, as the consequence of that , abound with proverbs, many of which are very expressive, quick, and home to the purpose; and, indeed, this humor prevails among the better sort of the commonalty, none of whom will discourse with you any considerable time, but he will affirm every assertion and observation with a Scottish Proverb.

From this statement we can see what a massive sea-change has taken place in society as regards the 'proverbial' mode of intercourse. In Kelly's day it was common practice in conversation to strengthen an argument or illustrate a point by using a proverb. According to Lord Bacon proverbs:

> serve not only for ornament and delight, but also for active and civil use; as being the edge tools of speech which cut and penetrate the knots of business and affairs.

Likewise Motherwell attests to the popular use of proverbs thus

> Among old and young in Scotland, not many years ago, it was a
> common country pastime of a winter's night to while time away by
> repeating proverbs, telling tales, and reciting songs and ballads.

Proverbs can be seen in some ways as the germ of moral and
political science. However they are the product of ordinary
common people, and do not owe their origins to the ivory towers
of academia or the baronial mansions. As Motherwell puts it:

> Proverbs are, to the vulgar, not merely a sort of metaphysical language,
> but a kind of substitute for philosophical principles. A man whose
> mind has been enlarged by education, and who has a complete
> mastery over the riches of his native language, expresses his ideas in his
> own words; and when he refers to any thing beyond the matter under
> his view, glances towards an abstract principle. A vulgar man, on the
> other hand, uses those proverbial forms which tradition and daily use
> have made familiar to him; and when he makes a remark which needs
> confirmation, he clinches it by a proverb. Thus both, though in a
> different way, illustrate the observation of Lord Bacon, that – 'The
> nature of man doth extremelye covet to have something fixed and
> immoveable, and as a rest and support for the mind'.

For this reason the use of proverbs was considered vulgar by later
generations of educated Scots, and their formal application was
almost prohibited by the rules of polite society. The coming of a
more educated and industrialised society also brought about a
change in the method of communication. Oral transmission of a
society's knowledge ceased to be the preferred method of communication and was instead replaced by the written and printed word.
On surveying those proverbs still in current use, one would be
hard pressed to find one that dated from the last century. Sadly the
decay in the use of the Scots language has probably also resulted,
as an epiphenomenon, in a decline in the use of Scottish proverbs.
If we hear someone using a proverb today, it is probably an English
one. As our society has become 'more sophisticated' it has become
less fashionable to use what appear to be common platitudes
couched in old fashioned language. The rise of the scientific study
of man has resulted in a preference for 'discovering' universal
truths about people through empirical observation, rather than
through folk wisdom handed down in verbal form.

I am greatly indebted to the works of the great Scottish proverb
documentors of the sixteenth, seventeenth, eighteenth and
nineteenth centuries (Cheviot, Fergusson, Henderson, Hislop,
Kelly, and Ramsay), for many of the older proverbs.

The earliest paroemiographers (proverb editors/collectors),
perhaps not surprisingly, came from the clergy. There is some

rather sketchy and contradictory evidence to suggest that the first Scottish proverb collection was made by Archbishop James Beaton of Glasgow (1517–1603) around the time of the Reformation. However there is so little definite information regarding this work that it can hardly be regarded as one of the authorities on the subject, nor as having been of use to subsequent collectors and writers on the subject.

The first work of real importance and undoubted authenticity is the one made by the Rev. David Fergusson, who was a contemporary of Archbishop Beaton. He was among the earliest of the Scottish reformers, and although not a graduate of any university, he was appointed Minister at Dunfermline by the Committee of Parliament in July 1560. He retained this position until his death on 23 August 1598, having also served as Moderator of the General Assembly in 1573 and 1578. Although we do not know the exact date of his birth it is thought to be no later than 1525, as he was described as 'the auldest minister that tyme in Scotland'[5] only six months before his death. Fergusson's collection contained 911 proverbs,[6] and was put *ordine alphabetico* when he died in 1598, but not published until 1641. The proverbs are given without any explanatory comment, and many are couched in a very old form of Scots. The collection was printed in Edinburgh without an author's preface but instead with an address 'From the Printer to the merrie, judicious and discreet Reader'. There is a suggestion that the address may in all likelihood have been contributed by the Rev. John Row of Carnock, a son-in-law of Fergusson. This 'Printer's' address makes reference to the author in the following terms:

> Therefore manie in this Realme that hath heard of David Fergusson sometime Minister at Dunfermbline, and of his quick answers and speeches, both to great persons, and others inferiours, and hath heard of his Proverbs which hee gathered together in his time, and are now put downe according to the order of the Alphabet: and manie of all ranks of persons being verie desirous to have the saids Proverbs, I have thought good to put them to the presse, for thy better satisfaction . . . I know that there may be some that will say and marvell that a Minister should have taken pains to gather such Proverbs together; but they that knew his forme of powerfull preaching the Word, and his ordinar talking, ever almost using proverbiall speeches, will not finde fault with this that hee hath done.

---

5. *Autobiography and Diary of James Melvill* (Wodrow Society).
6. This is the number detailed in the first edition, though subsequent editions contain more. For an excellent and detailed study of his work see the edition edited by Erskine Beveridge in 1924.

This first collection was later published together with a larger manuscript collection of about the same period in Edinburgh in 1924 under the editorship of E. Beveridge. This is an excellent study of the earlier work which I would recommend anyone to read. Another collection was made by James Carmichael, Minister of North Berwick, about twenty tears later.[7]

In 1721 *A Complete Collection of Scottish Proverbs*, explained and made intelligible to the English reader by James Kelly MA, was published in London. It contains a short explanation or commentary attached to each proverb, along with some parallel sayings from other languages. In his introduction Kelly describes his own disappointment at making the discovery that for many of the proverbs it is difficult to distinguish exactly their nation of origin. He also says that he has 'omitted in his collection many popular proverbs which are very pat and expressive', giving the reason that 'since it does not become a man of manners to use them it does not become a man of my age and profession to write them'. Reading Kelly's collection makes one think that some of the 'expressive' proverbs omitted must have used fairly strong language indeed, as many that he includes were dropped by later collectors who considered them unsuitable material to reproduce in print. Given that proverbs are the product of the common tongue it would be surprising if many of them did not employ choice language. Unfortunately, many of these have probably been censored from written record by previous collectors. As with his antecedents, Kelly made full use of the literature of his day, when searching for proverbs for his collection. According to Kelly several of his collected proverbs are 'taken out of an ingenious Scottish Book, called the Cherry and the Slae, a book so commonly known to Scottish men, that a great share of it passes for proverbs. It is written in native genuine Scotch, and, to them who understand it, very fine and taking.'

Allan Ramsay, the famous poet, published *A Collection of Scots Proverbs* in 1737, bearing the appropriate motto on the title page: 'That maun be true that a' men say'. Unlike Kelly's collection, which was written for the English reader, Ramsay's collection is deliberately very Scottish in its style, not only with the proverbs themselves, but also his dedication to the 'Tenantry of Scotland, Farmers of the Dales, and Storemasters of the Hills' prefixed to the collection, which is written in pure Scots dialect. In this dedication he says:

> As naething helps our happiness mair than to have the mind made up
> wi' right principles, I desire you, for the thriving and pleasure of you

7. James Carmichael, *Collection of Proverbs in Scots*, edited by M. L. Anderson (Edinburgh, 1957).

and yours, to use your een and lend your lugs to these guid auld saws,
that shine wi' wail'd sense, and will as lang as the world wags.

From his knowledge of the pastoral shepherding life, Ramsay was
able to add many proverbs peculiar to the sheep farming districts
of Scotland, which were not found in earlier collections. He also
alludes to the practice among shepherds of exercising their
memories by keeping up a conversation with these proverbs. As an
adjunct to recommending his readers to make themselves masters
of the contents of his collection, he adds the following:

How usefou will it prove to you (who hae sae few opportunities of
common clattering) when ye fergather wi' your friends at kirk or
market, banquet or bridal? By your proficiency you'll be able, in the
proverbial way, to keep up the soul of a conversation that is baith blyth
and usefou.

Ramsay refers to Kelly's work as a 'late large book of them, fou of
errors, in a style neither Scots nor English'. His own collection
contains a total of 2,464 proverbs, and although smaller than
Kelly's it attempts to restore many of the versions to their original
Scots form. However, whilst his criticisms of Kelly's changes to the
Scots language may be well founded, Ramsay's own collection is
less well known, and Kelly's notes are the standard annotations on
the proverbs which have been used by later writers.

It was nearly a hundred years before a major new work
appeared. Andrew Henderson, a Glasgow painter, published his
collection *Scottish Proverbs*, with an excellent introductory essay by
his lifelong friend the poet William Motherwell, in Edinburgh in
1832. This collection was largely a compilation from previous
printed collections as later was Alexander Hislop's *The Proverbs of
Scotland* (1862), to which he made large additions from the works
of Sir Walter Scott, Galt, Hogg, and other national writers.

In 1896 the largest collection of all was published. *Proverbs,
Proverbial Expressions and Popular Rhymes of Scotland* by Andrew
Cheviot (Rev. J. H. Watson) contains roughly five thousand entries.

This present collection draws heavily upon the excellent work
of these earlier collectors. I have also made an attempt to include
some of the 'earthier' proverbs of bygone generations which were
expunged by later collectors who considered them unsuitable. As
William Motherwell put it:

It has been a common error with the paroemiographers of this
fastidious age, to purge their collections so far as their sense of
conventional delicacy reaches, of all impureness of expression. We are
not partial to obscenity of any description, but as honest students of
human nature, and national character, we cannot sympathise in this

affected regard for the purity of morals, or rather of written language, which the verbal refinements of a particular day seek to enforce . . . A spade is a spade all the world over, and is so understood, however it may be expressed.

I have arranged the dictionary in an easily accessible alphabetical format, according to the first word of each proverb. This method is not ideal, as many proverbs vary in their initial word depending upon the part of Scotland in which they are being used. However, the alternatives seem even less so. In the past, some scholars have attempted to arrange proverbs according to their subjects, but this has never been entirely satisfactory, because many proverbs are too difficult to classify. For example, in Hislop's collection, the second part of the book contains the proverbs classified by subject, of which there are 148. He says of his classification that it:

> has been a work of very great labour and, indeed, attended with most unsatisfactory results.The difficulty of reducing a great number of proverbs, of almost universal application, into distinct, individual subjects can only be understood by those who have attempted the operation; while the greater number, which absolutely defy classification, add greatly to the difficulties of the task.

In his collection of over three thousand proverbs made in 1832, Andrew Henderson also attempted to classify them. He managed to put half of them into 130 different categories, but was then forced to list the other half under the heading 'Truisms and Miscellaneous'.

Most of the proverbs in the present collection are listed with an attendant note or explanation of their meaning. I will apologise in advance for any inadequacies in these explanations; it is not always possible to provide accurate and succinct alternatives for finely tuned phrases of 'distilled wisdom'. However, I hope that they may be of occasional use to the reader.

It is never easy to prove that any proverb or saying belongs to one particular country, or district, unless of course it contains a place-name or some distinctive feature. Even then a true proverb is never parochial; its true meaning has no boundaries. Nations are constantly borrowing proverbs from each other. The original stock of proverbs with which a nation starts are either orally handed down to it, or made part of its own stock by those early writers who brought the present into living communication with the past. Hence the common traditions of the civilised world have been preserved and passed down, ensuring that many Greek, Latin, and medieval proverbs are kept alive in many modern nations of the world. I have carefully selected those proverbs which

I believe contain some truly Scottish essence. Some, but not all, of the proverbs are exclusively Scottish – some are common to several different countries. Nevertheless, the language used gives them a peculiarly Scottish slant, or way of looking at the world, and I have included them for this reason.

At the end of the book I have provided a simple glossary of the Scots words used, to act as an aid for those unfamiliar with the language.

This book is not intended as an academic dictionary, recording each and every Scottish Proverb, its meaning, origins, and first date of written documentation. In some respects that would miss the real essence of proverbs themselves. The present volume has been compiled in the same spirit as those of previous amateur paroemiologists, keen to keep alive an essential part of the great oral tradition of the Scots language. I am well aware that the collection is not complete, and am constantly turning up new examples and sources. However, sheer pragmatism demands that something be put into print at sometime. Likewise, much more time could be spent researching the origins and meanings of each particular proverb. Hopefully this book might stimulate the reader to carry out some research of his or her own.

In the present volume there may be some variation in the spelling of certain words. I have not attempted to render them into some 'standard' form of Scots, as I believe it helps to illustrate the changes that have ocurred within the language over preceding generations. Likewise the reader will probably find a few redundacies or repetitions of proverbs with slight changes. I apologise for these, which have occurred partly as a result of the period over which the collection has been made. Hence I would ask the reader to view the present book as a work in progress. I hope that it does something to spread further the fertile seeds of our marvellous language and to ensure a vibrant and lively future for this rich and distinct aspect of Scottish culture.

ACKNOWLEDGEMENTS

The present work owes much not only to the proverb collectors mentioned in the introduction, but also to the works of some of Scotland's greatest writers: Burns, Galt, Henryson, Montgomerie, and Scott – to name a few. I am also grateful to Charlene Nash who miraculously translated my hieroglyphics into Scots, to my colleagues at Blackwell's who have fielded calls from an exasperated publisher, to Hugh Andrew for patience beyond the call of publishing, to my parents for their interest, and to Anne for her constant support and encouragement in everything I do. Finally, mention must be made of my dog Sorkie (named after a dog in a proverb: see 'Nae equal to you etc.'). He has taught me a new way of looking at books of proverbs – namely as something to be eaten. Bon appetit!

A

A' ae oo.
It's all for a common end. The above saying is a demonstration of the peculiarly powerful use of vowels in the Scottish dialect. An anecdote is recorded of the conversation between a shopkeeper and a customer relating to a plaid hanging at the shop door.
Cust. (inquiring of the material): *Oo? (Wool?)*
Shop.: *Aye oo (Yes, it's made of wool)*
Cust.: *A' oo? (All wool?)*
Shop.: *Aye, a' oo (Yes, all wool)*
Cust.: *A' ae oo? (All the same wool?)*
Shop.: *Aye a' ae oo (Yes, all the same wool)*

A' are good lasses, but where do the ill wives come frae?
A suggestion that marriage changes some women.

A' are no friends that speak us fair.
You cannot trust to the friendship of everyone who pays you a compliment.

A bad servitor ne'er made a gude maister.
A similar proverb is first recorded in Fergusson's collection.

A bad wound may heal, but a bad name will kill.
It is possible to recover from physical injury, but not if injury has been caused to one's reputation.

A bairn maun creep afore it gangs.
A learner must master the basics, before trying something more difficult. Perfection is only to be attained through practice.
First recorded in Fergusson as 'A bairne mon creip or he gang'.

A bald heid is soon shaven.
A slight task is soon completed.

A bannock is a gude beast, ye may eat the guts o't on a Friday.
There is no religious prohibition against eating bannocks on Fridays.

A bastard may be as gude as a bowstock by a time.
Bastard kail are a sort of cabbage that never close; those that close are called bowstocks. The meaning is that a bastard may prove as worthy a person as the full begotten. (Kelly 1721).

A bawbee cat may look at a King.
In Fergusson's Proverbs of 1641 the version is recorded as 'A half-pennie cat may look to the King'. According to a Fifeshire tradition, an infant King was exhibited to the public on a payment proportioned to the rank of the spectator. The lower classes were allowed to view the young monarch on presentation of a small coin equal to the English half-penny, which was consequently called a bawbee – i.e. a baby.

1

A beggar's wallet is a mile to the bottom.
This is because it generally contrives to contain all he gets.

'A begun turn is half ended,' quo' the wife when she stuck the graip in the midden.
Half the battle with work is getting it started. First recorded in Fergusson's Proverbs as 'A begun work is half ended'.

A beltless bairn cannot lie.
A very young child is too innocent to tell untruths.

A bird in the hand's worth twa fleeing bye or in the bush.
A small certainty is of more use than a larger uncertainty.

A bit but and a bit ben maks a mim maiden at the board end.
A joke aimed at women who eat little at the dinner table, suggesting that they would have a keener appetite if they had not already sampled the food in the kitchen.

A bit is often better gi'en than eaten.
On certain occasions it is better to give than receive. Recorded in Fergusson's Proverbs as 'Better apple given nor eaten'.

A black beginning maks aye a black end.
In 'Storms', James Hogg relates the following border tale. In 1620 a memorable snowstorm still spoken of as 'the thirteen drifty days', almost annihilated the sheep in the south of Scotland. On one large farm in Selkirkshire, on the estate of Sir Patrick Scott of Thirlestane, all the flock died except one black ewe, from which the farmer had high hopes of preserving a breed, but unfortunately this sole remnant of a good flock was chased by some idle boys into a lake and drowned. When John Scott, the farmer – commonly called 'Gouffin Jock' – heard of this, he is reported to have said, 'Ochon! ochon! an' is that the gate o't. A black beginning maks a black end.'

A black shoe mak's a blythe heart.
This proverb suggests that the supply of work and hence happiness will continue to be given to those who can be seen to be industrious, e.g. those who clean their shoes.

A blate cat maks a proud mouse.
When those who are in charge are not very forceful, those they are supposed to be leading are apt to take advantage. First recorded in Fergusson's collection this proverb is closely related to 'Weel kens the mouse when the cat's oot o' the house'.

A blaw in my lug.
Said of someone who is a flatterer.

A blind man has nae need o' a looking-glass.

A blind man's wife needs nae painting.

A boaster and a liar are near akin.

A body lives lang after they're laughed at.

A body's no broke while they hae a gude kail stock.
When all is not lost, it is still possible that all may be saved. A 'gude kail stock' means a good kitchen garden.

A bold foe is better than a cowardly friend.
At least you can judge how the former will behave in a given situation.

A bonny bride is soon buskit, and a short horse soon wispit.
A good-looking bride needs little in the way of adornment, and a small horse is soon groomed, i.e a slight task is soon finished. This proverb is first recorded in Fergusson thus: 'A fair bryde is soon buskt, and a short horse soone wipt'.

A bonny gryce may mak an ugly old sow.
A warning to young girls that their beauty may not last with age.

A borrowed len' should gae laughing hame.
A cautionary note to look after borrowed goods and to return them in good condition and with a good grace. First recorded in Fergusson's collection.

About the moon there is a brugh;
the weather will be cold and rough.
A weather warning if you see a halo effect around the moon.

A broken kebbuck gangs sune dune.
Once started, food does not last long.

Absence is a shrew.

Absence maks the heart grow fonder.

Abundance o' law breaks nae law.
It is less likely that people who know the law will break it than those who are ignorant of it.

A bund seck and set by.
Literally a bound sack put aside in storage. The phrase is applied to those who are engaged to be married.

A bushel o' March dust is worth a king's ransom.
A dry March foretells of a good harvest later in the year.

A careless watch invites the thief.

A' cats are grey i' the dark.

A cauld needs the cook as muckle as the doctor.
Many say the best remedy for a cold is to feed it.

A causey saint and a house deil.
A saint abroad and a devil at home.

A churl will savour a churl's kind.

'A clean thing's kindly,' quo' the wife when she turned her sark after a month's wear.

A closed mou' catches nae flees.
The person who keeps their mouth shut will also keep out of trouble.

A cock's aye crouse on his ain midden head.
It's much easier for people to be courageous on their own territory. This proverb was first recorded by Fergusson as 'A cock is crouse in his own midding'.

A' complain o' want o' siller, but nane a want o' sense.
The cheeky suggestion that if the complainants were more intelligent they would not want for money in the first place.

A covetous man is gude to nane, but warst to himsel.
Avarice does nobody any good, least of all the person who feels it.

A coward's fear maks a brave man braver.

A crackit bell will never mend.
It is pointless wasting effort trying to mend things which are irretrievably damaged.

A' cracks maunna be trew'd.
You shouldn't believe all that you hear.

A crammed kyte maks a crazy carcase.
A man is more likely to enjoy himself on a full stomach than on an empty one.

A craw is nae whiter for being washed.
The Scottish equivalent of the leopard and his spots.

A Crook in the Forth
Is worth an Earldom in the North.
When it reaches the low carse lands near Stirling, the River Forth pursues a very meandering course giving rise to many 'crooks' of land. This land is also very fertile, hence owning a small piece of it will bring in an equivalent income to a large estate in the Highlands.

A crooked man should sow beans, and a wud man peas.
The one agrees to be thick sown, and the other thin – Kelly.

A crooning coo, a crawing hen, and a whistlin' maid were ne'er very chancy.
To make sure their behaviour was seemly, young girls were told that these three things were unnatural, and hence to be avoided.

A cruel king ne'er reigns lang.
A warning to any malevolent monarchs.

A day to come seems langer than a year that's gane.
Waiting for something in the future seems to take forever.

A deaf man will hear the clink o' money.

A dear ship lies lang in the harbour.
First recorded by Fergusson in 1641, this proverb is often applied to unmarried women who are very exacting in their choice of partner.

A dink maiden oft maks a dirty wife.
Some neat maidens forget their neat habits when they get married.

A dirty hand maks a clean hearthstane.

A dish o' married love right sune grows cauld, and dosens down to nane as folk grow auld.
An early piece of unsentimental Scottish marriage guidance, from Ramsay's 'Gentle Shepherd'.

A dog in a deer's den.
Spoken when a widow or widower marries a person inferior to their former match – Kelly.

A dog's life – muckle ease an' muckle hunger.

A dog wi' a bane kens nae freens.

A dog winna yowl if ye fell him wi' a bane.
You will not hurt a dog by throwing bones at him.

A doucer man ne'er broke warld's bread.
A saying expressive of unqualified respect.

A drap and a bite's but a sma' requite.
A request to friends to have some food and drink, which is but small recompense for their friendship.

A dreigh drink is better than a dry sermon.
The first you can leave if it is not to your taste, the second you have to endure.

A drink is shorter than a tale.
An excuse given by some for drinking during the telling of a tale. This proverb first appears in Ramsay's collection of 1736.

A drucken doctor is aye clever.

A drudger gets a darg, and a drucken wife the drucken penny.
Kelly explains this proverb thus: 'They that are free and liberal will have to spend, when the saving and penurious will get hard labour.'
However Hislop defines it as 'a willing labourer manages to get work, and a drunkard contrives to get drink somehow or other'. In other words each will strive to get what they want and will probably end up with their just rewards.

A dry summer ne'er made a dear peck.
A dry summer is usually a sign of a good crop. A peck is a dry measure, and presumably if the crop was poor, due to heavy rain, its price would increase.

According to Kelly: 'I do not know any observation of weather, or seasons, that holds so true as this in these nations; for though the straw in such years be short, yet the grain is good and hearty. I remember no remarkable dry summers but three, 1676, 1690, 1713, and all of them very plentiful.'

A dumb man hauds a'.
A dumb man cannot disclose anything.

A dumb man wins nae law.
A talkative advocate is more likely to win his case than a taciturn one. Sometimes this proverb has the word land substituted for law.

Ae fine thing needs twa to set it aff.

'A'e gude turn deserves another,' as the deil said to the loon o' Culloden, when he hauled him doun screaming to the place ye ken o'.
A well-known proverb adapted to include the infamous Duke of Cumberland.

Ae half o' the world disna ken how the ither half lives.
Sadly one wonders sometimes if they even care, let alone know.

Ae hand winna wash the ither for nowt.

Ae hour i' the morning is worth twa after noon *or* at night.

Ae man may bring a horse to the water, when twenty winna gar him drink.
You cannot force people to change their minds or ways if they do not want to. This proverb is first recorded in Fergusson where the number quoted is even higher – 'fore and twentie'.

Ae man may steal a horse where anither daurna look ower the hedge.
This saying is used to demonstrate the value of having a good name and reputation. A man with a blameless character can get away with murder, whereas an individual with a poor reputation will always be suspected of being up to no good.

Ae saint maks twenty sinners.

Ae scabbit sheep will smit a hail hirsel.
It only takes one rotten apple to spoil the barrel. Fergusson recorded this proverb as 'A skabbit sheep flees all the flock'.

Ae scone o' that baking's enough.
One can tell from the example the quality of the rest.

Ae shook o' that stook's enough.
One is enough as a sample.

Ae year a nurish, seven years a daw.
A warning that after one year of nursing, a woman will have become used to feeding well and doing little. I think many mothers might disagree.

A fair maid tocherless will get mair wooers than husbands.
A sceptic's view that a Scotsman's wallet is more powerful than his heart.

A' fellows, Jock, and the laird.
Spoken when unworthy persons intrude themselves into the company of their betters – Kelly.

A fey man and a cursour fears na the deil.
A predestined man and a stallion fear nothing.

Affront your friend in daffin', and tine him in earnest.
Do not offend a friend even in jest or you may lose him for good.

A fidging mare should be weel girded.
A warning not to trust those who have caused trouble in the past.

A findly bairn gars his daddy be hang'd.
According to Kelly a 'findly bairn' is 'one who finds or steals'.

A fire that is all out is evil to kindle.
A warning against trying to rekindle relationships with old flames.

A fisherman's walk – twa steps an' owerboard.

A fleyer would aye hae a follower.
A coward, or someone who does wrong, generally likes to involve another person in their actions. However, 'A flier gets a follower' dates back to Robert Henryson and is explained by Kelly as 'Girls run away to be pursued'.

A flittin' stane gaithers nae fog.

A fool is happier thinking weel o' himsel than a wise man is of ithers thinking weel o' him.
A caution to the self-obsessed.

A fool may earn money, but it taks a wise man to keep it.
A fool and his fortune are soon parted.

A fool may gie a wise man counsel.
This proverb is first recorded by Fergusson. It also appears in Scott's Heart of Midlothian –

> *'Fair and softly gangs far,' said Meiklehose; 'and if a fule may gie a wise man counsel, I wad hae him think twice or he mells with Knockdunder.'*

A fool of a nurse maks a wise child.
Said as an excuse for the nonsensical bawling of nurses to their children – Kelly.

A fool's bolt is soon shot.
Some people lacking in wisdom do not hesitate to give their opinions on important matters without giving them serious consideration first.

A fool winnae gie his toy for the Tower o' London.
A reference to an incident in the life of Charles II, who according to the Earl of

Rochester, 'Never said a foolish thing, and never did a wise one'; the allusion being to the monarch chasing butterflies in his garden for the amusement of the ladies of the court, while the Dutch fleet was threatening his capital.

A foul fit maks a fu' wame.
A dirty foot implies the wearer has been out working in the field and hence can afford to eat.

A friend at Court is worth a penny i' the purse.

A friend's dinner is soon dished.
Recorded by Fergusson as 'A friend's dinner is soon digtht', i.e. a true friend can be treated like a member of the family, is easily served, and will not readily take offence.

A friend to ane is a friend to nane.

A frosty winter, a dusty March, a rain about April,
Another about the Lammas time when the corn begins to fill,
Is worth a pleuch o' gowd, an a' her pins theretill.
When asked what would buy a plough of gold, the poet George Buchanan answered with this rhyme.

Aft counting keeps friends lang thegither.
People with short accounts make long friendships with each other.

After cheese, naething.

After dinner sit a while, after supper walk a mile.
In his collection, Kelly says of this proverb 'The first I approve of, the other is ridiculous'.

After this we will hear the gowk.
An expression of extreme surprise/incredulity.

After words come weird: fair fa' them that ca's me Madam.
Roughly this means that after libel comes proof – let them that speak ill of me look to themselves. A similar meaning is given in Jamieson's Dictionary.

Aft ettle, whiles hit.
Try often, occasionally succeed. An exhortation to perseverance.

A fu' cup is ill to carry.

A fu' heart is aye kind.

A fu' heart never lied.
The truth generally comes out when a person is governed by their feelings.

A fu' man and a hungry horse aye mak haste hame.

A fu' man's a true man.
This is said because drink tends to lessen a speaker's inhibitions.

A fu' man's leavins.
i.e. precious little.

A fu' purse maks a haverin' merchant.
A man with a full purse who is engaged in a commercial transaction is likely to haver, or gossip, because he does not feel financially compelled to urgently conclude the deal.

A fu' sack can bear a clout i' the side.
A well to do person can afford to take a few knocks from those less fortunate.

A fu' wame maks a straight back.
A proverb of similar sentiment to the last one.

A gaun fit aye gets gate aneuch.
A willing worker never wants for a job.

A gaun fit's aye getting, were it but a thorn or a broken tae.
As with the above proverb, an industrious person will never want for work, but the proverb warns that it might not always be what the person desires.

A gi'en game was ne'er won.
A conceded game may be of no tribute to the skill of the opponent.

A gi'en piece is soon eaten.
A small favour is soon forgotten.

A gnarled tree may bear gude fruit, and a harsh nature may gie gude counsel.

A gowk at Yule'll no be bright at Beltane.
Literally this means that the person who is a fool at Christmas will not be wise in May, i.e you cannot change a person's inherited character.

A great rooser was ne'er a gude rider.
A boaster is rarely a good performer.

A greedy ee ne'er got a gude pennyworth.

A greedy ee ne'er got a fu' wame.
A warning that the greedy are never satisfied.

A green turf is a gude gudemother.
An old mother-in-law joke, i.e. the best place for her is in the churchyard.

A green wound is half game.
According to Kelly – 'because it commonly smarts more afterwards'.

A green Yule and a white Pasch mak a fat kirkyard.
A rather unfeeling proverb, reflecting the effects of the seasons on the frail human frame.

A grunting horse and a graneing wife seldom fail their master.
A case of the 'creaking gate' syndrome. Those who constantly complain that they are on their last legs, often contrive to live as long as their neighbours.

A gude calf is better than a calf o' a good kind.
The former is good already whereas the latter might possibly turn out bad.

A gude day's darg may be done wi' a dirty spade.

A gude dog ne'er barkit aboot a bane.
First recorded in Fergusson's collection, this proverb suggests that only fools complain about some small matter. Good servants aren't always looking for big rewards.

A gude face needs nae band, and an ill face deserves nane.
An honest face needs no recommendation and a dishonest one does not deserve one.

A gude fellow is a costly name.
A good reputation has to be hard earned.

A gude fellow ne'er tint but at an ill fellow's hand.
Only a dishonest person would cheat another person.

A gude friend is worth many relations.

A gude goose may hae an ill gaislin'.
First noted in Fergusson, this proverb warns that one cannot always rely upon offspring to turn out like their parents.

A gude grieve is better than an ill worker.

A gude hairst makes men prodigal, and a bad ane provident.

A gude ingle maks a roomy fireside.
Those who are welcoming will never be short of visitors.

A gude lawyer may be an ill neighbour.

A gude name is sooner tint than won.
It only takes one bad act to ruin a reputation.

A' gude or a' dirt.
It's either one extreme or the other.

A gude Scotch louse aye travels South.
A jibe at those Scots who seek their fortune south of the border.

A gude steel is worth a penny.
A good article is always worth a fair price. You only get what you pay for.

A gude tale is no' the waur o' bein' twice tauld.
Good advice can never be given too often. This proverb appears in Scott's Old Mortality: *'It's very true the curates read aye the same words ower again; and if they be right words, what for no? – a gude tale's no' the waur o' being twice told, I trow; and a body has aye the better chance to understand it.'*

A gude year winna mak him, nor an ill year mar him.
i.e. The person thus addressed is already comfortably off. However, Kelly says this phrase is – 'spoken of slothful, idle lazy fellows, who live from hand to mouth, and are equally poor all years'.

A hair in one's neck.
A weak spot, an Achilles heel.

A hair to mak a tether o'.
A small excuse to make a big fuss.

A hairy man's a geary man, but a hairy wife's a witch.
In the sixteenth and seventeenth centuries it was the fashion for successful and wealthy men to wear beards. This was also the era for witch hunting. Hence we can say that this saying dates from around this time.

A Hallow Fair horse and a Sunday wife.
A saying applied to things which are all dressed up. Common advice was always not to judge a potential wife on a Sunday when she is looking her best, but on another day when her true qualities can be seen. The Hallow Fair was held annually at Edinburgh on the second Wednesday of November.

A handfu' o' trade is worth a gowpen o' gold.
A little knowledge of a trade will pay dividends in the end.

A hantle cry Murder! and are aye upmost.
It is often the case that those who are least hurt cry the loudest.

A hard beginning is a gude beginning.
This fits in with the commonly held belief that you will only get out of life what you put in.

A hasty man is ne'er lusty.

A hasty man is no better than a fool.

A hasty meeting, a hasty parting.
Another piece of marriage guidance suggesting that a hot passion might soon cool.

A haveral woman's tongue is nae scandal.
A foolish gossip's tales will not be believed.

A Hawick hug.
When someone grips another round the waist. Taken from Border wrestling.

A head full of hair, a kirtle full of hips, a breist full of papes are three sure marks of a daw.

A hearty hand to gi'e a hungry mellith.
A jibe at those who profess to be liberal and generous, but in practice give very little.

A heavy purse maks a light heart.
Money does dispel some of life's worries. Conversely 'A light purse maks a heavy heart.'

A hen that lays thereout should hae a white nest egg.
A suggestion that an effort should be made to make the home attractive to those who are apt to wander.

A Hieland Welcome.
Said when given a particularly warm and generous welcome by a host. Burns wrote:

> *When death's dark stream I ferry o'er*
> *A time that surely shall come*
> *In heaven itself I'll ask no more*
> *Than just a Hieland welcome.*

A Highlander's privilege.
Rob the rich to help the poor.

Ahint that a cat in cuitikins!
Cuitikins are gaiters. An exclamation of great surprise used in the North East.

A' his buz shakes nae barley.
All his talking changes nothing.

A hook is weel tint to catch a salmon.
It generally pays off if one is prepared to lose a little in order to win a lot.

A horn spoon holds nae poison.
It is generally safe to eat at a humble table, because the less well-off do not attract poisoners.

A horse hired never tired.
This saying alludes to the fact that many people tend to look after their own possessions better than those which they may have hired or borrowed.

A houndless hunter and a gunless gunner see aye routh o' game.
You only see what you want when you can't have it.

A house built and a garden to grow ne'er brought what they cost.

A house fu' o' folk and a pouch wi' three fardens i' the corner o't dinna sort weel thegither.
Poverty and a desire to keep up appearances in front of others is an uneasy combination.

A house in a hastrie is dounricht wastrie.

A house wi' a reek, and a wife wi' a reard, will mak a man rin to the door.
Two things said to be enough to drive a man out of his own house.

A hungry man has aye a lazy cook.

A hungry man's an angry man.
Fergusson also records a similar proverb: 'A hungrie louse bytes sair'.

A hungry man sees far.

A hungry man's meat is lang o' makin' ready.
The watched pot never boils, or at least never seems to.

A hungry wame has nae lugs.
Those who are hungry are deaf to reason.

A' I got frae him I could put i' my e'e, and see nane the waur for it.
A saying used by a person who feels that they have not received a just reward for their efforts for another.

A' ills are guid untried.

A Januar haddock, a Februar bannock, and a March pint o' ale.
These three things were supposed to be at their best during these three months. However the first part is contradicted by a Mearns proverb which says :

A cameral haddock's ne'er gude
Till it gets three draps o' May flude.

A joke has sometimes mair wisdom in't than the pulpit oration o' a greetin' minister.
Many a true word is spoken in jest.

A kindly colt will ne'er mak a gude horse.

A kindly word cools anger.

A kinsman is part of a man's body, but a foster brother is a piece of his heart.

A kirkyaird deserter.
Said of someone whose appearance is deathlike.

A kiss and a drink o' water mak but a wersh disjune.
'Disjune' is breakfast. A warning to those who might marry for love without thought of their future means.

A landward lad is aye laithfu'.
A country lad is always shy or bashful.

A lang gathered dam soon runs out.

A lass that has mony wooers aft wales the warst.

A laughing faced lad often maks a lither servant.
A smiling boy rarely proves a good servant.

A lawyer's ee has twa lenses.
Presumably one is needed to read the small print.

A layin' hen is better than a standin' mill.
The first may be small but it at least makes a profit, whereas the latter does not.

A leaky ship needs muckle pumping.

Ale-sellers shouldna be tale-tellers.
It is expected that publicans will listen but not repeat all that they hear, and it is prudent that they do so if they wish to keep their customers.

A light-heeled mother maks a heavy-heeled dochter.
An active and industrious mother can sometimes do too much work around the home and hence leave little for the daughter to do so that she grows up being less industrious. This saying obviously predates any thoughts of equal opportunities for the sexes. This proverb was first recorded by Fergusson as 'An oleit mother makes a sweir daughter'.

A little wit ser's a lucky man.

All bite the bitten dog.

All craiks, all bears.
First recorded by Fergusson in 1641, Kelly gives the following meaning to this proverb – 'Spoken against bullies who keep up a great hectoring and blustering, yet when put to it, tamely pocket an affront'.

All hechtis should be haudin'.
Hechtis are promises; i.e. all promises should be kept.

A Locharbrigg lad or lass.
Used to describe someone as a warlock or witch, or later as someone of doubtful character. Locharbrigg hill was the noted tryst of the Nithsdale and Galloway warlocks and witches.

A loup-the-dyke Jenny Cameron.
Used to describe a woman of bad character – taken from Galt's The Entail.

A loving heart and a leal within
Are better than gowd or gentle kin.

Amaist and very near hae aye been great liars.

A man canna bear a' his kin about on his back.
No man can be expected to support all of his relations.

A man canna wive and thrive in the same year.
An unsentimental comment upon the cost of marriage.

A man cannot sell his tinsel.
Said when a person has turned down a good price for a commodity and then fails to make any improved deal for the goods. It is said as a warning not to be greedy.

A man may be kind, yet gi'e little o' his gear.

A man may haud his tongue in an ill time.

A man may see his friend in need that winna see his pow bleed.

A man may speir the gate to Rome.
Said of those who, on being asked to go on an errand, excuse themselves because they don't know the way.

A man may spit in his nieve and do but little.
A person may make a great show of their intentions to work, but actually do very little.

A man may woo where he will, but maun wed where his weird is.
A suggestion that marriage partners are already decided by fate.

A man of five may be a fool at fifteen.

A man of straw is worth a woman of gold.

A man o' words, but no o' deeds, is like a garden fu' o' weeds.

A man's a man for a' that.
The refrain from Robert Burn's song of brotherhood.

A man's aye blind in his ain cause.
Fergusson's collection lists a similar proverb: 'A man is a lyon to his ain cause'.

A man's aye crouse in his ain cause.

A man's hat in his hand ne'er did him ony harm.
A suggestion that it never does any harm to be polite.

A man's head is safer in a steel cap than in a marble palace.
This proverb implies that it is always safer to be in a constant state of readiness to defend oneself against attack.

A man should ride where he may not wrestle.

A man's mind is a mirk mirror.
This proverb is an early one which appears in Douglas' 'Aeneis' of 1513.

A man's o' little use when his wife is a widow.

A man's weel or wae as he thinks himsel' sae.

A man's worst friends are those he brings with him.
If they disparage him they are believed, as being supposed to know him. Spoken also when they whom we thought to have been our friends in such a case, were against our interest – Kelly.

A man was once hanged for leaving his drink.
This saying took its rise from the villain that assassinated the Prince of Orange. 'The saying is spoken when men proffer to go away before their drink be out'. – Kelly.

A man wha lippens to a strae rope may hang himsel'.
A cautionary note that it is safer to run no risks.

A mear's shoe will fit a horse.

A mein pot ne'er played even.
'Prospects in which many have a share often prove failures' – Kelly, i.e too many cooks spoil the broth.

A merse mist alang the Tweed
In a harvest mornin's gude indeed.
G. Henderson (1856).

A midge is as big as a mountain amaist.
'Amaist' is almost. This proverb is used to show the latitude afforded the word almost, when people are stretching a point.

A mile o' Don's worth twa o' Dee;
Except for salmon, stane and tree.
An Aberdeenshire saying expressing the differences in the terrain surrounding the two rivers. The banks of the Don are very fertile, whereas Deeside tends to be more wilderness and forest.

A mind that's scrimpit ne'er wants some care.
From Ramsay's 'Gentle Shepherd'.

A misty May and a dropping June
Brings the bonny land of Moray aboon.
Owing to its gravelly soil, it is said that Moray looks the better for early Summer rains.

A misty morning may be a clear day.

A morning's sleep is worth a fauld o' sheep to a hudderin' dudderin' daw.

A mote in a gunner's ee is as bad as a spike i' the gun.

A mouthfu' o' meat may be a tounfu' o' shame.
That is, if a small thing has been procured by foul means, it may bring great disgrace upon the offender.

A muffed cat was ne'er a gude rattan taker.
Appears in Fergusson as a gloved cat, i.e. restraint or caution will achieve nothing.

An Aberdeen man ne'er stands to the word that hurts him.
An old saying and an affront to all Aberdonians.

A nag wi' a wame and a wame wi' nane are no a gude pair.
Opposites do not get on well with each other, be it a well-fed person and someone who is hungry, or an intelligent and an ignorant pairing.

A naked man maun rin.
An extremely poor man must exert himself, if he is to survive.

An auld body's blast's sune blawn.
The elderly soon get out of breath.

An auld gum broken oot again.
Said when an old grievance is revived.

An auld pock needs muckle clouting.
Old things generally are often in need of repair. Another example sometimes given is 'An auld pock is aye skailing [leaking]'. These are both recorded in Fergusson's collection.

An auld tout on a new horn is little minded.
An old story or complaint will receive little attention, even if it is told in a different way, or by a different person.

Ance awa, aye awa.
Once a person has gone away from home for a while, there is always a feeling that it will not take too much to persuade them to leave again.

Ance is nae custom.

Ance provost, aye My Lord.
Once a person has been Provost they get to keep their title even when they have left office. Hence this proverb suggests that once a good or bad name has been attached to someone, it is very difficult to get rid of thereafter. Scott uses this proverb in Redgauntlet *when Peter Peebles says 'Was I a burgess? and am I not a burgess even now? I have done nothing to forfeit the right, I trow, once provost, and aye my Lord.'*

Ance there, and awa' wi' care.
Said when one has secured safe and comfortable quarters.

Ance wud, ne'er wise.

An eating horse ne'er foundered.
Said as an excuse for eating a hearty meal.

An elbuck dirl will lang play thirl.
'An elbuck dirl' is a knock or blow to one's elbow which has a very stunning effect for a time, i.e. a particular cause will have a particular effect.

Ane at a time is gude fishin'.
The suggestion is that slow and steady wins the race.

Ane flear gets ane follower commonly.

Ane leal man is nae ta'en wi' hauf a tail.
A loyal person waits to hear both sides of the story in order to determine the truth.

Ane may bind the sack afore it's fu'.
A reminder given when a particular process can be safely stopped at any time.

Ane may like a haggis weel enough that wadna like the bag bladded
on his chafts.
A warning not to take things to extremes.

Ane may like the kirk weel enough, and no ride on the riggin' o't.
*A jibe at fanatical churchgoers. One can be keen on something without taking it
to extremes.*

Ane o' the court, but nane o' the council.
*Although the person thus addressed may be asked for their opinion, it is only for
form's sake.*

Ane wad like to be lo'ed, but wha wad mool in wi' a moudiewort?
Another proverb warning that we should avoid extremes.

A new mantle or a new hood,
Poor brownie, ye'll ne'er dae mair gude.
*If a house was occupied by a brownie (household sprite), it was said the only way
to get rid of them was to leave out a new coat. Hence this is the phrase supposedly
spoken by the brownie on taking its leave from the house.*

A new pair o' breeks will cast down an old coat.
*Literally this means that wearing a new item of clothing will only serve to make
the other items look old and shabby. This saying was sometimes used when an old
man married a young girl. Hislop however gives the meaning as 'The acquisition
of a new friend may tend to lower our esteem for those of longer standing'.*

'A' new things sturts,' quo the gudewife when she gaed lie wi' the
hired man.

An ilka-day braw maks a Sabbath-day daw.
*A person who wears their best outfit everyday, will have nothing suitable for
special occasions.*

An ill cook should hae a guid cleaver.

An ill cow may hae a gude calf.
*i.e. Bad parents may produce good children. However Cheviot also records the
contrary proverb 'An ill bird maun hae an ill brood.'*

An ill custom is like a gude bannock – better broken than kept.

An ill-gated coo had aye short horns.
*A suggestion that for bad people, their will to do wrong is often greater than their
power.*

An ill plea should be well pled.

An ill shearer ne'er got a gude heuk.
It is a poor workman who blames his tools.

An ill wife an' a new-kindled candle should hae their heads
hadden doun.

An ill willy cow should hae short horns.
Fergusson.

An ill won penny will cast doun a pound.

An inch o' a nag is worth a span o' an aiver.

An olite mither maks a sweird dochter.
A mother who is over -industrious is apt to leave little for her offspring to do,
leading them to grow up lazy.

An ounce o' wit is worth a pound o' lear.
An ounce of natural wit is worth a pound of learning.

An unhappy fish gets an unhappy bait.
You get what you deserve in life.

An unlucky man's cart is eithly coup'd.
First recorded in Fergusson but with 'unhappie' substituted for unlucky.

A' owers are ill, but ower the water and ower the hill.
A warning to take all things in moderation. A similar saying appears in
Alexander Montgomerie's 'The Cherrie and the Slae':

> *All owres are repute to be vyce,*
> *Owre hich, owre low, owre rasch, owre nyce,*
> *Owre het, or zit owre cauld.*

A partridge frichted is hauf cooked.

A peesmeal o' clishmaclavers.
A load of nonsense.

A penny in the purse is better than a crown spent.

A poor man maks a poor marriage, and there's nae meat for him.
According to Kelly, this proverb is spoken when people in a mean condition are
meanly treated.

A primsie damsel maks a daidlin' dame.
Another version of 'A dink maiden, etc.'

A proud heart in a poor breist has muckle dolour to dree.
First recorded by Fergusson, this proverb tells us that pride and poverty do not sit
well together. The bearer of these feelings is bound to suffer.

A proud mind and a poor purse gree ill thegither.

A pun o' oo is as heavy as a pun o' leid.

A quarrelsome tyke comes limping hame.

A quern stone is the better o' being pitted and indented wi' mony
blows, so that you dinna break it.
This proverb dates back to the days of using hand querns for grinding in the

Highlands. It was applied to criminals and wrongdoers, suggesting that they be punished with due severity but that the end goal was the reformation of the culprit and not their death.

A raggit cowte may prove a gude gelding.
An unpromising colt may turn out to be a fine horse, i.e one cannot always tell how something will develop in the future.

A reckless houssie maks many thieves.

A red nose maks a raggit back.
A warning against the evils of too much drinking, which will lead to poverty.

A regular Pate Stewart.
A saying originating in Orkney said to denote any cruel tyrant. The reference is to Earl Patrick Stewart, son of Earl Robert, who received a grant of the Orkney islands from his sister Queen Mary. Patrick Stewart was a tyrant of the worst kind and was eventually hanged in Edinburgh in 1615.

A rent is better than a darn.
A mistake is often made worse by trying to cover it up. Honesty is the best policy.

A reproof is nae poison.

'Are they no a bonny pair?' as the deil said to his hoofs.

A rich man has mair cousins than his father had kin.
Money always attracts a group of hangers-on.

A rich man's wooing's no lang a-doing.

As a carl riches, he wretches.
A warning that as some people become wealthier they also become meaner.

As a'e door shuts anither opens.
New opportunities are always coming along.

As ane flits anither fits, and that keeps mailins dear.
The law of supply and demand tends to keep prices (or in this case farms) relatively stable, i.e. they don't get any cheaper.

As auld as the Moss o' Meigle.
Said of very old things. The more usual saying 'As auld as the hills' is often supplemented in the Highlands with the phrase 'and the MacArthurs'.

As auld as the three trees o' Dysart.

A's but lip – wit that wants experience.

As caigue as a pyat picking at a worm.

As cankered as a coo wi' ae horn.

A scar'd head is soon broken.
It does not take much to completely ruin the name of someone whose reputation has already been called into question before.

A schored man lives long.
Being forewarned, he is able to evade danger.

A Scotch warming pan.
This saying refers to the fact that at one time many Scots could not afford a set of warming pans and so would send a serving lass to warm up the bed.

A Scots mist will weet an Englishman to the skin.
A proverb arising from the frequent complaints of English visitors of the heavy mists which hang about the Highlands of Scotland.

A Scotsman is one who keeps the Sabbath – and any other darned thing he can lay his hands on.

A Scotsman and a Newcastle grindstane travel a' the world ower.
Both these things are known for their fine qualities, and hence are welcomed throughout the world.

A Scotsman is aye wise ahint the hand.

As bare as the birk at Yule e'en.
Said of somebody who is in absolute penury or indigence.

As caller as a kail-blade.
'Caller' means fresh.

As course as cat's dirt.
Said of something that is very disagreeable.

As daft as a yett on a windy day.
Yett means gate. Said of a scatterbrained person.

As day brake, butter brake.
Said when a person or object which is desired, suddenly arrives opportunely.

A secret foe gi'es a sudden blow.
A warning to be vigilant at all times.

A seven years maiden is aye at the slight.
An unmarried woman of a certain age was apt to be made fun of in previous times.

A's fair at the ba o' Scone.
No holds barred. Taken from the Statistical Account of Scone in Perthshire (1798): 'In the course of the play (in the annual football match between the married men and the bachelors of the parish) one might always see some scene of violence between the parties.'

As flat i' the fore as a farrow cat.
Spoken of a hungry-looking person.

As greedy as ten cocks scraping a midden for ae barley pickle.

As gude eat the deil as sup the kail he's boil'd in.
It is as well to do something (perhaps commit a sin) in an obvious manner as to try to achieve the same results by stealth.

As gude may haud the stirrup as he that loups on.
One cannot judge a man merely by his position in life. In his Border
Memories, *W. R. Carre relates the following tale:*

> *An illegitimate son of Elliot of Larriston in Liddesdale – the head of the family
> – served as a stable-boy with his relative Elliot of Stobbs. His master, who knew
> the connection, was in the habit of saying, as he mounted his horse, 'Better he
> that holds the stirrup than he that rides.' The young man entered the army, made
> a fortune in India, and on his return to Scotland purchased the ancestral estate.*

As gude to ye tak' a millstane oot o' Penan.
*A saying originating from the quarry at Penan, which at one time supplied a
large part of the North East with millstones. It is applied to any difficult
undertaking requiring formidable strength, and comes from the difficulty of
moving these heavy objects.*

A shave aff a new-cut loaf's ne'er missed.

A shor'd tree stands long.

A short grace is gude for hungry folk.

A shower in July when the corn begins to fill
Is worth a plough of oxen and all belongs theretill.
More weather-lore for the farmer.

As I gaed up the Canongate, And through the Netherbow,
Four and twenty weavers Were swinging in a tow;
The tow ga'e a crack, The weavers ga'e a girn,
Fie, let me doun again, I'll never steal a pirn;
I'll never steal a pirn, I'll never steal a pow,
O fie, let me doun again, I'll steal nae mair frae you.
*A rhyme from Robert Chambers' collection, which casts more aspersions on the
character of weavers.*

A sillerless man gangs fast throught the market.
Because he doesn't have the necessary money with which to buy or bargain.

A silly man will be slily dealt wi'.
Unscrupulous people will always take advantage of the lesser-abled.

A sinking maister aft maks a rising man.

A Skairsburn warning.
*No warning at all. A Kirkudbrightshire saying where the River Skairsburn was
noted for very sudden flooding.*

A skittering cow in the loan wad aye hae mony marrows.

As lang as the bird sings afore Candlemas, he greets after it.

As lang as ye serve the tod, ye maun bear up his tail.
We must help those who help us. One good turn deserves another.

As lang as ye stand, ye don't stay.

As lang lasts the hole as the heal leather.

As lang lives the merry man as the wretch, for a' the craft he can.

As learn't as a scholar o' Buckhaven College.
A sarcastic saying from Fife suggesting that the person thus addressed is ignorant.

A slothfu' hand maks a slim fortune.
A warning to the lazy.

As menseless as a tinkler's messan.
As ill-bred as a tinker's dog.

As muckle upwith, as muckle downwith.
The higher one gets, the further there is to fall.

A's no gowd that glisters, nor maidens that wear their hair.
Not everything is as it first appears. In seventeenth and eighteenth century Scotland it was the fashion for virgins to go bareheaded. The speaker of this proverb is questioning the honesty of some of the women not wearing headdresses. First recorded by Fergusson.

A's no tint that fa's bye

A sooth bourd's nae bourd.
A true jest is no jest at all.

A spindle o' bourtree, a whorl o' caumstane;
Put them on the housetop, and it will spin its lane.
These things were supposed to deter witches from a household.

A spoonfu' o' stink will spoil a patfu' o' skink.
We are perhaps more familiar with the proverb about one rotten apple spoiling the barrel.

A spur in the head is worth twa in the heel.

As sair fights the wren as the crane.
All are equally courageous or earnest in extremity – Hislop.

As sair greets the bairn that's paid at e'en as he that gets the paiks in the morning.
Punishment or misfortune is just as bad whatever time it occurs.

As sib as a sieve to a riddle.
Spoken of people who have much in common.

As slow's the Tweed at Muir House.
A saying local to Melrose, evidently used in a sarcastic sense because the river runs swiftly at this point.

As sure's death.
A common expression signifying either the truth or certainty of a fact, or to pledge the speaker to a performance of his promise. In the Eglinton Papers *the Earl gives an amusing anecdote illustrating this latter sense of the phrase. One day the Earl found a boy climbing up a tree, and called him to come down. The boy declined, because, he said, the earl would thrash him. His lordship pledged his honour that he would not do so. The boy replied, 'I dinna ken onything about your honour, but if you say as sure's death I'll come down.'*

A staffy-nieved job.
A saying indicating a task which requires physical force, i.e. sticks and fists.

As the auld cock craws, the young ane learns.
A proverb denoting the legacy of learnt behaviour. First recorded by Fergusson, Cheviot records an expanded version which appends the phrase 'aye tak' care what ye do afore the bairns'.

As the day lengthens the cold strengthens.
A proverbial weather warning. As the days start to get longer in February and March, the weather can be even colder than in December or January.

As the soo fills the draff sours.
The more we have of something the less attractive it can become.

As the wind blaws seek your beild.
Suit your way of life to your circumstances.

A's tint that's put in a riven dish.
Favours bestowed upon unworthy recipients are wasted.

As tired as a tyke is o' langkail.
Literally, as tired as a dog is of the same kind of meat every day.

A' Stuarts are no sib to the King.
People may have the name and appearance of greatness without the reality.

A sturdy beggar should ha'e a stout naesayer.

As weel be sune as syne.
A saying used to suggest that a thing is as well done now rather than put off until later.

As weel try to stop the North wind coming throu' the Glens o' Foudland.

As weel try to sup sour dook wi' an elshin.
The two preceding proverbs are used to denote something which is impossible.

As wight as a wabster's doublet, that ilka day taks a thief by the neck.
An allegation that the weaving fraternity tended to be dishonest. For some unknown reason this particular trade comes in for a lot of abuse in proverbs.

As ye brew weel, ye'll drink the better.
You only get out what you put in to begin with.

A's yours frae the door oot.
You have no right to claim anything in my house, but you can claim what you like outside it.

A tarrowing bairn was ne'er fat.
A child that does not eat will not thrive. This proverb is used as a warning to people not to neglect their opportunites or they will not prosper. First recorded in Fergusson.

A terrier tyke and a rusty key,
Were Johnny Armstrong's Jeddart fee.
A border thief of the above name was promised a free pardon on disclosing what he thought would be the best crime preventative. This was his reply.

At fasten e'en the maiden was fou'
She said she would fast all Lentren through.
Spoken when people in plenty command temperance – Kelly.

A' that's said shouldna be sealed.
Don't believe everything you hear.

A' that ye'll tak wi' ye will be but a kist and a sheet after a'.
A warning that no matter how wealthy you are, you can't take it with you when you die. Death is the great leveller.

A' the better since you speir'd, speir o'er again.
Said in reply to the question 'How do you do?'

A' the corn's no shorn by kempers.
Kempers were the best harvesters. The proverb is meant to console those who are not so strong or fast as the kempers, by letting them know that their contributions are still needed and valued.

A' the keys of the country hang na in ae belt.
All the power is not in one person's possession.

A' the months wi' an R in them.
A proverbial rule denoting in which months household fires were permissible in Scotland.

A' the truth shouldna aye be tauld.
A warning that sometimes the truth can hurt, and is better left unsaid.

A' the wealth o' the warld is i' the weather.

A' the winnings in the first buying.
The better the original deal, the better the eventual outcome.

A' the wit i' the warld's nae in ae pow.

A' things anger ye and the cat breks your hert.
A rebuke offered to those who are put out by the unalterable perversity of nature.

A' things sturt, no wonder you be old like.
A warning to people not to make a fuss over small trifles.

A' things thrive but thrice.
Third time lucky. First recorded in Fergusson.

A thoughtless body's aye thrang.

A thrawn question should hae a thrawart answer.

A thread will tie an honest man better than a rope will do a rogue.
An honest man's word is as good as his bond and can always be relied upon.

A Tinkler was never a toun taker,
A Taylor was never a hardy man,
Nor a Wabster leal o' his trade,
Nor ever was since the warld began.
A rhyme proclaiming the vagrant life of the first, the sedentary life of the second and the thievish disposition of the third.

A' to ae side, like Gourock.
Said when something is squint.

A tocherless dame sits lang at hame.
According to this proverb a financially poor beauty will find more lovers than husbands.

A tocher's nae word in a true lover's parle.
True love is not mercenary – money is of no consequence.

A tongue that wad clip clouts.
Spoken of someone who is either sharp-tongued, or who talks a lot.

A toom hand is nae lure for a hawk.

A toom pantry maks a thriftless gudewife.
When the cupboard is bare, there is nothing for the housewife to be thrifty with.

A toom pooch gaes quickly through the market.

A toom purse maks a blate merchant.

A traivelled man has leave to lie.
In days of old, travellers' tales were acceptable as entertainment, and so poetic licence was granted them.

A turn well done is twice done.

At Yule, and Pasch, and high times.
Such a thing must be done, worn or expended only on extraordinary occasions.

Auld acquaintance is kindly, like clean linen.

Auld men are twice bairns.
A saying suggesting that old men behave like they did when they were young children.

Auld saws speak truth.

Auld sparrows are ill tae tame.
Another version of trying to teach an old dog new tricks, i.e. the older one gets, the more set in one's ways one becomes.

Auld wives and bairns mak fools o' physicians.
The elderly can do so by virtue of experience, and children through ignorance.

Auld wives were aye guid maidens.
A satire on the observation made by older members of society that they were never as bad in their day as the youth of today.

A wa' between best preserves friendship.
It is sometimes best for friendship if the parties remain separate. A warning against friends entering into a partnership.

A wee bush is better than nae beild.
A small shelter is better than nothing.

A wee house has a wide mouth.
A warning that no matter how small a household is, it still takes more than one thinks to support it.

A wee mouse will creep beneath a muckle corn stack.
Said in fun when a small woman marries a larger man.

A wee spark maks muckle wark.

A wee thing puts your beard in a blaze.
Said of someone who can get worked up by the smallest thing.

A wife is wise enough when she kens her gudeman's breeks frae her ain kirtle.
A strong suggestion for women not to try to take the dominant role in a relationship. This proverb clearly predates any notion of equality for the sexes.

A wife's ae dochter is neither gude nor gracie.

A wilfu' man maun hae his way.

A winkin' cat's no aye blin'.

A winter night, a woman's mind, and a laird's purpose aften change.

A wise man carries his cloak in fair weather, an' a fool wants his in rain.
A word of encouragement to the cautious. Be prepared.

A wise man gets learning frae them that hae nane o' their ane.
A clever person can learn from the mistakes of others.

A wise man ne'er returns by the same road if anither is free to him.
This was sound advice in the days of brigands who would rob people on their return from market.

A wise man wavers, a fool is fixed.
A wise person will always keep an open mind on matters under discussion.

A woman's wit is in her forehead.
A saying from William Alexander's 'Johnny Gibb of Gushetneuk', which implies that women are guided by their senses rather than by judgement when it comes to matters of the heart.

A' would hae a', a' would forgie.
Those who expect too much should be ready to compromise.

A yeld sow was never gude to gryces.
A proverbial expression insinuating that those who are childless are rarely good with the children of others.

Aye as ye thrive your feet fa's frae ye.

Aye in a hurry; aye ahint.

Aye keep something for a sair leg.

Aye keep your bonnet on: sheep's heids are best warm.
Said as a rebuke to a man who forgets to take his hat off in the presence of a lady.

Aye tak the fee when the tear's i' the e'e.

Aye to eild, but never to wit.
A description of someone who continues to grow older, but no wiser.

A young cowte will canter be it uphill or doun.
You cannot suppress youthful enthusiasm.

A young plant ne'er throve that was watered wi' an auld man's blood.
A warning that disrespect to age brings bad luck.

A' you run you win.
Taken from playing the game of bowls, this proverb is applied to any seemingly unfeasible project, in which what you make is clear profit.

A Yule feast may be done at Pasch.
Festivities although normally practised at Christmas need not be confined to any particular season if a suitable occasion demands.

B

Bachelors' wives and auld maids' bairns are aye weel bred.
A reply to those who give advice on matters of which they have no personal experience.

Back to auld claes and parritch.
Said when we have come to the end of a holiday/luxury and will have to return to the normal routine.

Bad legs and ill wives should aye stay at home.

Bairns are certain care, but nae sure joy.
A warning of the realities of parenthood.

Bairns speak i' the field what they hear i' the ha'.
A warning to all parents to mind what they say in earshot of children.

Bairns and fools speak at the cross what they hear at the ingleside.
A similar warning to that given above.

Bairns' mither bursts never.
Said because a mother's instinct is always to feed her children before herself.

Baith weel and woe come aye wi' the warld's gear.
Wealth brings with it both joys and woes.

Baken bread and brown ale winna bide lang.
Good food and drink are soon consumed.

Bank's fou', braes fou'
Gather ye a' the day, ye'll no gather your nieves fou'.
An enigmatic rhyme about 'mist' collected by Robert Chambers.

Bannocks are better than nae bread.
Half a loaf is better than no bread at all. First recorded in Fergusson's collection as 'Bannoks is better nor na kin bread'.

Barefooted folk shouldna tread on thorns.
Another version of the English 'Those who live in glass houses should not throw stones'.

Bare gentry, bragging beggars.

Bare legs need happing.
The poor need assistance.

Bare shouders mak' burned shins.
According to Kelly – 'When a boy is ill clothed he will sit so near the fire that his legs will burn.'

Bare words mak' no bargains.

Bastard brood are aye proud.

Be a friend to yoursel' and ithers will.

Bear and forbear is gude philosophy.
One should be prepared to give and take.

Bear wealth weel, poortith will bear itsel'.

Beauty but bounty availeth nothing. *or*
Beauty, but bounty's not bauch.

Beauty draws more than oxen.
Kelly says 'This is an English proverb, the Scottish one that answers it is smutty'.

Beauty is but skin deep.

Beauty's muck when honour's tint.
Beauty no longer has any worth when honour is lost.

Beauty'll no mak' a man's parritch.
A warning to young men not to choose their partners purely on looks.

Be aye the thing ye would be ca'd.
Always try to live up to the standards you would want to be known by.

Be blyth in sorrow, for that is best remeid.

'Because' is a woman's reason.

Beds are best, quo' the man to his guest.
This saying was presumably used in the interests of economy, i.e. the host wanted his guest to go straight to bed and hence would avoid having to supply him with any supper.

Beefsteaks and porter are gude belly mortar.

Bees that hae honey in their mouths hae stings in their tails.
A warning to be wary of silver-tongued individuals who are often up to no good.

Before an ill wife be gude, even if she was a' turn'd to tongue.
Used when we promise to do a thing soon, tho' the promise need not oblige us to haste, for it will be a considerable time before a woman reforms an ill tongue – Kelly.

Before I ween'd: but now, I wat.
This phrase is spoken when we finally find evidence of some wrongdoing of which we could only suspect beforehand, i.e. Before I suspected, now I know for certain.

Before the deil gaes blind, and he's no blear e'ed yet.
A reply informing the questioner that what they request will be at some time in the future – if at all.

Before ye choose a friend, eat a peck o' saut wi' him.

Be gaun the gate's afore ye.
A humorous or surly hint to go.

Beg frae beggars and you'll ne'er be rich.

Beggars breed, and rich men feed.

Beggars douna bide wealth.

Beggars shouldna be choosers.

Begin the warld at the richt end.

Begin wi' needles and preens, and end wi' horn'd nowte.
Small beginnings can often lead onto much greater things. The saying is used here as a warning against dishonesty.

Being gude naturally leads to the getting o' gude.

Be it better, be it worse, be ruled by him that has the purse.

Be it sae, is nae banning.
Spoken when yielding a point in an argument because you are either unwilling or unable to go further, but also indicating that you still think yourself to be in the right.

Be lang sick that ye may be sune hale.
Take time to recover. Do not get out of your sickbed too soon.

Believe a' ye hear, an' ye may eat a' ye see.
Said as a warning to mock a gullible person.

Belyve is twa hours and a half.
The person who says that they will do something immediately, or shortly, will probably take longer than anticipated.

Be quick, for you'll never be cleanly.

Be ready wi' your bannet, but slow wi' your purse.
A suggestion that if you are busy raising your hat to be polite you may get out of dipping your hand into your purse to pay for things.

Be slow in choosing a friend, but slower in changing him.

Be still taking and tarrowing.
Take all that you can get, though not all that is due.

Best not handle the horse shoe til it cools.

Best to be off wi' the auld love before we be on wi' the new.
A warning of the dangers of 'two-timing'.

Be thou weal, or be thou wae, thou wilt not aye be sae.
One cannot always predict what one's circumstances will be in the future.

Better a bit in the morning than fast a' day.
Breakfast is the most important meal of the day.

Better a clout in than a hole out.
An item of clothing with a patch is preferable to one full of holes.

Better a deil as a daw.

Better a dog fawn on you than bark at you.

Better ae ee than hail blin'.

Better ae wit bought than twa for nought.
You only get what you pay for.

Better a finger aff than aye waggin'.
It is better to face the worst than to always have some evil hanging over you.

Better a fremit friend than a friend fremit.
Better a strange friend than a friend turned stranger.

Better a gude fame than a fine face.
Beauty is only skin deep, and a good reputation counts for more. What you do is more important than how you look.

Better alane than in bad company.

His absence is guid company.

Better a laying hen than a lying crown.
Better a small thing which gives you something, than a greater thing which lies idle and does nothing for you.

Better a lean horse than a toom halter.
It is better to have something, no matter how small, than nothing at all. One should always count one's blessings.

Better a moose in the pot than nae flesh.
Advice to count one's blessings.

Better an auld maid than a young whore.
The retort given when a young woman calls an older unmarried one an old maid.

Better an auld man's darling than a young man's warling.
A saying sometimes used to induce young girls to marry an older man.

Better an even doun snaw than a driving drift.
Things are better in moderation than in extremes.

Better an old woman wi' a purse in her hand than three men wi' belted brands.
Money can talk louder than threats on occasion.

Better a saft road than bad company.
It is preferable to make a difficult journey than to be stuck with bad company.

Better a sair fae than a fause friend.

Better a shameless eating than a shamefu' leaving.
An encouragement to eat up.

Better a sma' fish than an empty dish.

Better at a time to gie than tak'.
Policy is sometimes necessary.

Better a thigging mither than a riding father.
Thigging means begging or borrowing. The proverb suggests that it is better to have a mother who is prepared to beg or borrow for her children than a sporting father who is only interested in himself.

Better a tight girth than a loose saddle.
It is better to be safe than sorry.

Better a tocher in her than wi' her.
Better the woman with good qualities and no money than vice versa.

Better a toom house than an ill tennant.

Better auld debts than auld sairs.

Better a wee bush than nae beild.
Better to have something, no matter how small, than nothing at all.

Better a wee fire to warm you than a big fire to burn you.
Moderation in all things is best.

Better bairns greet nor bearded men.
This saying was commonly used in the past to justify stern measures, especially when punishment was being handed out to children. This old saw was apparently repeated in 1583 when the Ruthvens seized a seventeen-year-old King James VI. When he burst into tears the Master of Glamis is said to have uttered the above phrase to the young king. According to another story John Knox used an amended form of this proverb when he made Mary Queen of Scots cry in his attempts to convert her to Protestantism. He substituted the word 'women' for 'bairns'.

Better be a coward than a corpse.

Better be a fool at a feast than a wise man at a fray.

Better be before at a burial than ahint at a bridal.

Better be blythe wi' little than sad wi' naething.
Better be merry with something, as sad with nothing.

Better be envied than pitied.

Better be friends at a distance than enemies at hame.

Better be happy than wise.

Better be idle than ill employed/occupied.

Better be John Thomson's man than Ring and Dinn's *or* John Knox's man.
'John Thomson's man is he who is complaisant to his wife's humours, Ring and Dinn is he who his wife scolds; John Knox is he whom his wife beats' – Kelly.

Better be kind than cumbersome.

Better be oot o' the warld than out o' fashion.

Better be sonsy than soon up.
It's better to be naturally fortunate than to have to get up early to make one's fortune.

Better be the head o' the commons than the tail o' the gentry.
It is always preferable to be the one in control than the follower. A coarser version is given in Kelly thus: 'Better the head of the yeomanry, as the arse of the gentry.'

Better be the lucky man than the lucky man's son.

Better belly burst than gude meat spoil.
A saying used by gluttons to justify their greed, on the grounds of economy.

Better bend than break.

Better buy than borrow.

Better cry 'Feigh Saut' than 'Feigh Stink'.
'An apology for having our meat too much powdered, as otherwise it would stink' – Kelly. Better to have something overpreserved than rotten.

Better day the better deed.

Better deaf than hear ill tales of oneself.
This saying appears in Scott's Fortunes of Nigel.

Better do it than wish it done.
A suggestion that it is always better to take command of a situation and decide what you are going to do to other people before they decide what they are going to do to you.

Better dogs are born in the kennel than in the parlour.

Better eat brown bread in youth than in eild.
It is better to be in poor circumstances when young and fit than in old age. In days gone by brown bread was cheaper than white. Kelly uses the word 'grey' rather than 'brown'.

Better fed than bred.
Said of someone with bad table manners.

Better fill'd than prick'd.
According to Kelly this saying is 'Taken from blood puddings, apply'd jocosely to them who have often evacuations'.

Better find iron than tine siller.

Better fish saut than fish stinkin'.

Better fleech a fool (the deil) than fight him.
To 'fleech' is to flatter.

Better gang about than fa' in the dub.
It is sometimes safer to take the long way round than to try the shortcut.

Better gang to bed supperless than rise in debt.

Better gi'e the slight than tak' it.

Better greet ower your gudes than after your gudes.
It is better not to sell your wares than to sell them and not receive any payment.

Better gude sale than gude ale.

Better guide weel than work sair.

Better hae than want.

Better hain weel than work sair.
It is better to economise than to toil for a greater subsistence.

Better half egg than toom doup.
Another version of 'half a loaf etc.', exhorting everyone to count their blessings.

Better half hang'd than ill married.

Better hand loose nor bound to an ill bakie.
'Bakie' – The stake to which an ox or cow is tethered in the stall.

Better hands loose than in an ill tethering.
Better to be single and free than part of an unhappy relationship.

Better happy at Court than gude in service.
'Luck often raises a courtier when good service is not rewarded' – Kelly. A saying applied to people when they get a lucky break.

Better haud at the brim than at the bottom.
It is better to live sparingly while we have something, than spend lavishly and afterwards have nothing.

Better haud by a hair than draw by a tether.

Better haud out than put out.
Prevention is better than cure.

Better haud wi' the hounds than rin wi' the hare.
Sometimes it is best to act politically and side with the stronger/winning party.

Better in Spring the work of one day,
Than three at Hallowmass, work as you may.
A West Highland saying.

Better keep the deil oot than hae to pit him oot.
It is easier not to weaken to some temptation in the first place than to try to give up a bad habit later on.

Better keep weel than mak' weel.

Better ken'd than car'd for.

Better kind friend than fremit kindred.

Better kiss a knave than cast oot wi' him.

Better lang little than sune naething.

Better late thrive than ne'er do weel.

Better laugh at your ain pint stoup, than greet, an' gather gear.
It is better to be happy spending money, than miserable acquiring it.

Better learn frae your neebor's skaith than frae your ain.
It is better to learn from others' mistakes than from your own.

Better leave than lack.
It is better to have too much than too little of some things.

Better leave to my faes than beg frae my friends.

Better live in hope than die in despair.

Better mak your feet your friends.
Said as a warning, meaning run for your life!

Better marry than do worse.

Better master ane than fight wi' ten.

Better meddle wi' the deil than the bairns o' Falkirk.

Better my bairns seek frae me than I beg frae them.

Better my friends think me fremit than fashious.
It is better to visit friends seldom than to be such a constant caller that you become a nuisance.

Better nae man than an ill man.
It is better to be single than to be married to a bad husband.

Better nae ring nor the ring o' a rash.

Better ne'er begun than ne'er ended.
Do not start what you cannot finish.

Better ower't than in't.
It is better to be beyond the fear of danger than in it.

Better play for nought, than work for nought.

Better plays the fu' wame than the new coat.
Given the choice between having food or having new clothes, the person who chooses the former is likely to be the happier.

Better ride safe in the dark, than in daylight wi' a cut-throat at your elbow.
A warning to choose one's friends carefully.

Better rough an' sonsy than bare an' donsy.
It is better to be a fortunate rough diamond, than to be an unlucky person from a genteel background.

Better rue sit than rue flit.
It is better not to move house at all than to move and then regret it.

Better saucht wi' little aucht than care wi' mony cows.
It is better to have little and peace of mind than to have a lot and all its worries. Recorded first by Fergusson.

Better saut than sour.

Better say 'Here it is' than 'There it was'.
It is better to take what is on offer than to lament the loss of it when you have let it pass by.

Better short and sweet than lang and lax.
In his collection, Kelly applies this saying to sermons.

Better sit idle than work for nought.
The implication is that if you work for nothing once, you will never be able to charge for your services again.

Better sit still than rise an' fa'.
It is sometimes better to continue in a low position than to be promoted and later fall from grace.

Better skaiths saved than mends made.
It is better not to offend to begin with, than to have to apologise later.

Better sma' fish than nane.

Better soon as syne.

Better spared than ill spent.
There is no point in waste.

Better speak bauldly oot than aye be grumphin'.
Speak your mind rather than harbour a grudge.

Better stay wi' ken'd friends than gang farther and fare waur.
The grass always appears greener on the other side. Many drivers will be familiar with the roadside services at Stracathro which bear the legend 'Ye may gang far and fare waur'.

Better stumble in the path than be upheld by the arm of a thief.
It is better to struggle on than to live off immoral earnings.

Better that ae heart brak than a' the warld wunners.
It is better to keep your sorrows to yourself.

Better the barn filled than the bed.
This saying dates back to the times when mattresses were stuffed with straw and chaff. Hence one would rather have the corn to fill the barn than the chaff to stuff the mattress.

Better the end o' a feast than the beginning o' a fray.

Better the ill ken'd than the gude unken'd.
Better the devil you know. A known trouble is easier to deal with than an unknown one.

Better the lean lintie in the hand than the fat finch on the wand.
Another version of 'A bird in the hand etc.'

Better the mother wi' the poke than the faither wi' the sack.
According to Kelly, a poor mother is generally more kind to her offspring than a father in a similar condition.

Better the nag that ambles a' day than him that maks a brattle for a mile, and then's dune wi' the road.
Slow and steady gets there in the end.

Better thole a grumph than a sumph.
It is preferable to be troubled by an intelligent, though surly, man, than by a stupid one.

Better tine life, since tint is gude fame.
Take away someone's good name and they would be better off dead.

Better tine your joke than tine your friend.

Better to haud than draw.
Possession is nine-tenths of the law.

Better to rule wi' the gentle hand than the strang.

Better to wed ower the midden than ower the moor.
It is better to marry a neighbour than a stranger. This proverb is very old as it is recorded in M. L. Anderson's Proverbs in Scots *as 'Better to wow over middin, nor over mure'. Fergusson likewise record this proverb as 'Better wooe over midding nor over mosse'.*

Better twa skaiths than ae sorrow.
'Losses may be repaired, but sorrow will break the heart' – Kelly.

Better unborn than untaught.
Kelly: 'An hyperbolical expression of our esteem of learning'.

Better unkind than ower cumbersome.

Better wade back mid water than gang forward and droun.
Sometimes it is better to withdraw part way than to proceed with something which is foolhardy.

Better wait on cooks than leeches.
See below.

Better wait on the cook than on the doctor.
Said when someone is getting impatient waiting for their meal.

Better wear shoon than wear sheets.
It is better to be wearing shoes in the first place than end up ill in bed i.e. prevention is the best kind of medicine.

Better well beloved than ill-won gear.

Better you laugh than I greet.
I would rather be ridiculed for not doing a thing than do it and be sorry for it.

Better your feet slip than your tongue.

Between Martinmas and Yule, water's wine in every pool.

Between the deil and the deep sea.
Said when one is caught between two equally dangerous extremes.

Between three and thirteen thraw the woodie when its green.
Train the minds of children when they are young.

Between twa steels feels fa' through.
An Aberdeenshire saying. Kelly gives the saying thus: "Between two stools, arses fall down". Commonly he that depends upon two contrary parties, will be disappointed by both.'

Between you and the lang day be't.
Said to someone who has committed an offence but refuses to own up to it.

Be what ye seem, and seem what ye are.
Be true to yourself.

Bid a man to a roast and stick him wi' the spit.
Said when someone pretends a kindness which in fact hides a less well intentioned act.

Bide amongst the mists and the crows.
A saying expressing the policy of Highlanders when they were in danger, i.e. they lost themselves in their surroundings.

Bide weel, betide weel.
If you wait patiently you will fare well.

Biggin and bairns marrying are arrant wasters.
Building houses and children marrying are expensive undertakings.

Bind the sack ere it be fu'.
Advice not to push one's luck too far.

Birds o' a feather flock thegither.

Birk will burn be it burn drawn,
Sauch will sab if it were simmer sawn.
Birch will burn even if it is soaking, but willow will hiss even if it has been sawn in the summer and allowed to dry for the winter. Basically this means that everything will revert to its natural type.

Birth's gude but breeding's better.

Bite not my bannock.
Do not interfere in my affairs.

Bitin' and scartin' are Scotch folk's wooin'.
First recorded by Fergusson.

Bitter jests poison friendship.

Bitter pills may have blessed effects.

Black arse quoth the pot to the caldron.
'Spoken when others upbraid us with those faults that they are guilty of themselves.'

Black dog, white dog, what shall I ca' thee?
Keek i' the kail pat and glower i' the awmrie.
Said when someone is found helping himself to food out of the cupboard.

Black's my apron, and I'm aye washing it.
Said when somebody who has got a bad name finds it difficult to redeem it.

Black will tak nae ither hue.

Blaw the wind as it likes,
There's beild about Pitmilly dikes.
A local Fife saying suggesting there is shelter in this particular area.

Blaw the wind ne'er sae fast, it will lown at the last.

Blind horse rides hardy to the fecht.

Blind men shouldna judge o' colours.
Advice to stick to what you are good at.

Blue and better blue.
That is, there may be a difference between things of the same kind and persons of the same station (Kelly).

Blue are the hills that are far away.
Distance improves how things appear. In John Buchan's Watcher by the Threshold *(1902), he mentions that this 'is an owercome in the countryside'.*

Blue's beauty, red's a taiken,
Green's grief, and yellow's forsaken.

Bluid's thicker than water.

Boasters and liars are cousins.

Bocht wit maks folk wise.
We learn by the cost of our mistakes.

Bode for a silk gown and ye'll get a sleeve o't.
Set your sights high if you hope to achieve anything.

Bode a robe and wear it
Bode a poke and bear it.
*As you make your bed so you must lie on it. A saying suggesting that we make
our own fortunes in life and cannot blame others for our own situations but must
accept them.*

Bode gude and get it.

Bode weel and hae weel.

Boden gear stinks.
*'The theory of the fox and the grapes; it stinks because we cannot obtain it.' –
Hislop.*

Bonnet aside! How sell you your maut?
A joke upon anyone who is wearing something at a crooked angle.

Bonnie silver is soon spent.
Fergusson (1641).

Bonny birds are aye the warst singers.

Bonny cooks ne'er made gude broth.

Bonny feathers dinna aye mak' bonny birds.
A warning that beauty is only skin deep.

Bonny sport to fare weel, and pay naething for't.
We often enjoy most those things which have cost us nothing.

Boot who better has.
He that has the best bargain, give the boot.

Borrow as I did.
*Kelly – 'A facetious answer to a man who asks his loan before I have done with
it.'*

Borrowing days.
*A proverbial expression for the last three days of the old month of March, i.e. if
the weather is bad on these days it is as if March has borrowed from April.
Superstitious people refused to lend and were not keen to borrow on these days.*

*Apparently when the borrowing days are stormy the rest of the season will be good,
and conversely if they are fine it will be a bad summer. There are many local
Scottish rhymes regarding this period, including:*

> *March borrowed frae Aprile*
> *Three days an' they were ill;*
> *The first of them was wind and weet,*
> *The second of then was snaw and sleet,*
> *The third o' them was sic a freeze,*
> *That the bird's legs stack to the trees.*

Bourdna wi' Bawtie lest he bite ye.

*Bawtie is a dog's name. A warning not to fool around or take liberties with
certain people lest it end in disaster. The saying appears in Montgomerie's
Sonnets as 'Quhom Bawtie byts, he dier that bargain byis.'*

Bourdna wi' my ee nor wi' mine honour.

Don't joke about delicate subjects such as character, etc.

Bowked brides should hae bor'd maidens.

*According to Kelly, 'They who are with child before they are married should be
attended by whores'.*

'Bread and cheese is fair to see,
 But man keep thou thine honestie.' – Said the landlady
'Bread and cheese is gude to eat,
 When folk can get nae ither meat.' – Replied the Guest

*From Kelly's collection of 1721. 'The one implies the excellency of modesty, in the
midst of plenty. The other, the necessity of eating, when a man is hungry.'*

Bread and milk is bairn's meat: I wish them sorrow that loe it.

Bread's house skail'd never.

A full or hospitable house never wants visitors. Recorded by Fergusson.

Break my head and syne draw on my how.

Break the legs o' an ill custom.

Breeding wives are aye beddie.

Breeding wives are aye greening.

They are always wanting something; greedy.

Bridal feasts are soon forgotten.

Brig o' Balgownie, wicht's your wa,
Wi' a wife's ae son and a mear's ae foal,
Doun ye sall fall.

*'wicht' means stout, sturdy. A prophecy that the Brig o' Balgownie over the River
Don in Aberdeen would collapse if it were crossed by a woman's only son, or a
mare's only foal. The poet Lord Byron, who was educated at Aberdeen, quotes the*

prophecy in his Don Juan, substituting the word black for wicht. He further wrote 'I still remember, though perhaps I may misquote, the awful proverb which made me pause to cross it, and yet lean over it with a childish delight, being an only son, at least by my mother's side.'

Bring the head of the soo to the tail of the grice.
Balance your loss with your gain. Used in Scott's Rob Roy.

Broken bread maks hale bairns.

Broken friendship may be souther'd, but ne'er found.

Buchannan's almanack, long foul, long fair.
A suggestion that a long spell of bad weather will be followed by a long spell of good weather.

Burn a candle at both ends, and it will not last long.

Burn whins, a' whins; how whins, nae whins.
If you burn whins they will spread, but if you uproot them with a hoe they will die.

Burning a halfpenny candle seeking for a farthing.
Said when someone is making a false economy.

Burn't bairns dread the fire.

Busy folk are aye meddling.

But beginning yet, as the wife did that rin wud [went mad].
Kelly – 'A woman being mad and raging furiously stopped a little; some said, she has done now; but she answered, I am but beginning yet. It is since an answer to them who ask us if we have done.'

But bonny o't like Bole's gude-mither
Spoken when we think a thing little – Kelly.

Butter and burn trouts are kittle meat for maidens.

Butter is gold in the morning, silver at noon, and lead at night.

Butter's king o' a' creesh.

Butter to butter's nae kitchen.
Like to like provides no relish. Often used by cheeky males when they see women kissing each other.

Buy a thief frae the widdie and he'll help hang ye.
Don't trust wrongdoers. A warning that if you try to help them they will abuse your help and cost you dearly in the end.

Buy friendship wi' presents and it will be bought frae you.

Buy in the market and sell at hame.

Buy what you dinna want, and ye'll sell what ye canna spare.

By chance a cripple may grip a hare.
All things are possible, if unlikely.

By doing naething we learn to dae ill.
The devil will find work for idle hands.

C

Ca' a cow to the ha' and she'll rin to the byre.
People feel more comfortable in familiar surroundings.

Ca' again you're no a ghaist.
A welcoming invitation for a person to call again, i.e. their visits are not unwelcome like those of a ghost.

'Ca' away callant! for the deil a bit o' yon man I like,' as Robin A—
said when coming frae the Dron moss wi' the stolen peats.
Robin A—, a basket-maker of Reston, Berwickshire, on returning home from the moss with a cartload of stolen peats, saw the owner approaching and at once called out to the boy who was driving the cart 'Ca' away callant etc.' This saying is applied jocularly when labourers notice their master entering the field – Henderson.

Ca' canny and flee laigh.

Ca' canny and ye'll break nae graith.
Take care and you won't come a cropper. Literally, drive slowly and you won't overstrain your harness.

Ca' canny, lad, ye're but a new-come cooper.
A warning to those who are new at a profession to take things cautiously, hinting that more experience or information might be needed than is immediately apparent.

Cadgers are aye crackin' o' creels.
i.e. talking shop.

Cadgers are aye cracking o' crook-saddles.
'Crook-saddles' are those used for supporting panniers. Professionals are very apt to talk too much of their profession.

Cadgers hae aye mind o' lade saddles.
Similar to the above two proverbs.

Caff and draff is gude enough for aivers.
Caff and draff are brewers' grains, and are plenty good enough for horses. A suggestion that common food suits unsophisticated people.

Ca'ing names breaks nae banes.

Cake day.
In Fife, the last day of the year is proverbially known as cake day.

Ca' me what ye like but dinna ca' me ower.

Can do is easily carried about wi' ane.
Knowledge accompanies you wherever you are.

Canna has nae craft.
To the person who is unwilling, instruction is useless.

Canny stretch, soon reach.
i.e. luck in leisure.

Cap for cap, and clean cap oot.
i.e. drink fair – Cheviot.

Care will kill a cat, and yet there's nae living without it.

Careless folk are aye cumbersome.

Carena would hae mair.

Carles and aivers win a', carles and aivers spend a'.
'Servants' wages, buying and keeping of horses, and purchasing the utensils, eat up the product of the farm' – Kelly.

Carrick for a man, Kyle for a coo, Cunningham for corn and ale, and Galloway for woo'.
A local saying from the southwest of Scotland.

Carry a lady to Rome, and give her one hatch all is done.
A reflection upon the character of some self-important types, whom if you oblige them in many things and disoblige them in one, will only remember the latter.

Carrying saut to Dysart and puddings to Tranent.
A Scottish version of the English 'Carrying coals to Newcastle', i.e. carrying out a redundant task.

Cast a bane in the deil's teeth.
Make a concession to an oppressor to save yourself from harm.

Cast a cat ower the house and she'll fa' on her feet.
Said of people on whom good luck always seems to shine.

Cast nae snawba's wi' him.
Do not play with or trust him.

Cast not a clout till May be out.
A warning not to get rid of one's winter clothing until the end of May.

Cast not out the foul water, till you bring in the clean.

Cast the cat ower him.
It was believed at one time that a cure for a raging fever was to cast a cat over the patient. The saying is applied to those heard telling such outrageous stories as if they were raving through fever.

Cast the glamour o'er her.
Impose upon her, as the witches did to their victims.

Cast ye ower the house riggin' and ye'll fa' on your feet.
Said of those who enjoy good luck.

Cast yer cloths thegither.
A suggestion to a couple to get married.

Castna out the dowed water till ye get the clean.

Cat after kind.

Cats and carlins sit i' the sun, but fair maidens sit within.
A suggestion that overexposure to the sun is not good for young girls. In olden days, girls were thought to look more attractive if they were pale and interesting.

Cats eat what hussies spare.

Cauld grows the love that kindles ower het.
A warning that strong passions can soon fizzle out.

Cauld kail het again is aye pat tasted.
Something generally does not improve by repetition. Often said when someone starts to tell the same story again.

Cauld kail het again, that I liked never:
Auld love renewed again, that I liked ever.

Cauld parritch are sooner het again than new anes made.
It is easier to repeat something you have done before than to do something original.

Cauld water scalds daws.
Used sarcastically to suggest that touching even cold water would be a shock to the systems of lazy people.

Cauldrife law wark.
A moral essay as opposed to a gospel sermon – Cheviot.

Chalk's no shears.
There is a great difference between merely marking out on the cloth a desired pattern from actually cutting it, i.e. planning to do something is not the same as actually doing it. This proverb is first recorded in Fergusson's collection as 'Calke is na sheares'.

Change o' deils is lightsome.

Change o' maisters, change o' manners.

Changes are lichtsome, and fools like them.
A warning that sometimes the old ways are the best and are changed at one's peril.

Changes o' wark is a lightening o' hearts.
A change in routine relieves the monotony and so revives flagging spirits. A change is as good as a rest. First recorded by Fergusson.

Charge nae mair shot than the piece'll bear.

Charge your friend ere ye hae need o' him.
i.e. so that you will know what to expect from him if you need his help.

Charity begins at hame, but shouldna end there.

Cheatery game will aye kythe.
Wrongdoing will always come to light. Be sure your sins will find you out.

Choose your bird oot o' a clean nest.
Old-fashioned marriage guidance – choose your wife from a respectable family.

Choose your wife on Saturday, not on Sunday.
A suggestion that a man should choose a wife for her good qualities and usefulness which are in evidence in her daily labours, rather than for her appearance and manners in her Sunday best outfit.

Choose yer wife wi' her nightcap on.
A proverb giving a warning similar to that above.

Christiecleek will come to ye.
This has been used as a phrase of terror for centuries in Scotland, particularly by parents trying to frighten unruly children into behaving themselves. In fourteenth-century Scotland, a combination of wars, famine and anarchy forced some Highlanders to turn to cannibalism. One such character was Christie, a gang leader, who according to stories attacked his victims using a large iron hook, or 'cleek', to drag them down. Hence he earned the terryifing nick-name 'Christiecleek'. He is said to have evaded capture and to have eventually prospered as a merchant when times improved.

Clap a carle on the cods, and he'll fart in your loof [hand].
Kelly: 'Shewing the ungrateful temper of mean and unmannerly curs, who often requite a kindness with an ill turn.'

Claw for claw, as Conan said to Satan, and the deil take the shortest nails.
Legend has it that Conan the jester, a Celtic hero, vowed that he would never take a blow without returning it. Having descended to hell he received a blow from the devil, which he instantly returned using the above expression, according to Scott's Waverley. *A proverb used by someone who is resolved to return fire with fire, no matter the strength of his opponent.*

Claw me and I'll claw thee.
Speak well of me/help me and I will speak well of/help you. We are perhaps more familair with the modern version 'You scratch my back and I'll scratch yours'.

Clawing and eating needs but a beginning.

Clean pith and fair play.
'Without a trick or cheat, taken from wrestling' – Kelly.

Clear in the South beguiled the cadger.
Said of people who turn out to be false weather prophets.

Clear in the South drown'd the ploughman.

Clecking time's aye canty time.
From Scott's Guy Mannering. *Hospitality was freely offered in the past to all comers on the occasion of a birth.*

Clipped arse, quoth Bunty.
Spoken when someone pulls us up for an act of which they are guilty themselves.

Clippet sheep will grow again.

Clout upon a hole is gude gentry, clout upon a clout is good yeomanry, but clout upon a clouted clout is downright beggary.
'Facetiously spoken to those who quarrel with a patch about you' – Kelly.

Cocks are aye gude will'd o' horses corn.

Cocks wi' red combs are good traders.
A joke made about people with red hair.

Comb sindle, comb sair.
If something is not cared for regularly it can become a problem. The phrase alludes to uncombed hair becoming entangled.

Come a' to Jock Fool's house and ye'll get bread and cheese.
This saying is spoken sarcastically to those who invite people indiscriminately.

Come back the morn, and ye'll get plack pies for naething.
A plack was a third of a penny.

Come day, go day, God send Sunday.
'Spoken to lazy, unconscionable servants, who only mind to serve out their time and get their wages' – Kelly.

Come it ere, or come it late, in May will come the cow-quake.
Cow-quake is a cattle disease caused by the cold easterly winds in May.

Come not to council unbidden.

'Come to the point,' as the cat said when she let claut at the dog's nose.

Come unca'd, sits unserved.
The uninvited guest is an unwelcome one. A warning to all gate-crashers.

Come up, my dirty cousin.
'A reprimand to mean people when they propose a thing that seems too saucy' – Kelly.

Come when ye're ca'd and ye'll no be chidden.

Come wi' the wind, and gang wi' the water.

Common fame, sindle to blame.

Common saw sindle lies.
Common sayings seldom lie. This would seem to be at variance with another proverb 'Rumour is a common liar'.

Condition makes, condition breaks.
Contracts must be kept to unless both parties agree to break them.

Confess and be hang'd, and syne your servant, smith.

Confess debt and crave days.

Confess'd faut is half amends.

Content is better than riches.
Wealth does not automatically bring happiness with it.

Content is nae bairn o' wealth.
As above, there's more to life than money.

Contented wi' little, and canty wi' mair.

'Contentibus,' quo' Tammy Tamson, 'kiss my wife, and welcome.'
'Spoken facetiously when we comply with a project' – Kelly.

Contentment kitchens wark.
To 'kitchen' is to give flavour to, therefore a contented person finds his/her work more interesting and satisfying.

Cool in the skin you het in.
A warning for someone to calm down.

Corbies and clergy are kittle shot.

Corbies dinna gather without they smell carrion.
There's no smoke without fire, i.e. there has to be a reason for something to happen.

Corbies dinna pike out corbie's een.
Wrongdoers tend not to wrong each other.

Corn him weel, he'll work the better.
Don't abuse those who work for you if you expect them to work hard for you.

Corn's no for styags.
Young people should not have luxuries.

Counsel is nae command.

Counsel will mak a man stick his ain mear.
A phrase spoken when we are over-persuaded to do a thing.

Count again is no forbidden.
Said when we physically check an amount of money we receive.

Count like Jews an' 'gree like brithers.

Count siller after a' your kin.
You cannot trust anyone.

Court to the town, and whore to the window.
Kelly – 'Persuading our daughters to stay within, and not be gadding, and gaping after every new sight: for such practice looked liker a whore than a modest virgin.'

Courtesy is cumbersome to them that kens it na.

Crab without a cause, mease without mends.
A person who is angry without cause will try to appease without making amends.

Crabbit was, and cause hadna.

Crack of wealth Watty.
'A jeering exclamation, when one has gotten something they did not expect, or far'd better than was supposed' – Kelly.

Craft maun hae claes, but truth gaes naked.
The former needs to be disguised whereas the latter is self-evident.

Credit is better than ill won gear.

Credit keeps the crown o' the causey.

Creep before ye gang.

Cripples are aye better planners than workers.

Cripples are aye great doers – break your leg and try.
Spoken to people who are quick to give advice, but slow to give actual help.

'Crookit carlin', quo' the cripple to his wife.
A warning to those who criticise others to look to their own faults first.

Cry a' at ance, that's the way to be served.

Curses mak the tod fat.
Curses and threats in themselves do not make anything happen; action is needed if things are to be resolved.

Custom is a second nature.

Cut a tale with a drink.
Spoken when a man preaches over his drink – Scott's Bride of Lammermoor.

Cut dwells in every town.
According to Kelly 'Cut is a dog's name, and Cut is a publick tax, and few towns want that.'

Cut your coat according to your claith.
Advice to be prudent with your spending.

D

Dae naething in a hurry but catching flees.
See 'Naething to be done etc.'

Daffin' and want o' wit mak' auld wives donnart.
Foolish behaviour in the aged is inconsistent/stupid.

Daffin' does naething.
Playing accomplishes nothing.

Daft clavers.
Foolish talk.

Daft folk dinna bide to be contradicted.

Daft folk's no wise, I trow.
Spoken when people advise what is not sensible, or promise what is not reasonable.

Daily wearing needs yearly beiting.
Constant use brings with it constant renewing, i.e. you cannot expect to wear the same clothes daily without having to renew them once a year.

Dame, deem warily, ye watna wytes yoursel.
Don't be hasty to judge others, when you are not sure who may find fault with yourself. First recorded by Fergusson, as 'Dame deim warilie'.

Dammin' and lavin' is gude sure fishing.
The technique of 'Dammin' and lavin'' is used by poachers as a way of catching fish in small rivulets, first by damming and thereby diverting the course of the stream, and then by laving or throwing out the water so as to get them.

Danger past, God forgotten.
Many people pray when facing adversity but soon forget their religion when the danger has passed.

Darkness waukens the owl.
Mystery brings out the inquisitive.

Daughters and dead fish are kittle keeping wares.
This saying suggests that daughters should be married and dead fish eaten otherwise they will both spoil.

Daughters pay nae debts.

Dawted bairns can bear little.
Spoilt children are easily hurt.

Dawted daughters mak dawly wives.
Daughters who have been doted upon tend to make untidy wives as they are unused to doing any work around the house.

Daylight has mony e'en.

Daylight will peep through a sma' hole.
Hope will always find a way.

Dead men are free men.

Dead men bite not.

Dead men do nae harm.

Deal sma' an' ser' a'.
Prudent advice to someone serving a meal.

Dear bought and far sought is good for ladies.

Dear bought, far sought, and little for the handling.

Dear o' little siller.
An object which is dear at any price.

Death and drink-draining are near neighbours.
Not so much a warning of the dangers of drinking to excess, as an allusion to the wakes or amount of drinking that used to be common after funerals.

Death and marriage make term-day.
Marriage frees a man from his service in Scotland, and death in all countries – Kelly.

Death at ae door and hardship at the other.

Death at ae door and heirship at the other.

Death comes in and speirs nae questions.
Death visits us unannounced and treats everyone alike.

Death defies the doctor.

Death pays a' scores.

Death's gude proof.

Deed shews proof.
The thing done shews how it was done, and what was done with it – Kelly.

Deil a bodle.
Nothing at all.

Deil a cowrie.
Not a farthing will you get.

Deil a fear o' me.
Certainly not.

Deil be in the house that ye're beguiled in.
Said as a compliment meaning that the person thus addressed is considered to be so shrewd that only the Devil in person could deceive them.

Deil be in the pock that ye cam in.
A wish that evil should befall the listener.

Deil made souters sailors, that can neither steer nor row.
'Spoken to them that take a thing in hand that they have no skill of' – Kelly.

Deil mend ye if your leg were broken.
A saying of similar sentiment to the above one.

Deil raise ye, and set ye doun wi' a rattle.

Deil ride to Turin on ye, for a lade o' sclates.

Deil speed them that speir, and ken fu' weel.
To the devil with those people who ask questions to which they already have the answers.

Deil stick pride – my dog died o't.

Deil tak' them wha hae nae shifts; and deil tak' them wha hae ower mony.

Deil's in oor bairns, they will not go to bed when their belly is full.
A rebuke to those who are discontented when they have every reason to be satisfied – Kelly.

Delays are dangerous.

Delays in love are dangerous.
Because either party might change their mind.

Did ye ever fit counts wi' him?
Do not count upon someone's friendship until you have had financial transactions with them.

Diet cures mair than the doctors.

Ding doon Tantallon, an' big a road tae the Bass.

Ding doon the nest and the rooks will flee away.
Destroy a villain's hideout and he'll soon disappear. Unfortunately this proverb was used during the Reformation with regard to the destruction of the collegiate churches, abbeys and cathedrals.

Dinna bow to bawtie, lest he bite.
Familiarity breeds contempt. See also 'Bourdna etc.'

Dinna cast awa' the cog when the cow flings.
Do not give up at the first misfortune – try, try again.

Dinna dry the burn because it wat your feet.
Do not remove a useful thing just because of some minor inconvenience.

Dinna empty your ain mouth to fill ither folk's.

Dinna forecast till ye ken; till ye ken, wait an' see.

Dinna gut your fish till ye get them.
Advice not to live on expectations, as one can never be certain what will happen in the future. Another version of 'Don't count your chickens until they've hatched.'

Dinna lee for want o' news.

Dinna let the multure be ta'en by yer ain mill.
This proverb refers to the old custom by which farmers were thirled (i.e. legally obliged as part of a tenancy agreement) to particular mills. It is a hint to people to look after their own interests.

Dinna lie in yer bed an' lippen tae yer neebor.

Dinna lift me afore I fa'.
Don't find fault with me until you have good cause.

Dinna meddle wi' the deil and the laird's bairns.
In both cases it was known that anyone doing so was sure to come off worst.

Dinna open yer mooth tae fill ither fowks'.
A warning against gossiping.

Dinna scald your mouth wi' ither folk's kail.
Don't poke your nose into other people's business – it will only end up hurting you.

Dinna scald yoursel' wi' yer ane ladle.

Dinna sell yer customers wi' yer gudes.

Dinna sigh for him, but send for him: if he be unhanged he'll come.
A cry against procrastination. Do not just wish for something or speak about it – do it.

Dinna speak o' a raip to a chiel whase faither was hang'd.
Think before you speak, or you may inadvertantly put your foot in it.

Dinna straik against the hair.

Dinna stretch yer airm far'er than yer sleeve'll let ye.

Dinna tak the doo or ye hae the doocot.
Marriage advice – don't get married until you have sorted out the accommodation.

Dinna tell your fae when your foot sleeps.
Don't show any weakness to your opponent. This is sometimes appended by the phrase 'nor your step-mither when thou'rt sore hungry'.

Dinna tie a knot wi' yer tongue that ye canna lowse wi' yer teeth.

Dinna touch him on the sair heal.
A plea for tact and diplomacy. Do not speak to him about a certain subject on which he is known to be sensitive.

Dinna tread on his corns.
As above.

Dirt bodes luck.

Dirt defies the king.

Dirten arse dreads ay.
Kelly – 'When people are sensible that they have done amiss, they are still apprehensive of discovery.'

Dirt pairts gude company.
Said of unwelcome intruders.

Dit your mouth wi' your meat.
Close your mouth with your food. A suggestion that someone stop gossiping.

Do a man a gude turn, and he'll ne'er forgie ye.
Most people do not like feeling indebted to another.

Do as the collier did when he met the deil, hae naething to say to him, if he has naething to say to you.
A warning to speak as little as possible to certain people.

Do as the coo o' Forfar did, tak a stannin' drink.
A cow in Forfar stopped while passing a doorway and drank a tub of ale which had been placed on the doorstep to cool. The owner of the ale tried to sue the owner of the cow for the value of the ale consumed by the beast. However, a local baillie gave the decision in favour of the cow's owner, because he decreed that since the ale had been drunk by the cow while it was standing by the door, it must be considered as a deoch-an-doruis (Stirrup cup) for which no charge could be made, according to the rules of ancient Scottish hospitality.

Do as the lassies do – say 'No', – but tak' it.

Do as the miller's wife o' Newmills did – she took what she had and she never wanted.

Dogs and bairns are aye fain o' fools.
Fools attract the attention of children and animals.

Dogs bark as they are bred.

Dogs will redd swine.
'Redd' is used here to mean put in order.

Dolour pays nae debts.

Donald Din, built his house without a pin.
An Ayrshire saying referring to Dundonald Castle built by Donald Rin. Originally a poor man, Donald Rin found treasure in his kail-yard and acquired great wealth.

Dool and an ill life soon mak an auld wife.
Sorrow and an evil life soon age a woman.

Do on the hill as ye wad do in the ha'.
Be consistent in your actions. Do in public as you would in private.

Doos and dominies leave aye a foul house.

Do't by guess, as the blind man fell'd the dog.

Do the likeliest, and God will do the best.

Do the likeliest an' hope the best.

Double charges rive cannons.
Moderation in all things is the best policy, as excesses can be dangerous.

Double drinks are gude for drouth.
The more you drink, the more you want.

Do weel and doubt nae man, do ill, an' doubt a' men.
Those who do wrong live in fear of others doing wrong to them.

Do weel and dread nae shame.

Do weel and hae weel.

Do what ye ought and come what can; think o' ease but work on.
The first clause is commonly seen, but the second is only found in A. Henderson's collection of 1832.

Do what ye ought and let come what will.

Dowie dowie Dean, ilka seven years gets e'en.
Said of the River Dean in Forfarshire, implying that someone is drowned in it every seven years.

Do your turn weel, and nane will speir what time ye took.
A suggestion that well done work is appreciated rather than the speed at which it is done.

Draff he sought, but drink was his errand.
While asking for one thing, a person may really be after something else.

Draff is gude enough for swine.
A man will be treated according to his conduct.

Dree out the inch, when ye have thol'd the span.
When you have suffered patiently for a long while, don't give up just as the end is in sight.

Driest wood will eithest lowe.

Drink and drouth come na aye thegither.
Things do not always occur when you want them to. First recorded by Fergusson as 'Drink and drouth come sindle together'.

Drink little, that ye may drink lang.
A plea for moderation.

Drive a cow to the ha' an' she'll rin to the byre.

Drive the swine through't.

Drucken joy brings sober sorrow.

Drunk at e'en, and dry in the morning.

Drunk folk seldom tak' harm.

Dry bargains bode ill.
In the past, a deal was considered unlucky unless it was ratified with a drink.

Dummies canna lee.

Dunse dings a'.
'It may be mentioned that this is only the opinion which the people of Dunse entertain of their town' – Robert Chambers. There are several local additions to this saying, such as 'Dunse dings a' for braw lads and drunken wives'; 'for gude yill and bonnie lasses.'

E

Eagles catch nae fleas.
A saying applied to conceited people who affect disdain for small details.

Eagles dinna hunt for bees.

Eagles flee alane, but sheep herd thegither.

Early birds catch the worms.

Early crooks the tree, that good cammock should be.

Early maister, lang knave.
A suggestion that if a young person is given the responsibilities of a master too soon they will not be up to the task and so will end up a servant.

Early pricks that will be a thorn.
Children soon show their inclinations.

Early rising is the first thing that puts a man to the door.
A joke against those who make a virtue of rising early based upon the phrase 'to be put to the door' which also means to be ruined.

Early sow, early mow.

East and wast the sign o' a blast; north and south the sign o' a drouth.
Weather forecasting according to the direction of the prevailing wind.

East or west, hame is best.
Often said after returning from a journey or holiday.

Easy learning the cat the road to the kirn.
It is easier to learn something when your natural inclinations lie along similar lines.

Eat and well come, fast and twice as welcome.

Eaten meat is eith to pay.
First recorded by Fergusson as 'Eaten meat is gude to pay'. However, there is also the following proverb:

Eaten meat is ill to pay.
We do not like having to pay for things already consumed and forgotten.

Eating and drinking tak' awa' a man's stomach.

Eating and drinking wants but ae beginning.

Eating, drinking and cleaning need but a beginning.

Eat in measure and defy the doctor.
For a healthy life – moderation in all things. First recorded by Fergusson in 1641.

Eat peas wi' a Prince and cherries wi' a chapman.

Eats meat, an's never fed; wears claes, an's never cled.
No matter how well some people are provided for, they never appear to look any the better for it.

Eat till ye sweat and work till ye freeze.

Eat-weel's Drink-weel's brither.
Good eating and drinking should go side by side.

Eat your fill, but pouch nane is gardener's law.
The person that is overly greedy might be caught with the evidence.

Edinburgh Castle, town, and tower,
God grant ye sinke for sinne,
And that even for the black dinner
Earl Douglas gat therein.
In the reign of James II, Lord Douglas was invited to a banquet at Edinburgh Castle, and there treacherously put to death in 1440 at the instigation of Chancellor Crichton.

Edinburgh's big, but Biggar's bigger.

E'en as ye won't sae ye may wear't.
As you have won it, so you may wear it. This can be applied either in a good or bad sense.

E'en pickle in your ain poke neuk.

E'ening grey and a morning red,
Put on your hat or ye'll weet your head;
E'ening red an' a morning grey
Is a taiken o' a bonny day.
Red sky in morning, shepherd's warning;
Red sky at night, shepherd's delight.

E'ening orts are gude morning's fodder.
'Orts' are rejected foodstuffs, i.e. a thing which is rejected just now may be acceptable or even desirable at a later date. – Fergusson.

Eident youth maks easy age.
A person will reap the rewards of a hard working youth in later years.

Eild and poortith are a fair burden for ae back.
Old age and poverty are a sore burden for one person to bear.

Eild and poortith's sair to thole.

Eild should hae honour.

Eith keeping the castle that's no beseiged.
It is easy to be in charge when there are no problems to face.

Eith learned, soon forgotten.
What is soon learned is forgotten just as quickly.

Eith to that thy ain heart wills.
See below for a similar proverb.

Eith working when will's at hame.
It is easier to get work done when the heart is willing.

Either live or die wi' honour.

Either prove a man or a mouse.
Either succeed or fail in an undertaking.

Either the tod or the bracken bush.
Spoken to silly people when they speak with uncertainty – Kelly.

Either win the horse or tine the saddle.
All or nothing.

Ell and tell is gude merchandise.
'Ell and tell' refers to good measure and prompt payment.

Ell and tell is ne'er forgotten, and the best pay's on the peck bottom.
Kelly explains the latter part of this proverb thus: 'The grain is emptied from the "peck" measure, the measure is inverted, and payment for the grain is "told" on the bottom of it.'

Empty barrels mak maist din.

Eneuch's as gude as a feast.
To have enough is all one should want.

Enough's enough o' bread and cheese.
Too much of a good thing is not good.

Envy aye shoots at a high mark.

Envy ne'er does a gude turn but when it means an ill ane.

Even a haggis will run downhill.
Spoken when a cowardly action is observed. It does not take a particularly brave soldier to charge downhill.

Even as ye win't, so may you wear't.

Even a young fit finds ease in an auld bauchle.

Even stands his cap the day, for a' that.
This saying is used when we consider that all that we can say against a great person cannot possibly do them any harm. It was reputedly used by a minister in

concluding a sermon in which he had most fervently preached against the
supremacy of the Pope.

Even your heels to your arse, and your arse to the muck midden.
According to Kelly, this is 'A phrase of great contempt and indignation, to them
that say, in anger, that they are as good as us, as if we should say, compare things
that are alike; compare your heels to your breech, and that to the dunghill.'

Ever busy, ever bare.
A simple version of the proverb 'Great cry and little wool' i.e. some things are more
trouble than they are worth.

Every ane loups the dyke where it's laighest.
Everyone does what comes easiest to them.

Every bean has its black.

Every best his bottle.
According to Kelly 'This is only spoken when people are drinking, and propose
that everyman shall have his pint, quart etc.'

Every bird thinks its ain nest best.
i.e. there's no place like home.

Every cheese maun keep its ain chisset.
We must all keep our place.

Every cock craws crousest on his ain midden head.

Every craw thinks his ain bird whitest.
Every parent thinks well of their own children.

Every day is no Yule day – cast the cat a castock.
A castock is a cabbage stalk. Hence the saying is used satirically to suggest one is
being generous by giving something of little value.

Every dog hath his day, and a bitch twa afternoons.

Every dud bids another good day.

Every fault has its fore.

Every flow hath its ebb.

Every house which a man, not a lawyer, builds out of Edinburgh,
enables a man, who is a lawyer, to build one equally comfortable in
Edinburgh.
A comment upon the fees of the Edinburgh lawyers.

Every land has its laigh; every corn has its ain cauff.
This proverb has been given two meanings. In Kelly's Scottish Proverbs
(1721), it is recorded as meaning that 'every country hath its own laws, customs,
and usages'. However Hislop's Proverbs of Scotland *(1862) gives a different*

interpretation, namely 'everything may be found fault with; and silly objections be raised against the most valuable and useful things'.

Every man as he loves let him send to the cook.
Let every man choose according to his liking.

Every man bows to the bush he gets beild frae.
Everyone has to pay their respects to those who protect them.

Every man buckles his belt his ain gate.
Every one works in their own way.

Every man can guide an ill wife weel but him that has her.
It is always easy for those not in a particular situation to comment upon it.

Every man can tout best on his ain horn.
Everyone knows best how to tell their own story.

Every man flamms the fat sow's arse.
Kelly – 'They will be sure to get most gifts that least want them'.

Every man for himself, and God for us a'.

'Every man for himself,' quo Saint Martin.
This is the earliest recorded version of the proverb collected by Fergusson.

Every man for his ain hand, as Henry Wynd said.
Around 1392 two clans fought a battle with thirty a side, in the presence of the King, on the North Inch of Perth. One man went missing and his place was filled by a wee bandy-legged citizen called Henry Wynd (or Gow Chrom as the Highlanders called him). He fought well and greatly contributed to the outcome of the battle without knowing on whose side he had fought.

'Every man for himself,' as John Jelly focht.
This is the version of the above proverb recorded by Kelly in 1721.

Every man has his ain bubbly-jock.
We all have our own problems and crosses to bear. According to popular folk legend, a man described as a simpleton working for a farmer was asked by a visitor if he was happy. He said that he was comfortable, well fed and well provided for, but upset because the turkey-cock didn't like him and would chase him on sight.

Every man has his ain draff poke, though some hang eider than others.
Every person has their own faults, though for some these are more apparent than in others.

Every man is a fool sometimes, and none at all times.

Every man is no born wi' a siller spoon in his mouth.
Not everyone is born with privileges.

Every man kens best where his ain sair lies.

Every man kens best where his ain shoe binds him.

Every man's blin' in his ain cause.
A warning against self-love which can sometimes obscure our view of what is real and true.

Every man's dog will be as full of him as mine.
Kelly – 'Spoken when we are blam'd for riding our horse too hard; as if you would say, I'll get no other use for him, for when he is dead, he will be a common feast for every dog.'

Every man's man had a man, and that gar'd the Treve fa'.
The Treve or Threave, was a very strong castle which belonged to the Black Douglases. The governor of the castle left a deputy in charge, and he in turn a substitute, by whose negligence the castle was taken and burned.

Every man's nose winna be a shoeing horn.
Certain things can only be used for certain purposes.

Every man's tale's gude till anither's tauld.

Every man thinks his ain craw blackest.

'Every man to his ain trade,' quo' the browster to the bishop.

Every man to his taste, as the man said when he kiss'd his cow.

Every man toots his ain horn best.

Every maybe hath a may not be.
There are two sides to everything.

Every miller wad weise the water to his ain mill.
Everyone has their own interests at heart.

Every pea helps to fill the peck.

Every play maun be played, and some maun be the players.

Every shoe fits not every foot.

Every sow to her ain trough.
Every one to their own place, i.e. you should not depend upon others.

Everything has a beginning.

Everything has an end, and a pudding has twa.

Everything has its time, and sae has a rippling-kame.
A 'rippling-kame' is a coarse comb used in the flax industry. The proverb means that there is a proper time for everything.

Everything is the waur o' the wear.

Everything wad fain live.
Kelly – 'Spoken in excuse of man or beast, who make their best endeavour to get a living.'

Every wight has his weird, and we maun a' dee when our day comes.
No person can avoid what is destined to happen to them.

Evil words cut mair than swords.
The pen is sometimes more powerful than the sword.

Experience is good, but often dear bought.

Experience keeps a dear school, but fools will learn in nae ither.

Experience teaches fools.

F

Facts are chiels that winna ding.
Facts cannot be denied. Used by Robert Burns in 'A Dream'.

Faint heart ne'er wan fair lady.

Fair an' foolish, black an' proud, lang an' lazy, little an' loud.
A groundless proverb upon women's different statures and complexions.

Fair and softly gangs far.

Fair exchange is nae robbery.

Fair fa' gude drink, for it gars folk speak as they think.
Good luck to good drink, for it causes people to speak their minds.

Fair fa' the wife, and weel may she spin, that counts aye the lawin'
wi' a pint to come in.
*Good luck to the hostess who includes a pint still to come when it is time to reckon
up.*

Fair fa' you, and that's nae fleaching.
Good wishes meant sincerely.

Fair folk are aye foisonless.
*Kelly says that the word 'foisonless' means 'without strength or sap'. Sir Walter
Scott uses it in* Old Mortality *meaning 'unsubstantial' in the moral sense.*

Fair gae they, fair come they, and aye their heels hindmaist.
*According to Kelly this phrase was originally applied to fairies, but is now applied
to disreputable persons with whom the speaker wishes to have no dealings.*

Fair hair may hae foul roots.
A warning that outward appearances can be deceptive.

Fair hechts mak fools fain.

> *Hope puts that haste into zour heid,*
> *Quhilk boyls zour barmy brain;*
> *Howbeit fulis haste cums huly speid,*
> *Fair hechts will mak fulis fain.*

> *– from 'The Cherrie and the Slae', by Alexander Montgomerie.*

Fair in the cradle may be foul in the saddle.
One cannot always tell from looking at the child how the adult will turn out.

Fair maidens wear nae purses.
*Despite their legendary meanness, this was a phrase commonly used by Scotsmen
at one time, when a woman offered to pay in mixed company.*

Fair words are nae cause o' feuds.

Fair words canna mak' amends for foul actions.

Fair words hurt ne'er a bane, but foul words break mony a ane.

Fair words winna mak the pat boil.
Flattery will not get you anywhere.

Falkirk bairns dee ere they thrive.

Falkirk bairns mind naething but mischief.

Falset never made a fair hinderend.
Falset means deceit.

Fancy flees before the wind.

Fancy was a bonnie dog, but Fortune took the tail frae't.

Fancy may kill or cure.
A testament to the power of the mind.

Fann'd fires and forced love ne'er did weel.
A warning not to force things that do not come naturally.

Fa' on the feeblest, the beetle amang the bairns.
According to Kelly, this proverb is 'spoken when we do a thing at a venture, that may be good for some and bad for another; and let the event fall upon the most unfortunate'.

Far ahint maun follow the master.

Far ahint that mayna follow, an' far before that canna look back.
A warning not to let oneself stray too far from the mainstream.

Far-awa fowls hae fair feathers.
Sometimes the further away something is or the harder it is to get, makes it appear more desirable than it actually is. First recorded in Fergusson's collection as 'Far fowles hes fair feathers'.

Far frae court, far frae care.

Far frae my heart's my husband's mither.
Spoken when a loss is mentioned with which one has little or no concern. First mentioned in Kelly's collection.

Far sought and dear bought is gude for ladies.
The harder it has been to obtain something the more favourably it will be looked upon.

Farewell frost, fair weather neist.

Fare-ye-weel, Meg Dorts, and e'en's ye like.
A jocular goodbye to those who leave in a sulk.

Farmer's fauch gars laird's laugh.
'Fauch' is fallow ground. As part of good crop husbandry, one should let a field lay fallow occasionally – thus pleasing the landlord who can see that the land is being looked after and can still collect the rent even although the tenant will make no money from it.

Farther east, the shorter west.
There are always two ways of looking at any problem.

Farthest frae the kirk aye soonest at it.
This saying is in contradiction to those who are 'near the kirk but far frae grace.'

Fart on this side of the sea, and fart on the other side.
According to Kelly – 'Change of climates doth not always change manners'.

Farts in erse is dirt in Latin.
Kelly – 'A byword expressing contempt and scorn of any person, or thing.'

Fashious fools are easiest flisket.
Troublesome people are most easily offended.

Fast bind, fast find.

Fat flesh freezes soon.

Fat fowls hae fair feathers.

Fat hens are aye ill layers.

Fat housekeepers mak lean executors.
Because they spend everything during their lifetime.

Fat paunches bode lean pows.
Overfull stomachs lead to empty skulls.

Fause folk should hae mony witnesses.
Don't trust a liar unless he pledges himself before many witnesses.

Fausehood maks ne'er a fair hinder-end.
Falsehood is bound to be exposed in the long run.

Favours unused are favours abused.

Fear has lang legs.
Scared people can run quickly.

Feather by feather the goose is plucked.
Said when urging someone to tackle a job a bit at a time. Slow and steady wins the race.

Febrawar will fill the dyke,
Be it black, or be it white.
A weather warning for February.

Fecht awa' wi' the fou' hand and the toom purse.

Feckfu' folk can front the bauldest wind.

Feckless folk are aye fain o' ane anither.
Silly people are always fond of each other.

Feckless fools should keep canny tongues.
Silly people should watch what they say, lest it land them in trouble.

Feed a cauld, but hunger a colic.
Homespun medical advice.

Feeding out o' course mak's mettle out o' kind.
'Good pasture will make a small breed of cattle larger' – Kelly.

Feeling has nae fellow.

Few get what they glaum at.

Fey folk run fast.

Fiddlers, dogs, and flesh-flies come aye to feasts unca'd.
Those who live off others will always turn up uninvited. First recorded in Fergusson.

Fiddler's fare – meat, drink and money.

Fiddlers' wives and gamesters' drink are free to ilka body.
The suggestion is that the fiddler and gamester are both too preoccupied to look after their own things properly.

Fight dog, fight bear; wha wins deil care.

Fill fu' and haud fu', maks a stark man.
Plenty of food and drink makes a strong man.

Findin's keepin'.
Finders keepers.

Fine feathers mak fine birds.

Fine to fine maks a bad line.
Another version of 'Butter to butter's nae kitchen'.

Fine words mak foolish maidens fain.

Fire an' water are gude servants, but ill maisters.

Fire is gude for the fireside.
All things are good when they are in their proper places or put to their proper uses.

First come, first ser'd.

First comes Candlemas, and then the new moon,
The next Tuesday after is Fasten's e'en.

Fish guts and stinkin' herrin',
Are bread and milk for an Eyemouth bairn.
From Henderson's collection.

Fish maun soom thrice.
First in water, second in sauce, and third in wine.

Fleas and a girning wife are waukrife bedfellows.
A man will get little sleep if he shares his bed with fleas or a fretful wife.

Flee as fast as you will, your fortune will be at your tail.
You cannot escape your destiny.

Fleying a bird is no the gate to grip it.
Literally – frightening a bird is not the way to catch it. This saying is often applied to bringing up children, implying that constant threatening will not improve their behaviour.

Fling at the goad was ne'er a gude ox.

Flit an auld tree an' it'll wither.

Flitting o' farms mak' mailins dear.
Another version of 'As ane flits etc.'

Folk are aye free to gie what's no their ain.

Folk aye like them that are opposite to themsel's.
Opposites attract.

Folk maun grow auld, or dee.

Folks' dogs bark waur than themsels.

Folk should ne'er ask for mair than they can mak' a gude use o'.
A warning against being greedy.

Folks sometimes get a gude meal out o' a dirty dish.
Sometimes good can come from a tainted source.

Folks wat not, sometimes, whether to run fast, or go at leisure.

Folk that see your head dinna see a' your heicht.

Folk wha count afore the change-keeper have often to count twice.

Follow love and it will flee thee; flee love and it will follow thee.

Folly is a bonny dog, but a bad ane.
Being foolish can seem attractive, but usually ends in trouble.

Fools and bairns ne'er ken when they are weel aff.

Fools and bairns should ne'er see half done wark.
They may mistakenly judge the finished product by the state of the incomplete project.

Fools are aye fleet and fain.
In a great hurry and in good spirits.

Fools are aye fond o' flittin', and wise men o' sittin'.

Fools are aye fortunate.

Fools are aye seein' ferlies.

Fools are fain o' flattery.

Fools are fain o' naething.

Fools are fond o' a' they foregather wi'.

Fools aye see ither folks' fauts, and forget their ain.
It takes a wise person to know their own faults.

Fools, bairns, and drunken men tell a' that is in their minds.
Usually said as a warning to the latter category.

Fools big houses and wise men buy them.

Fools' haste is nae speed.

Fools laugh at their ain sport.

Fools look to tomorrow, and wise men use tonight.
A warning against procrastination.

Fools mak feasts and wise men eat them.
This was reputedly said to the Duke of Lauderdale by a rude guest. Being a great wit he immediately retorted 'Aye and wise men mak proverbs, and fools repeat them! So beware!' First recorded by Fergusson in 1641.

Fools ravel and wise men redd.
Fools get entangled, or wound up, in situations which it takes wise men to sort out.

Fools set far trysts.

Fools shouldna hae chappin' sticks.

Fools tie knots, an' wise men loose them.
According to Kelly, 'Spoken when people, for want of skill or management, have spoil'd and entangled a business, which will require wisdom to set right again.'

For a hen's gerss
They'll flit i' the Merse.

For as gude again, like Sunday milk.
A respectable countrywoman would not sell her milk on a Sunday, but would give it for as good again. This saying is applied to those whose kindness we suspect to be mercenary in its origins.

For a' that's come and gane yet.

For a tint thing, carena.
Do not waste your time worrying about lost opportunities. – Fergusson.

'For better acquaintance' sake,' as Sir John Ramsay said when he drank to his father.
On returning home after many years abroad, Sir John Ramsay accidentally met his father, who did not know him. He invited him to take a glass of wine with him and drank to better acquaintance.

Forbid a fool a thing, an' that he'll do.
Said when someone acts against good advice.

Force without foresight aften fails.

Forewarned is forearmed.
One who expects a misfortune will prepare against it.

For fashion's sake, as dogs gae to market.

For faut o' wise men fools sit on binks.
Due to the carelessness of those in authority, sometimes fools can end up in positions of power.

Forgotten pains, when follow gains.
We soon forget hardship if it yields pleasant results.

For gude cheese and gude cheer mony haunt the house.
Many people will frequent the house just for what they can get to eat and drink.

For my ain pleasure, as the man thrashed his wife.
Used to be said when someone was doing something purely for their own pleasure.

For puir folk they seldom ring.

For saints' blood, and saints harried,
The third generation will ne'er inherit.
According to Cheviot, this was a Covenanting prophecy made with reference to the persecutors, and which was, in many cases fulfilled.

Forsake not God till you can find a better maister.

Forth bridles the wild Highlandmen.
An old saying dating from the time when the River Forth acted as a line of defence for the Lowlanders against raids from the Highlanders.

For the same reason that the Aberdeen cats never drink cream.
i.e. because they never get the chance to.

Fortune and futurity are no to be guessed at.

Fortune aye favours the active and bauld.
You only get out of life what you are willing to put in.

Fortune favours the brave.

Fortune gains the bride.

Fortune helps the hardy.
This saying is taken from Montgomerie's 'The Cherrie and the Slae':

> *For I haif aft hard suith men say,*
> *And we may see oursells,*
> *That fortune helps the hardy aye,*
> *And pultrones aye repels.*

For want o' a steek a shoe may be tint.
A stitch in time saves nine.

Foster the guest that stays, further him that maun gang.

Foul fa' nought, and then he'll get naething.
Used to make fun of those who expect to inherit a legacy from a highly improbable source.

Foul water will slocken fire.
Even tainted things can be put to good use.

Four an' twenty tailors cannot mak a man.
In this phrase the joke is upon the word make. Although each tailor can show himself to be a man, he cannot make one in cloth!

Four churches together and only one steeple,
Is an emblem quite apt of the thrift of the people.
A witty description of Dundee by Thomas Hood.

Frae Buchaness to Ardnamurchan;
Frae the Mull o' Galloway to John o' Groats.
From one end of the country to the other.

Frae Maiden Kirk to John o' Groats.
Same as above. The Mull of Galloway is in the parish of Kirkmaiden.

> *Hear land o' cakes and brither Scots,*
> *Frae Maiden Kirk to John o' Groats.*
>
> *— Burns*

Frae saving comes having.

Frae the greed o' the Campbells
Frae the ire o' the Drummonds
Frae the pride o' the Grahams
Frae the wind o' the Murrays
Good Lord deliver us!
The Grace said by the eccentric Highland laird Maxtone of Cultoquey.

Frae the teeth forward.
Said of someone who speaks without great conviction, i.e. he speaks from the lips and not from the heart.

Freedom's a fair thing.
Friends frae the teeth outwith.
Friends not to be trusted.

Fresh fish and puir friends soon grow il saur'd.

Fresh fish and unwelcome guests stink before they're three days auld.

Friday flit short time fit.
It was considered unlucky to move house on a Friday.

Friday rules Sunday.

Friends are like fiddle-strings, they maunna be screwed ower ticht.

Friends 'gree best at a distance.

Friends 'gree best sindry.

Friendship canna stand aye on ae side.
We must learn to give as well as take.

Frost and fausehood hae baith a dirty wa' gang.

Frosty winter, misty spring, chequered summer, and sunny autumn, never left death in Scotland.

Fry stanes wi' butter, and the broo will be gude.
Even the most useless things can appear better if much is spent on them. Sometime this phrase was used sarcastically of a plain-looking woman who wore expensive clothes.

Fu' o' courtesy, fu' o' craft.

G

Gae hop and hang yoursel', and then you'll die dancing.

Gae kiss your lucky – she lives in Leith.
According to Allan Ramsay this is 'A cant phrase, from what rise I know not, but it is made use of when one thinks it is not worth while to give a distinct answer, or think themselves foolishly accused.'

Gae shoe the goose.

Gae to bed wi' the lamb and rise wi' the laverock.
Early to bed, early to rise!

Gae to Scotland without siller, and to Ireland without blarney.
Used ironically.

Gae to the deil and he'll bishop you.
Said to somebody who is considered to be so bad that the devil would grant them high office.

Gae to the deil for his name's sake.

Gair-gaithert siller will no haud thegither;
The heir will be careless, his wife maybe waur;
Their weans will be fearless and fa' in the glaur.
Gair means thriftily.

Gane is the goose that laid the muckle egg.

Gang farther and fare waur.
A plea to join one's company. You may travel further and fare worse.

Gape while you get it.
Spoken to those who expect something without good reason.

Gar wood's ill to grow, chuckie stanes are ill to chow.

Gardener's law – Eat your fill, but pouch nane.

Gather haws before the snaws.

Gathering gear is weel liket wark.
Acquiring wealth is pleasant employment.

Gaunting bodes want o' ane o' three things – sleep, meat, or gude companie.
Yawning was traditionally said to be caused by a lack of one of the above three things.

Gaunting gaes frae man to man.
Yawning is infectious.

Gawsie cow, gudely calf.
Handsome mother, goodly daughter.

Gaylie is sing walloway's brither.
'Spoken when we ask how a thing is done, and are answered "gaily", that is, indifferently, as if indifferent were next to bad' – Kelly.

Gaylie would be better.
Said when a person is not feeling well, i.e. gaylie or 'pretty well' would be better than they presently feel.

Gear is easier gain'd than guided.
It is easy to get something but more difficult to then look after it.

Geese tae the sea, guid weather tae be;
Geese tae the hull, guid weather tae spill.
A popular weather rhyme from Angus.

Gee ways, as Geily pish'd.
'Gee' means toward one side and 'Geily' is a woman's name. Kelly gives the meaning as 'A senseless bauble when a thing is crooked, or looks awry.'

Gentle deid maks gentle bleid.

Gentlemen are unco scant when a wabster gets a leddy.
Another proverbial slight against the weaving fraternity, suggesting that there must be few men around when one actually attracts a woman.

Gentle partans hae lang taes.

Gentle servants are poor men's hardships.

Gentle servants are rich men's tinsel.

Gentry's dowff wi' an empty purse.

Gentry sent to the market will not buy a peck of meal.
'Spoken when a bare gentlewoman is proferred in marriage to the son of a wealthy yeoman' – Kelly.

Get and save and thou wilt have.

> *Get and saif and thou salt haif,*
> *Len and grant and thou salt want;*
> *Wha in his plenty taks not heid,*
> *He sall haif falt in tyme of neid.*
>
> — *Ramsay's 'The Evergreen'.*

Get the word o' soon rising an' ye may lie in bed a' day.
Obtain a good reputation and you can get away with misbehaving without people suspecting you.

Get weel, keep weel.

Get what you can, and keep what you hae, that's the way to get rich.

Get your rock and spindle ready, God will send the tow.
You can only do your duty, the rest is up to God.

Gibbie's grace – deil claw the clungiest.
Devil take the hungriest.

Gie a bairn his will, and a whelp its fill, and nane o' them will e'er do weel.
Giving in to the demands of children will only spoil them.

Gie a beggar a bed, and he'll pay you wi' a louse.
It is pointless trying to help some people.

Gie a carl your finger and he'll tak your hail hand.

Gie a dog a bad name an' ye may hang him.

Gie a gaun man a drink, and a rising man a knock.
The former is leaving the gathering, the latter is getting up to make a disturbance.

Gie a greedy dog a muckle bane.
Said when we give someone something which is large but rather coarse.

Gie a man luck, and cast him in the sea.

Gie a strong thief a stark name.
According to Kelly, this phrase was used as a ridicule upon the hard names doctors gave their remedies.

Gie a thing, tak a thing, Auld man's gowd ring;
Lie but, lie ben, Lie amang the dead men.
Said in reproach to those who ask for a gift to be returned. Sometimes also recorded as below:

Gie a thing, tak a thing, and that's the ill man's ring.

'Gie her her will, or she'll burst,' quo' the man when his wife kamed his head wi' the three-legged stool.

Gie him a hole and he'll find a pin.
Give the person a chance or opportunity and he will take advantage of it.

Gie him an inch, and he'll tak' an ell.
Said of someone who takes advantage of others.

Gie him tow enough and he'll hang himsel'.

Gie is a gude fellow, but he soon wearies.
One becomes tired of always giving.

Gie losin' gamesters leave to talk.
Allow those who have suffered wrongs and losses a chance to express their resentments.

Gie my cousin kale enow and see my cousin's dish be fou'.
His room is better than his company — Kelly.

Gie ne'er the wolf the wedder to keep.
Do not put temptation in front of those who might do wrong.

Gie ower when the play's gude.
Quit when you are ahead.

Gie't about, it will come to my faither at last.
According to Kelly, a young fellow sitting in company received a blow from his father, which he passed on to his neighbour along with the above expression.

Gie the deil his due and ye'll gang to him.

Gie the Lord's leather to the Lord's weather.
Do not wear gloves, but use your bare hands instead.

Gie ye a use and ye'll ca't a custom.
Said to those who take advantage.

Gie ye meat, drink, and claes, and ye'll beg among your friends.
Said to unreasonable people who get everything and are still not satisfied.

Gie yer tongue mair holidays than your heid.
Think before you speak.

Gie your heart to God, and your alms to the poor.
This proverbial saying first appears in Andrew Henderson's collection.

Gif we did as we sould we mycht haif as we wald.
If we did as we should, we might have as we would. This inscription is taken from a building opposite St Peter's pend in Edinburgh's Cowgate.

Giff gaff maks gude friends.
Give and take between people helps to build a good relationship.

Gin a' stories be true, that ane's nae lie.

Gin ye dinna see the bottom, dinna wade.

Gin ye hadna been amang the craws ye wadna hae been shot.
Those who associate with folk who are up to no good must expect to land in trouble.

Gin ye hae pain tae yer pech ye're sair made.

Girn when ye bind, and laugh when ye lowse.
Be firm when necessary and relaxed when it is not. Kelly says this idea is taken from the binding of sacks. If you are careful to begin with you will be able to laugh later on.

Glasgow for bells, Lithgow for wells, an' Falkirk for beans an' peas.

Glasgow people, Greenock folk, and Paisley bodies.

Glasses and lasses are brittle ware.
Both can be fragile to handle.

Gleds and corbies will ne'er pair.
Kites and ravens will never pair.

Glib i' the tongue is aye glaiket at the heart.
Don't trust those who are silver-tongued, as it betrays a deceitful heart.

Glowering in the lum ne'er filled the pot.

Glowering is nae gainsaying.

Glum folk's no easily guided.
It is difficult to manage morose people.

Gluttony gaes haund-in-haund wi' drunkenness.

God be wi' the gude laird o' Balmaghie, for he ne'er took mair frae a poor man than a' that he had.
The good laird was obviously not noted for his generosity.

God comes wi' leaden feet, but strikes wi' iron hands.

God doth not measure men by inches.
A person's worth is not measured by their height.

God forgie ye for gallopin', when trottin's nae a sin.

God gies, and the deil misgies.

God helps them that helps themsels.

God help them that gets them with one, and brings them up with anither.
Spoken about those who have motherless orphans brought up by a stepmother.

God help the poor for the rich can help themsels.

God help the rich for the poor can beg.

God help you to a hutch, for ye'll never get a mailing.
Said to someone considered to be incompetent: that they may be able to scratch a small living, but their lack of abilities will never secure them a fortune.

God keep ill gear out o' my hands; for if my hands ance get it, my heart winna part wi't, – sae prayed the gude Earl of Eglinton.
A prayer not to be led into temptation.

God keep me from the man that has but one thing to mind.

God keep my tongue for my tale was ne'er sicker.
You could say something but consider it more sensible to hold your tongue.

God keep the cat out o' our gate, for the hens canna flee.
A plea to be spared danger, because the speaker cannot defend himself.

God ne'er sent the mouth, but he sent the meat wi't.
A plea to trust in God to provide what is necessary in life.

God sain your eye man.
According to Kelly, this phrase was 'Spoken when you commend a thing without blessing it, which my countrymen cannot endure, thinking that thereby you will give it the blink of an ill eye: a senseless, but common conceit. If the person commending be an unworthy or inferior fellow, they will say, "Dee'l be in your een, and a pickle salt togither".'

God's aye kind to fu' folks and bairns.
A comment on how the flexibility of a drunk's limbs helps them to avoid injury.

God sends fools fortunes.

God sends meat and the deil sends cooks.

God sends men claith as they have cauld.
Originally recorded in Fergusson's collection of 1641.

'God send us siller, for they're little thought o' that want it,' quoth the Earl of Eglinton at his prayers.

God send us something of our ain when ither folk gae to their meat.
Spoken when we feel disappointed in something we have borrowed.

God send water in that well that people think will ne'er go dry.
Used when people are always asking for our help, as if we never get tired.

God send ye mair sense and me mair siller.

God send ye readier meat than running hares.
Spoken to people who harbour improbable expectations.

God send ye the warld you bode, and that's neither scant nor want.

God shapes the back for the burden.
Spoken when people predict ill things to us.

God's help is nearer than the fair e'en.

God's will be done; but dee'l bedrite the speeman.

Gold's gude, but it may be dear bought.

Go to Hecklebirnie.
A phrase used in reply when someone says to you 'Go to the devil'. Hecklebirnie is said to be a place three miles beyond hell.

Go thy way, lad, and gie thy wife naething.

Grace gangs no by generation.
Good manners have to be learned.

Graceless meat maks folk fat.

Grass grows nae green in the common road.

Gratitude is a heavy burden.

Gratitude preserves auld friendships and begets new.

Great barkers are nae biters.
Don't be frightened of those who make a lot of noise about things – their bark is worse than their bite, i.e. their actions are not as drastic as their words.

Great bodies move slowly.

Great gains maks wark easy.

Great pains and little gains soon mak a man weary.

Great tochers makna aye the greatest testaments.

Great winning maks wark easy.
Work seems easier when it brings successful results.

Gree like tykes and swine.

Greed is envy's auldest brither: scraggy wark they mak thegither.

Greedy folk hae lang arms.

Greening wives are aye greedy.

Grey-eyed, greedy; brown-eyed, needy; black-eyed ne'er blin' till it shame a' its kin.

Gude advice is ne'er out o' season.

Gude ale needs nae wisp.
In days gone by, a wisp of straw was stuck on the roof of a country house to show that ale was sold there. But if the ale was good, no such advertising was necessary as word of mouth would guarantee a full house.

Gude bairns are eith to lear.

Gude bairns get broken brows.
A warning that good children are just as liable to physical injury as bad ones.

Gude be wi' auld langsyne, when our gutchers ate the trenchers.

Gude breeding an' siller mak our sons gentlemen.

Gude cheer and cheap gars mony haunt the house.
A hospitable house will never want for visitors.

Gude claes open a' doors.

Gude counsel is abune a price.
Good advice is priceless.

Gude counsel ne'er comes too late.
It is never too late to follow good advice.

Gude Enough has got a wife, and Far Better wants.
Those who are too choosy might end up with nothing.

Gude folk are scarce – Tak' care o' me.

Gude folks are scarce, you'll take care of one.
This saying is spoken to those who carefully protect themselves against bad weather, or who cowardly shun any dangers or problems.

Gude foresight furthers the work.

Gude gear gangs into little bouk.
Good things come in small packages.

Gude gear's no to be gaped at.

Gude health is better than wealth.
If you haven't got the former, the latter is useless.

Gude kail is hauf meat.

Gude memories have ill judgements.
Said to those who mention something from the past at an unsuitable time or before inappropriate company.

Gudeness ne'er grows cauld.

Gude news are welcome to some folk if they cam' frae the deil himsel'.

Gude night, and joy be wi' you a'.

Gude reason and part cause.
Signifying that a person has both good reason and cause to complain.

Gude to begin well, better to end well.

Gude to be merry and wise.
Spoken when people's mirth borders upon folly.

Gude to fetch sorrow to a sick wife.
Spoken to those who stay long, when sent on an errand.

Gude to fish in muddy waters.
According to Kelly, 'A cursed saying, of them who expect to find their private interests in the public disturbance'.

Gude wares hae often come frae an ill market.

Gude wares mak a quick market.
Quality items will always be in demand.

Gude watch hinders harm.
Better safe than sorry.

Gudewill ne'er wants time to show itsel'.

Gudewill should aye be ta'en in part payment.

Gude wit jumps.

Gude words cost naething.
It costs nothing to be civil/polite.

Gude! Ye're common to kiss your kimmer.

Guessed wark's best if weel done.

'Gulp!' quo' the wife when she swallowed her tongue.

Gunpowder is hasty eldin.
You don't need to use a sledgehammer to crack a nut.

Gust your gab wi' that.

Gut nae fish till ye get them.
Another version of 'Don't count your chickens until they've hatched'.

H

Ha' binks are sliddery.
Literally this means that the benches in the entrance hall of a grand house are slippery, i.e. the favour of one's superiors is always uncertain, so don't get above yourself. This proverb appears in Robert Henryson's fifteenth-century moral fable 'The Taill of the Wolf and the Wedder' as 'Hall binks ar richt slidder'.

'Ha' ds' a'' quoth the herd's wife, 'kiss me first, for I am farrest frae hame.'
A silly saying meaning only that we are all content.

Had heather bells been corn o' the best,
Buccleuch had had a noble grist.
Refers to the wide extent and one-time unproductiveness of the Buccleuch estates.

Had I as muckle black spice, as he thinks himself worth of mice dirt, I would be the richest man of my kin.
Spoken satirically of proud people who we think hold too high an opinion of themselves.

Had I fish was ne'er gude to eat mustard.
'An answer to them that say, had I such a thing, I would do so or so' – Kelly.

Had it come in your arse, you would have gone to the midden wi't.
According to Kelly this proverb was 'Spoken in anger to them, who, being ask'd why they did or said such a thing, say, it came in my head.'

'Had I wist,' quo' the fool *or* beware of had I wist.
According to Hislop this phrase is 'Spoken when people say, Had I wist what would have been the consequence of such an action, I had not done it.'

Had you been in the midden you would not have seen that.
Spoken with resentment when people claim to have seen such a thing that was indecent.

Had you sic a shoe on ilka foot, it would gar you shackle.
If you had my troubles to bear you too would look miserable.

Hae a care o' the cattle.
An ironical warning to beware a feigned danger.

Hae, gars a deaf man hear.
Some people are only deaf when it is convenient.

Hae God, hae a'.

Hae is half fu'.

Hae lad, rin lad; that maks a willing lad.
Hislop says 'Give ready money for your service, and you will be sure to be well served.'

Hae you gear, or hae you nane, tine heart and a' is gone.
Without heart, everything is pointless.

Hain at the breard.
Literally, protect at the sprouting stage, i.e. look after your investment.

Hain'd gear helps weel.
Savings are of great assistance.

Hair and horn grows weel upon shargars.

Hair by hair maks the carl's head bare.
Little by little one can bring about complete destruction.

Hale claith's afore cloutit.

Hale sale is gude sale.
It is a good sale if we can get rid of everything in one lot. This phrase is often used humorously when someone takes all that is before them.

Half a tale is eneuch for a wise man.

Half acres bear aye gude corn.
Those who have least often make the most of it.

Half done, as Elgin was burned.
During the wars of the fifteenth century between the Douglasses and the Royal authority, Lord Huntly burned down that part of Elgin which belonged to the Douglasses.

Halloween bairns see far.
A superstition that those born at Halloween have special powers.

Hame's a hamely word.

Hame's aye kindlier than a strange place.

'Hame's hamely,' quo' the deil when he fand himsel in the Court o' Session.
The Court of Session is the supreme civil tribunal in Scotland which was established in 1532. In his introduction to Henderson's Scottish Proverbs *the poet William Motherwell said of this saying 'Nothing more bitter was ever uttered . . . against our Supreme Court of Judicature'. No comment!*

Hand in gear helps weel.

Hand-in-use is father o' lear.
Practical experience is the best way of learning something.

Handle the pudding while it is hot.
Strike while the iron is hot, i.e. sieze the opportunity.

Handle your tools without mittens.

Hand ower head, as men took the covenant.
This saying alludes to the manner in which the covenant was violently taken by over 60,000 people in Edinburgh in 1638.

Hands aff is fair play.

Handsome is that handsome does.

Hang a thief when he's young, and he'll no steal when he's auld.
According to Cheviot's Proverbs of Scotland *(1896) this was a favourite saying of Robert MacQueen (1722–99), Lord Chief Justice Braxfield, who invariably acted upon its teaching.*

Hang him that has nae shift, and hang him that has ower mony.

Hang hunger and droun drouth.

Hanging gaes by hap.

Hanging's nae better than it's ca'd.

Hanging's sair on the e'esicht.

Hankering an' hinging-on is a poor trade.
Relying upon the benevolence of others is a poor way to make one's living.

Hap an' a ha'penny is world's gear enough.
Happiness and modest means are all that one needs in this life.

Happy for the son when the dad goes to the deil.
This arises because the son will probably inherit a great estate which his father has committed bad deeds to gain in the first place.

Happy is the bride that the sun shines on; happy is the corpse that the rain rains on.

Happy is the wooing that's no lang o' doing.

Happy man be his dool.
A good wish – that happiness be the greatest affliction sent him.

Happy man, happy kavel.
A kavel or kevel is a lot. The phrase is spoken when one is drawing lots and it turns out well.

Happy's the maid that's married to a mitherless son.
An old fashioned jibe at mothers-in-law.

Happy the man that belongs to nae party, but sits in his ain house, and looks at Benarty.
Spoken by Sir Michael Malcolm of Lochore on hearing talk of the French Revolution.

Hard fare maks hungry bellies.

Hardships seldom come single.

Hareship in the Highlands, the hens in the corn,
If the cocks go in, it will never be shorn.
According to Kelly this is an ironical outcry made upon sustaining a small loss. Hareship or her'ship was plundering by armed force.

Haste and anger hinder gude counsel.

Haste maks waste, and waste maks want, and want maks strife between the gudeman and the gudewife.

Hasty meet, hasty part.
'An observation upon marriage suddenly contracted, as if it were ominous, and portended a sudden separation' – Kelly.

Hasty was hanged, but speed-o'-foot wan awa'.

Haud Taggie by the tail.
'Taggie' means a cow with a white tipped tail. A warning to look after what you have in your hand as it is worth more than what you might dream of having.

Haud the hank in your ain hand.
Do the difficult part yourself.

Haud yer feet Lucky Dad, auld folk's no scery.
Literally look to your feet, as you are not nimble. Spoken when someone stumbles.

Haud yer hand, your faither slew a whaup.
A taunt to someone who makes empty threats.

Haud yer hands aff ither folks bairns till ye get some o' yer ain.
Don't criticise until you have experienced the thing for yourself.

Hawks winna pike oot hawks' een.
Wrongdoers generally do not wrong each other.

Heard you the crack that gave.
Spoken when we hear a lie.

Hearken to the hinder end, aften comes not yet; and Hereafter comes not yet.
Said when we suspect that a certain action will produce an ill consequence.

Hearts may gree tho' heads may differ.

He ate the cow an' worried on the tail.

He aye keeps the coble heid doun the stream.
'Coble' means a small flat bottomed rowing boat. Said of someone who follows the tide.

He begs frae them that borrowed frae him.
A warning not to start lending things to others.

He bides as fast as a cat does to a saucer.
A saying applied to mercenary characters – that they will stay as long as there is something for them.

He blaws in his lug fu' brawly.
To 'blaw the lug' is to praise a person in an extravagant manner.

He blushes at it like a beggar at a bawbee.

He breeds o' the gowk that casts a' doun at e'en.

He brings a staff to break his ain head.
i.e. a rod for his own back. He brings his own trouble upon himself.

He cam' awa' as wise as he went.
He learned nothing from the experience.

He can do ill, and he may do gude.

He can draw a sneck weel.
He can take advantage. A sneck drawer is a bolt drawer or a sly fellow.

He can haud the cat and play wi' the kitten.
Spoken of those who can hold their own with their peers but also have fun with those holding lesser positions.

He can hide his meat and seek mair.

He can ill rin that canna gang.

He can lee as weel as a dog can lick a dish.
He is an accomplished liar.

He canna get brose without butter.

He canna haud a candle to him.
He cannot be compared to another.

He canna haud meal in his mouth and blaw.
Said when someone claims to be able to do two contradictory things at once.

He canna mak saut to his parritch.
He can't even earn the smallest amount to sustain himself.

He canna see an inch afore his nose.
He lacks foresight and general awareness.

He canna tell his bluid frae his banes.
Said when someone has received a thorough thrashing/beating.

He canna tell nicht frae day.
Cheviot calls this 'the acme of stupidity'.

He can say 'My Jo', and think it no.
He can be complimentary in his speech but not in his intentions.

He can wile the flounders oot o' the sea.
He is a possessor of great charm. A phrase used by Sir Walter Scott in Heart of Midlothian.

He caresna wha's bairns greet if his laugh.
He is only interested in himself and his own kin.

He ca's me scabbed because I winna ca' him sca'd.
A person has tried to make his opponent lose his temper but, in failing to do so, has ended up losing his own.

'Hech!' quo' Howie, when he swallowed his wife's clue.
A 'clue' is a ball of worsted.

He comes oftener wi' the rake than the shool.
Again, said of a mercenary type, who comes to take more often than to give.

He comes o' the gude, he canna do ill.

He complains early that complains o' his parritch.

He could eat me wi' out saut.

He couldna bite his thoom.
He was very drunk.

He counts his ha'penny gude siller.
A man may give a small gratuity but have an exaggerated idea of his own generosity.

He cuts awfu' near the wood.
To 'cut near the wood' is to drive a hard bargain.

He daurna say 'Bo' to yer blanket.
He is a very timid person.

He died o' ower muckle care, like Lucky Christie's chickens.

He does as the blind man does when he casts his staff.
He is helpless and can do nothing.

He doesna aye ride when he saddles his horse.
He does not always carry through everything that he starts.

He doesna ken a B frae a bull's foot.
He is exceptionally ignorant on the matter.

He doesna ken what end o' him's upmost.
He is in a state of utter confusion.

He doesna ken when the clatter comes frae him.
'He is a talkative fool' – Cheviot.

He doesna like his wark that says 'Now' when it's done.

He doesna need to scart a neebor's parritch pat.
Said of someone who is already well off.

He doubles his gift that gies in time.

He draws in his horns like a snail at a bairn's finger.

He drives a gude waggon-load into his farm that gets a gude wife.

He eats his kail in a riven dish.
Spoken of them who are lightly regarded – Kelly.

He eats the calf i' the cow's wame.
Said of someone who lives off their expectations.

Heedna 'says' or ye'll ne'er sit at ease.

He fell in the midden glowerin' at the mune.

He fells twa dogs wi' ae bane.
He succeeds in meeting two objectives with a single act.

He flings the helve after the hatchet.

He found himsel' in five-bladed clover.
He found himself in comfortable surroundings.

He fyles his neebor's cog to get the brose himsel'.
Spoken when someone is mean enough to injure the character of a neighbour/friend just to secure an advantage for himself.

He gaed oot for woo', but cam hame shorn.

He gangs awa' in an ill time that never comes back again.

He gangs awa' wi' borne heid.
Literally, he carries his head high, i.e. he is proud.

He gangs early to beg ['steal' in some versions] that canna say nae.
A warning to the greedy that they will end up in unfortunate circumstances.

He gangs far about seeking the nearest.
Spoken of one who makes false economies.

He gangs frae the jilt to the gellock.
To 'jilt' is to throw or dash water upon a person and a gellock or gavelock is an iron bar. Hislop suggests that it possibly means that a man's temper is such that he passes from the extremes of playfulness to that of passion very quickly.

He gangs lang barefoot that waits for dead men's shoon.
Spoken as a warning to those who expect to inherit on the death of another.

He gars a'body dance after his fiddle.

He gars a deaf man hear.

He gars his ain wand ding him.
He makes a rod for his own back, i.e. he brings his own troubles upon himself.

He gave no green barley for't.

He gies nae whitings without banes.
He gives away nothing without there being a condition attached.

He girns like a sheep's heid in a pair o' tangs.

He gives no other milk.
According to Kelly this saying was used to refer to a horse you are said to have overworked. His work is all you can get from him.

He glacket my mittens.
He gratified me, or gave me money.

He glowers like a duck hearkenin' to thunner.

He got his mother's malison the day he was married.
Said of a man who has a bad wife.

He got the knight's bone aff her.
'Intimating that he debauch'd her before she was married' – Kelly.

He grudges ilka drap o' water that gaes by his ain mill.
Spoken of a mean/miserly person.

He had gude skill o' horse flesh wha bought a goose to ride on.

He had nae help but in his ten fingers.
He did everything with his own two hands.

He hangs his fiddle up at his ain door check.
Spoken of someone who has much to say when in company, but who is very quiet at home.

He harps aye on ae string.
He always gives the same message.

He has a bee in his bonnet-lug.
Said of somebody who has a particular preoccupation of their own.

He has a cauld coal to blaw at.
Spoken of someone who has a lowly position with poor prospects. The phrase appears in both Sir Walter Scott's Old Mortality *and Galt's* Sir Andrew Wylie.

He has a crap for a' corn.

He has a gude judgement that doesna lippen to his ain.

He has a hearty hand for gieing a hungry meltith.
He is very charitable.

He has a' his ain back teeth.
He is no fool.

He has a hole beneath his nose that winna let his back be rough.
He is so fond of his food that he does not have the money left to make his back 'rough', or well clothed.

He has a lang clue to wind.
He will be busy for sometime yet.

He's an ee in his neck.
Spoken of cautious/wary people.

He has an ill look among lambs.

He has an ill-scrapit tongue.
He has a foul mouth.

He has a saw for a' sairs.

He has a sliddery grip that has an eel by the tail.
Used when speaking about those who deal with cunning fellows.

He has a steady fit wha ne'er maks a slip.
He must have firm principles if he never goes wrong.

He has a' the ill laits that ever followed swine.
Spoken of someone who is lazy, greedy, dirty, obstinate and mischevious.

He has been rowed in his mither's sark tail.
The Scots equivalent of saying that a man is tied to his mother's apron strings.

He has broken his face on the aumrie.
According to Kelly this phrase was used to describe bluff and fat-cheeked boys.

He has brought his pack to a braw market.
He has made the most advantage of his resources.

He has brought his pack to the preens.
He has squandered his resources.

He has come to gude by misguiding.

He has coosten his cloak on the ither shouther.
He has changed his opinion/ways.

He has coup'd the muckle pat into the little.
Said sarcastically of those who claim to have achieved the impossible.

He has drouned the miller.
Meaning that in mixing liquids, as in making a toddy, too much water has been added.

He has faut o' a wife that marries mam's pet.

He has feathered his ain nest; he may flee when he likes.

He has gane ower the tow.
He has gone wrong. Taken from a farming phrase for a horse getting its legs over the traces.

He has gane without taking his leave.
He has left abruptly.

He has gi'en up a trade and ta'en to stravaigin'.
To stravaig is to walk about idly. This saying is said in fun of those who have retired from business to live comfortably.

He has got a bite o' his ain bridle.
He is suffering for his own misconduct. He has got a taste of his own medicine.

He has got a wing o' Wauchope's moorhen.
He is in a peevish or querulous humour, i.e. in a bad mood. Taken from The Hunt of Eildon *by the Ettrick Shepherd.*

He has gotten his heid under his belt.
He has got him in his power.

He has gotten his kail through the reek.
To meet with severe reprehension.

He has gotten the boot and the better beast.
Said when someone has got an advantage out of an exchange.

He has gotten the whip hand o' him.

He has got the heavy end of him.
In an argument he has the better of his opponent.

He has help'd me out o' a deadlift.
He has helped me in an emergency.

He has his nose in every man's turd.
He pokes his nose into everyone's business.

He has hit the nail on the head.
He has got to the heart of the matter.

He has it o' kind, he cost it not.
Meaning that a person's bad qualities are inherited.

He has lain on his wrang side.

He has left the key in the cat-hole.
He has run off.

He has licket the butter aff my bread.
He has taken away my business.

He has made a moonlight flitting.
He has moved house in the middle of the night to avoid paying any rent owed.

He has mair floor than he has flail for.
Literally he has more work than he can complete. Said when someone has bitten off more than they can chew.

He has mair jaw than judgement.

He has mair wit in his wee finger than you hae in your hale bouk.

He has muckle prayer but little devotion.

He hasna a bauchle to swear by.
He is penniless. (A bauchle is an old shoe.)

He hasna a hale nail to claw him wi'.

He hasna a penny to buy his dog a loaf.

He hasna as muckle sense as a coo could haud in her faulded nieve.
The person thus spoken of is completely lacking in sense. Hogg uses another version in Katie Cheyne *– 'He hasna as muckle sense as a hen could haud in her steekit nieve.'*

He has nae clag till his tail.
A vulgar phrase signifying that there is no stain on one's character.

He has nae haud in his hand.
A saying applied to sprendthrifts.

He has nae mair sense than a miller's horse.

He has naething to crave at my hand.

He hasna the pith to pu' the heid aff a rotten herrin'.
He is somewhat lacking in strength.

He hasna the right grip o' his hand.
Spoken of those who let money fall through their fingers, i.e. he cannot keep money.

He has need o' a clean pow that ca's his neighbour nitty-now.
Do not criticise others unless you are perfect yourself.

He has neither stock nor brock.
i.e. neither money nor meat.

He has one face to God, and anither to the deil.
He is two faced, and not to be trusted.

He has other tow to tease *or* on his distaff.
A saying applied to a man who is suspected of two-timing his girlfriend, i.e. he has other work to do.

He has ower mony greedy gleds o' his ain.
A man has too many family claims upon his resources to enable him to help any strangers.

He has risen aff his wrang side.
He is in a bad mood.

He has skill o' roasted woo' – when it stinks it's ready.
Spoken of those who pretend to have a skill they do not possess.

He has some sma' wit, but a fool has the guiding o't.
A derogatory remark said about someone whose intelligence we hold in low regard.

He has soon done that never dought.
Said of people who are weak.

He has spur metal in him.

He has swallowed a flee.
Spoken of those who drink too much, as if they are trying to drown a fly which is caught in their throat.

He has ta'en the country on his back.
He has run away.

He has the best end o' the string.
He has the upper hand, or the better end of a bargain.

He has the gift o' the gab.
He is a ready speaker.

He hastit to his end like a moth to a candle.
Spoken about somebody who hurriedly approaches danger without a thought for their own safety.

He has wit at will that wi' an angry heart can sit still.
It takes an intelligent person to suppress their anger at times.

He hauds baith heft and blade.
He has a thing entirely at his own option.

He hearsna at that ear.
He turns a deaf ear to certain subjects.

He hears wi' his heels, as the geese do in hairst.

He hid a bodle and thought it a hoard.

He hides his meat and seeks for mair.
'Spoken when covetous people pretend poverty, and conceal their wealth to plead pity' – Kelly.

He is not a merchant bare, that hath either money, worth or ware.

He jumped at it, like a cock at a grosset.
He seized the opportunity without a moment's hesitation.

He keeps his road weel enough wha gets rid o' ill company.
A warning not to be influenced by bad company if you wish to stay out of trouble.

He kens a'thing that opens and steeks.

He kens his ain groats amang other folk's kail.
Said of someone who is acutely aware of his own interests.

He kens how mony beans mak five.
He kens how to butter a whiting.
Both of these phrases are applied to shrewd calculating people who know exactly what's what.

He kens how to turn his ain cake.
He knows how best to look after his own interests. Scott uses this phrase in The Bride of Lammermoor.

He kens muckle wha kens when to speak, but far mair wha kens when to haud his tongue.

He kens nae a mavis frae a madge howlet.
He knows nothing on the subject in hand.

He kens nae a selgh frae a salmon.
As above.

He kens nae the door by the door-bar.
He does not know and keep his place.

He kens nae the pleasures o' plenty wha never felt the pains o' poverty.
It takes someone who has experienced the pains of poverty to really appreciate the joys of wealth.

He kens the loan frae the croun o' the causey as weel as the duck does the midden from the aidle dub.
He knows what's what.

He kens whilk side his bannock's buttered on.
He knows who he is answerable to.

He kicks at the benweed.
Benweed is ragwort, i.e. he is headstrong/unreasonable.

He lay in his scabbard as mony a gude sword has done.
He decided that discretion was the better part of valour and let an insult pass without notice.

He left his siller in his ither pocket.
Said of people who try to get out of paying their fair share.

He likes nae beef that grows on my banes.
He does not like me.

He'll be a man afore his mither.
Spoken to ill-grown children.

He'll claw up their mittans.
Metaphorically, he will kill them.

He'll either win the horse or tine the saddle.

He'll gang mad on a horse wha's proud on a pownie.
Spoken of those who let the least bit of power go to their heads.

He'll gang nae farther than his tether's length.

He'll gang to hell for house profit.

He'll get some o' the blessings in the byegoing.
Good will come to those who give unselfishly.

He'll get the poor man's answer, 'No'.

He'll gie his bane to nae dog.
Spoken of someone who is particulary selfish.

He'll gie you the whistle o' your groat.

He'll girn in a tow yet.
He will end up on the gallows

He'll hae enough some day, when his mouth's fu' o' mools.
Spoken of greedy people who will never be satisfied as long as they are alive.

He'll hang up his hat on some ither pin.
He will marry someone else.

He'll hing by the lug o't.
He will keep a firm grip/hold of it.

He'll hing that ower my head.
He will hold that over me.

He'll kythe in his ain colours yet.
He will appear as himself, and not in disguise.

He'll lick the white frae your e'en.
'This phrase is always applied when people, with pretence of friendship, do you an ill turn, as one licking a mote out of your eye makes it bloodshot.' – Allan Ramsay.

He'll mak a spune or spoil a horn.
Spoons used to be made of horn. Therefore he will either be a success or a disaster.

He'll mend when he grows better, like sour ale in summer.
He will always get worse. This phrase is found in Sir Walter Scott's Waverley.

He'll need to dree the dronach o't.
i.e. he will need to suffer the penalty / take the consequences of his actions.

He'll ne'er go weel for he was foundered in his feet.

He'll ne'er mak saut to his kail.
He will never succeed.

He'll ne'er rue but ance, and that'll be a' his life.

He'll ne'er send you awa' wi' a sair heart.
See 'He winna send etc.'

He'll neither dance nor haud the candle.
He will neither join in nor let others do so.

He'll neither dee nor do weel.
Sarcastically applied to those who may be peevish or fretful through ill-health.

He'll neither haud nor bind.
He is in a state of violent excitement. According to Jamieson this is perhaps borrowed from the fury of an untamed beast which cannot be held long enough to be bound with a rope.

He'll neither hup nor wine.
As above. 'Hup' and 'wine' were two words used in guiding plough and cart horses.

He'll no gie an inch o' his will for a span o' his thrift.
His wishes must be satisfied, no matter the expense.

He'll no gie his bone to the dog.

He'll no gie the head for the washing
To 'keep the head for the washing' is to retain possession of an article which has either been made to measure, or handed in for repair, until payment is received.

He'll no haud doon his head to sneeze for fear o' seeing his shoon.
Said of very vain people. Scott uses it in The Antiquary.

He'll no let the grass grow at his heels.
He will not procrastinate.

He'll no lie where he's slain.
Spoken of cowards, as if even their corpses would flee.

He'll no sell his hen on a rainy day.
He will not sell his wares at an unpropitious time.

He'll pish i' the wisp.
A phrase of uncertain origin used to signify that one will not thrive in that trade.

He'll put o'er the borrowing days.
'Spoken upon some hopes of our sick friend's recovery; taken from the weak cattel, who if they outlive the first nine days of April, we hope they will not die.' – Kelly.

He'll rather rin a mile than fecht a minute.

He'll rather turn than burn.

He'll shoot higher that shoots at the moon, than he that shoots at the midden, e'en though he may miss his mark.
A plea for people to always aim as high as possible with their ambitions and plans.

He'll soon be a beggar that canna say 'No'.

He'll tell it to nae mair than he meets.
He will tell it to everyone he meets.

He'll think his breeks a burden.
He will become heartily wearied with such a thing.

He'll wag as the bush wags.
He will do as circumstances dictate, i.e. he will follow the popular line.

He'll wind you a pirn.
He will create difficulties for you.

He lo'ed mutton weel that lick'd where the ewie lay.
A humorous remark made to those who scrape the bottom of their dish or drink the very last drops from a glass.

He lo'es me for little that hates me for naught.
He has never had a very strong liking for me if he is prepared to turn against me for a small thing.

He looks as if he could swallow a coo.
This and the next four sayings are all expressive of personal peculiarities.

He looks as if the wood were fu' o' thieves.

He looks like a Lochaber axe fresh frae the grundstane.

He looks like a wild cat out o' a bush.
He looks fierce.

He looks like the far end o' a French fiddle.

He looks like the laird o' fear.

He loses his time that comes early to a bad bargain.

Help for help in hairst.
Said when one returns a favour.

Help is gude at a'thing, except at the cog.
Help is always appreciated, except when taking one's food.

He maks a puir mouth.
Said when someone complains to gain compassion.

He maks mickle o' his painted sheets.
He is proud.

He maks nae bairn's bargain.

He maun be a gude friend when ye dinna ken his value.

He maun be a poor gudeman that's ne'er missed.

He maun be soon up that cheats the tod.

He maun hae leave to speak that canna haud his tongue.
Addressed to people who talk idly or foolishly.

He maun lie as he's bigget.
He must take life as he has made it, i.e. take the consequences of his actions.

He maun lout that has a laigh door.
We must accommodate according to our circumstances.

He maun rise soon that pleases a'body.

He may be trusted wi' a house fu' o' unbored millstanes.
He cannot be trusted at all.

He may find faut that canna mend.

He may grow better, but he canna be worse.
*Said of someone who can but improve either in character or at performing a
particular task.*

He may laugh that wins.

He may lead, but he winna drive.
Said of someone who will never take full control of things.

He may tine a stot that canna count his kine.
Originally taken from Montgomerie's 'The Cherrie and the Slae':

> The man may ablens tyne a stot
> That canna count his kinsch,
> In zour awin bow ze are owre-schot
> Be mair than half an inch.

He may weel soom wha has his head hauden up.
A task is made easier when assistance is given.

He needs a lang-shanket spoon that sups kail wi' the deil, or a Fifer.
*Few people were thought to be as cunning and wily as those from the Kingdom of
Fife, and this proverb serves as a warning to be on one's guard with such people.*

He needs maun rin that the deil drives.

He needs not a cake o' bread o' a' his kin.
Spoken of a drunkard.

He ne'er did a gude darg that gaed grumbling about it.
*A gude darg was a good days' work, i.e. you will only work well if you enjoy
performing the task at hand.*

He ne'er had a hand to thraw a key wi'.
He is a spendthrift.

He ne'er lies but when the holly's green.
Holly being an evergreen, this saying is applied to a person who never tells the truth.

He ne'er tint a cow that grat for a groat.
He never lost a cow who cried for the loss of fourpence.

He nickers like a cursour at a caup o' corn.
He laughs as a stallion neighs at feeding time.

Henry Clark never slew a man till he come at him.
'A ridicule upon them that threaten hard and dare not execute.' – Kelly.

Hens are aye free o' horse corn.
Spoken about those who are free with what is not theirs.

Hen scarts and filly tails, mak lofty ships wear lowly sails.
'Hen scarts' and 'filly tails' were common names for types of cloud which were held to indicate stormy weather.

He owes a pudding to the gled [kite].
A phrase applied to a beast that is dying.

He owes me a day's shearing, the longest in hairst.
'Spoken of one to whom I have done a signal good turn.' – Kelly.

He picked it up at his ain hand as the cow learned the flinging.
He is self-taught.

He plays least in sight.
A phrase taken from card playing and applied to someone who likes to keep himself concealed.

He put it out o' my e'e, and into my arse.
'That is, he conceal'd it out of my sight, but apply'd it to my profit; spoken when servants steal corn to feed their master's horse, or such like.' – Kelly.

He puts his meat in an ill skin.
According to Hislop this phrase is said of someone whose appearance belies the fact that they actually take plenty of food and nourishment.

He puts in a bad purse that puts in his pechan [stomach].
Spoken of gluttonous people who would rather eat when unnecessary than save for the future.

Her auld tout will buy ye a new horn.
A rude punning remark said to a young man who has married an older woman because he thinks it will be financially advantageous to do so.

Herds wha count their hogs afore Beltane hae often to count twice.
Another version of 'Don't count your chickens etc.'

He reads his sin in his punishment.

Hereafter comes not yet.

Here comes John Black, and Gilbert Ram on his back.
Spoken when we see black clouds which threaten rain.

He reives the kirk to theek the quire.
Literally, he steals from the church to roof the choir, or robs Peter to pay Paul.

'Here's tae you a', arse o'er head', as the moor-bride drank tae her maidens.
A toast to the whole company.

Here's the wine, but whaur's the wa'nuts?

He rides on the riggin' o't.
He goes to a great extreme.

Here's the gear, but where's the money.
A proverbial exclamation made when showing some fine thing.

He rides sicker that never fa's.
The person who never makes a mistake is sure of himself.

He rides wi' a sark-tail in his teeth.
Said when a newly married man has been away from home for a while and makes haste to return.

He rises ower early that is hangit ere noon.

He rules easier wi' a saugh wand than wi' a sharp brand.

He's a bad hand at sic wark.
He is not good at dirty work.

He's a body o' the nick-stick kind.
One who behaves exactly according to rules.

He's a cake and pudding courtier.

He's a' fair gude e'en, and fair gude-day.

He's a fool that asks ower muckle, but he's a greater fool that gies it.

He's a fool that forgets himsel'.

He's a fool that marries at Yule; for when the bairn's to bear the corn's to shear.
Old-fashioned rural family planning advice.

He's aftener there than in the parish kirk.

He's a gentle horse that never cust his rider.
'A good servant that never disobliged his master' – Kelly.

He's a gude horse that never stumbled, and a better wife that never grumbled.
Kelly cheekily comments in his collection 'Both so rare, that I never met with either.'

He's a gude man when there's nae better by.

He's a gude piper's bitch; he comes aye in at meal times.

He's a gude shot that aye hits the mark.

He's a' guts and gab.
He is a big eater and a talker.

He's a hardy man to draw a sword at a haggis.
An ironical ridicule against anyone showing off their bravery.

He's a hawk o' a right nest.

He's a heavy handfu'.
He is a great trial or responsibility.

He's a landward loon.
He belongs to the district and therefore is not a stranger.

He's a mere cutchin carle for a' his manly looks.
Spoken of someone who is a coward.

He's an Aberdeensman takin his word again.
Someone who forswears himself.

He's an auld horse that winna nicker when he sees corn.

He's ane o' sna' ba's bairntime.
Kelly says 'That is such as wealth or prosperity make worse, or who insensibly go behind in the world'.

He's a poor beggar that canna gang by ae door.

He's a poor man that's ne'er miss'd.

He's a proud beggar that maks his ain awmous.

He's a proud horse that winna carry his ain oats *or*
He's a weak baist that downa bear the saddle *or*
He's a proud tod that winna scrape his ain hole.
Used to indicate pride and incapacity in someone.

He's a sairy cook that canna lick his ain fingers.
Applied satirically to receivers, trustees, guardians, and other managers, signifying that they will take a share of what is among their hands.' – Kelly.

He's as bare as the birk at Yule.
He is very poor indeed.

He's as blind as the silly blind body that his wife gart believe her gallant's horse was a milk coo sent frae her minny.

He's as bold as a Lammermuir lion.
He's not very bold at all. The Lammermuir hills is a pastoral area not noted for wild animals, but a 'lion' is a local nickname for a sheep.

He's a selfish skyte that cares but for his ain kyte [stomach].

He's as fu's a fiddler.
He's drunk.

He's as gleg as a gled.

He's as gleg as M'Keachen's elshin, that ran through sax plies o'
bend-leather into King's heel.
Used in Scott's Heart of Midlothian.

He's as happy as a dead bird.
Presumably not very happy at all.

He's as hard wi' me as if I had been the wild Scot o' Galloway.

He's a silly chiel that can neither dae nor say.

He's as stiff as if he had swallowed a poker.

He's as uplifted as a midden cock upon pattens.

He's as welcome as snaw in hairst.
He is not welcome at all.

He's as welcome as water in a riven ship.
As above.

He's as wise as Wudsie's calf, that kent milk frae water.

He's a twa legged cratur wi' a goose's head and a hen's heart.
He is a fool and a coward. A phrase used by Scott in Rob Roy.

He's auld and cauld and ill to lie beside.
*The satirical reply to this proverb is as follows: 'He is neither so auld, nor yet so
cauld, but you may heat your nose in his nether end.'*

He's awfu' big ahint the door.
He is very brave when there is no occasion for it.

He's a wise bairn that kens his ain faither.

He's a wise man that can make a friend o' a foe.

He's a wise man that can tak care o' himsel'.

He's a wise man that when he's weel can haud himsel' sae.

He's aye ahint the foremost.
Used in Galt's Sir Andrew Wylie.

He's aye wise ahint the hand.

He's aye for out o' the cheese-fat he was moulded in.

He's been at the kirk o' crackaboot, whaur the kailpat was minister.
Said when someone has been secretly eating.

He's blind that eats marrow, but far blinder that lets him.

He's but Jock the laird's brither.
A phrase applied to hangers-on.

He's cooling and supping.
He has nothing but from hand to mouth – Kelly.

He's cowpet the crans.
He has gone to ruin, like a pot on the fire when the cran upon which it stood is upset. This phrase appears in Scott's Rob Roy, chap. 24.

He's dead now, and it's better for me to eat off him than lie on him.

He seeks nae mair than a bit and a brat.
Spoken of someone who is quite content with little.

He's either a' honey or a' dirt.
He is either exceedingly kind and affectionate or quite the reverse. Sometimes the phrase is given as 'Ye're either a' dirt or a' butter'.

He sell't his soul for a cracket saxpence.

He's esquire o' nae place, and laird o' far less.
Spoken sarcastically of one who assumes great airs.

He's failed wi' a fu' hand.
Said when a person declares himself bankrupt and hence does not have to pay off creditors immediately.

He's fishing wi' Hoy's net *or*
His head's in Hoy's net.
The first is applied to someone who is courting, the second to someone who has got married.

He's fond o' barter that niffers wi' Auld Nick.

He's frae the tap o' the wing, but ye're a grey neck quill.
He's a better man than you.

He's free o' fruit that wants an orchard.

He's gane aff at the nail.
He has gone mad, or peculiar.

He's gane a' to pigs and whistles.
He has gone to ruin.

He's gane ower the buss taps.
To behave extravagantly. To go over the bush tops.

He's gane to seek his faither's sword.
According to Kelly this refers to vagrants who travel without any good design.

He's gane to the dog-drave.

He's got his leg ower the harrows.

He's got his nose in a gude kail pat.
Often said of someone who has married a person of wealth.

He's gude that ne'er failed.

He shall either girn or man fin'.
A phrase applied in a case of slander – that the person who uttered it shall give the name of the author or be punished for it himself.

He's his faither's better, like the cooper o' Fogo.
Fogo is a small decayed village near Dunse. 'It appears that each generation of its coopers improved upon the plans of workmanship of their ancestors, and the son became better than the father' – G. Henderson.

He's horn deaf on that side o' his head.
Meaning that he has made up his mind upon the matter in question. Sometimes the word 'born' is substituted for 'horn'.

He should be seldom angry that has few to mease him.

He's idle that might be better employed.

He's ill-faur'd that dogs bark at.

He's in the wrang when praised that glunshes.

He sits above that deals acres.
An appeal to Divine Providence.

He sits fu' close that has riven breeks.

He sits fu' still that has a riven breek.
Used by Scott in The Fortunes of Nigel, *chap. 35. Following Kelly, he ascribes this saying to the Earl of Douglas. According to legend, the Earl was wounded in the nether regions whilst fighting at the Battle of Shrewsbury in 1403. He apparently sat still waiting until his soldiers' wounds were seen to before speaking out the above proverb.*

He sits wi' little ease wha sits on his neighbour's coat tail.

He's laid down the barrow.
See 'He's cowpet the crans'.

He sleeps as dogs do when wives sift meal.
The person is very sharp and figuratively sleeps with one eye open.

He's lifeless that's faultless.
No one alive is without fault. This phrase is used to put down those who claim to be perfect.

He's like a bagpipe, ne'er heard till his wame's fu.

He's like a chip amang parritch, little gude, little ill.

He's like a cow in an unco' loan.
He is out of place.

He's like a crane upon a pair o' stilts.
He is very tall and lanky. This must be a fairly old proverb, as cranes have been extinct in Scotland for some time.

He's like a flea in a blanket, aye jumpin'.
He is an irritation that is not immediately obvious.

He's like a singet cat – better than he's bonny.

He's like the craws, he eats himsel' out o' ply.

He's like the smith's dog – so weel used to the sparks that he'll no burn.
Said of people who are so used to drinking alcohol, that they never seem to be the worse for it.

He's like the wife's bawty – kens naething about it.

He's like the witches o' Auchencraw, he'll get mair for his ill than his gude.
Said when someone is given something out of fear of a malevolent reprisal.

He slippet awa' like a knotless thread.
Spoken of an elusive person.

He's loose in the heft.
Literally this means he has a loose slate, i.e. he is insane.

He's mair buirdly i' the back than i' the brain.
Suggesting the person's strength is of a physical rather than a mental nature.

He's mair fleyed than hurt.

He's mair worth hanging than hauding.

He's nae a deacon o' his craft.
He is not very good at his job/business. In Scotland the president of a trade corporation is called a deacon.

He's nae gude weaver that leaves lang thrums.
He is a poor workman that wastes material or leaves work in an unfinished state.

He's nae sae daft as he lets on.

He's nae sae daft as he's daft like.

He's nae sae saft i' the horn as that.

He's nae sma' drink.
He is not insignificant.

He's ne'er at ease that's angry.

He snites his nose in his neighbour's dish to get the brose himsel.
An all too vividly expressive proverb, used when someone will harm others to benefit personally.

He's no a man to ride the water wi'.
He is not a man to be trusted.

He's no a stirk o' the right stock.
Said of someone who does not come from the right background. Galt employs this phrase in his novel Sir Andrew Wylie.

He's no gude to creel eggs wi'.
He is not easy/safe to deal with.

He's no nice but needfu'.
Said of someone who is making flattering remarks about another.

He's no steel to the bane.
This can be used to imply that someone is either not thoroughly trustworthy, or not very healthy.

He's no the berry nor yet the bush it grew on.

He's no the best wright that cast maist spails.
A reminder that quality is preferred to quantity in many cases.

He's no the fool that the fool is, but he that wi' the fool deals.

He's not the happiest man that has maist gear.
Money isn't everything.

He's no wise man who cannot play the fool by a time.

He's no worth kissing caps wi'!
To 'kiss caps wi'' is to keep company with, to associate together in drinking.

He's out and in like a dog at a fair.

He's ower auld a cat to draw a strae before.
He is not easily taken in. The phrase appears in Scott's Rob Roy.

He's ower shot wi' his ain bow.
Said of someone who has overstretched his own capabilities, or is hoist with his own petard. This originally appears in Montgomerie's 'The Cherrie and the Slae' as 'in your ain bow ye are owerschot'.

He's ower soon up that's hanged ere noon.

He speaks in his drink what he thinks in his drouth.
Drink loosens the tongue.

He speaks like a prent book.
Said of someone who speaks in a very formal manner.

He spoke as if every word would lift a dish.
Said of someone who addresses others in a pompous, affected manner.

He's poor enough wha's ill-faur'd.

He's poor that canna promise.

He's rich that has nae debts.

He's sairest dung that's paid wi' his ain wand.
He suffers most who suffers for his own mistakes.

He's silly that spares for ilka speech.

He's sometimes i' the air, but ye're aye on the grund.

He's taen the bent.
Bent is a species of grass. Hence this phrase means that the person referred to has taken to the fields, or run away.

He stands as near to the barn door.
He is closely related.

He starts at straes, and lets windlins gae *or*
He stumbles at a strae and loups ower a linn.
Said of nit-picking people who are intent on correcting trifling mistakes, but miss the important things.

He's the bee that maks the honey.

He's the best spoke o' your wheel.
He is the best member of your team.

He's the slave o' a' slaves wha ser's nane but himsel'.

He streaks reem in my teeth.
Said when we think someone is merely trying to flatter us.

He's unco fu' in his ain house, that canna pick a bane in his neighbour's.
Said as a joke to those who refuse a meal in a friend's house.

He's waur to water than to corn.
He is fonder of drink than food.

He's weel awa', if he bides.
Spoken when we are glad to leave someone's company that we do not care for.

He's weel eased, that has ought of his own.

He's weel stocket there ben that will neither borrow nor lend.
A person must be comfortably provided for if they can afford to dispense with any help.

He's weel worthy o' sorrow that buys wi' his ain siller.

He's wise that kens when he's weel enough.

He's wise that's timely wary.

He's worth gold, that can win it.

He's worth nae weel that can bide nae wae.

He taks a gude grip o' Scotland.
Said of someone who walks flat-footed.

He taks pepper in his nose.
Spoken to describe someone who is easily angered.

He tarrows early that tarrows on his kail.
He complains early who complains before he sees what his dinner is to be. Spoken of those who complain before they have just cause to do so.

He that ance gets his fingers i' the dirt can hardly get them out again *or*
He that deals in dirt has aye foul fingers.
A warning to people not to become involved in bad deeds or they will find it hard to shake them off.

He that bides weel betides weel.

He that bids me to meat wishes me to live.

He that blaws best bears awa' the horn.
To the victor the spoils.

He that blaws in the stour fills his ain een.
The individual who creates trouble is likely to end up in it himself.

He that borrows and bigs, maks feasts and thigs, drinks an's no dry, – nane o' these three are thrifty.

He that brings the gudes has a right to guide the gear.

He that buys a house that's wrought has mony a pin and nail for nought.

He that buys land buys stanes; he that buys beef buys banes; he that buys nuts buys shells; he that buys gude ale buys naething else.
A warning that money spent on drink is money wasted as there is nothing to show for it later.

He that can hear Dumbuck may hear Dumbarton.
A saying local to Glasgow. Dumbuck hill in Argyllshire is farther from Glasgow than Dumbarton. Hence, the saying is applied to those who are better acquainted with circumstances than they pretend to be, but who, in their search for even more information, give themselves away.

He that canna do as he would maun do as he may.

He that canna do better maun be a monk.
A proverbial saying attributed to Earl Douglas, who, being defeated at the battle of Lochmaben, was sent by James III to the monastery of Lindores as his punishment.

He that canna gie a favour shouldna seek ane.

He that canna mak sport should mar nane.

He that cheats in daffin' winna be honest in earnest.

He that cheats me ance, shame fa' him; he that cheats me twice, shame fa' me.
A reminder to learn by one's mistakes.

He that comes atween a fool and his ruin is like him wha interferes atween a man and his wife, he's sure o' the redding straik.
A warning not to get involved in certain situations, but to attend to one's own business.

He that comes first to the ha' may sit where he will.

He that comes o' the hens maun scrape.

He that counts a' costs will ne'er put plough i' the grund.
A plea for positive thinking. The person who weighs up all the possible difficulties, will never get around to doing anything.

He that counts a' the pins i' the plough will ne'er yoke her.
Same as above.

He that counts without his host may have to count twice.
Many folk reckon their debts to be smaller than they really are.

He that dares weel fares weel.
He who dares wins!

He that does as he's bidden deserves nae bannin'.

He that does his turn in time sits half idle.

He that does ill hates the light.
Wrongdoers use cover of darkness to do their bad deeds, and so escape detection.

He that doesna mind corn pickles ne'er comes to forpits.
A phrase used by Scott in The Fotunes of Nigel.

He that does you an ill turn will ne'er forgie you.
Presumably because each time they see you they will feel guilty.

He that drinks when he's no dry will be dry when he has nae drink.

He that eats a boll o' meal in bannocks eats a peck o' dirt.

He that eats but ae dish seldom needs the doctor.
Moderation in all things is best!

He that eats till he burst will be waur while he lives.
A cheeky reply to someone who urges us to eat.

He that eats while he lasts will be the waur while he die.

He that fa's in a gutter, the langer he lies the dirtier he is.
A warning to people not to keep bad company, or their own reputation will soon become tarnished.

He that fishes before the net, fishes lang or he fish get.

He that follows freits, freits will follow him.
The person who looks for portents of the future will find himself dogged by them. This proverb must date from around the sixteenth century, as it first appears in J. Pinkerton's Scottish Tragic Ballads *(1781) as 'Wha luik to freits, my master deir, Freits will ay follow them.'*

He that forecasts a' perils will win nae worship.

He that forsakes measure, measure forsakes him.
He that is immoderate in anything, shall meet with treatment accordingly.

He that gangs a borrowing, gangs a sorrowing.
A warning of the misery which borrowing can bring.

He that gapes till he be fed may gape till he be dead.
A warning not to wait for things to come to you.

He that gets forgets, but he that wants thinks on.

He that gets gear before he gets wit is but a short time maister o't.
A warning to any winner of the National lottery. A fool and his money are soon parted.

He that gies all his gear to his bairns
Tak up a beetle and ding out his harns.
According to Kelly this saying is taken from the story of one John Bell who, having given all his wealth to his children, was neglected by them. After his death, there was found in his chest a mallet with the following inscription:

> *I, John Bell, leaves here a mell, the man to fell,*
> *Who gives all to his bairns, and keeps nothing to himsel'.*

He that gies all, would gie naething.
A phrase applied when we suspect that we were only given everything because the giver was in a bad mood and gave it grudgingly.

He that grapes in the dark may fyle his fingers.

He that hains his dinner will hae the mair to his supper.

He that has a bonnie wife needs mair than twa een.
The suggestion is that he also needs eyes in the back of his head to be aware of the advances of unscrupulous suitors.

He that has a dog at hame may gang to the kirk wi' a clean breast.

He that has ae sheep in a flock will like a' the lave the better for't.
When our kith and kin enter a group or club, we wish all the other members well because of their relationship.

He that has a goose will get a goose.
Riches come to those who already possess riches.

He that has a gude crap may thole some thistles.
He that has enjoyed good fortune can easily put up with slight drawbacks.

He that has a muckle nose thinks ilka ane speaks o't.
People who have a secret to hide are always suspicious of others.

He that has an ill wife should eat muckle butter.
A joke based around the pronunciation of butter or but-her – meaning without her.

He that has a wide wame ne'er had a lang arm.
Said to try and shame greedy people. i.e. those who are greedy are not usually forthcoming in handing round food.

He that has a wife has a maister.

He that has but ae ee maun tent it weel *or*
He that hath but one eye, must look well to that.
Said when someone only has one of a thing and hence is reluctant to lend it.

He that has gall in his mou', canna spit honey.
A person with an unpleasant nature is not likely to speak pleasantries.

He that has gold may buy land.

He that has his hand in the lion's mou' maun tak it out the best way he can.
He who has placed himself in difficulties must sort it out for himself.

He that has horns in his bosom needna put them on his heid.

He that has just enough can soundly sleep; the owercome only fashes folk to keep.

He that has lost a wife and sixpence has lost sixpence.

He that has muckle wad aye hae mair.
Some people are never content with what they already have.

He that hasna purse to fine may hae flesh to pine.
A phrase from Rob Roy *by Sir Walter Scott. He that is not able to pay his fine may have to face corporal punishment.*

He that hasna siller in his purse should hae silk on his tongue.
A suggestion that either money or flattery will get you everywhere.

He that has routh o' butter may butter his bread on baith sides.
The person who is well supplied with a commodity can afford to be prodigal with it.

He that has siller in his purse may want a head on his shouthers.

He that has twa hoards is able to get a third.
All things come more easily to those who already have.

He that hath and winna keep it; he that wants and winna seek it; he that drinks and is not dry; siller shall want as well as I.

He that hews abune his head may get a spail in his e'e.
He who aims at things beyond his power or abilities may be injured in the process.

He that hides kens whaur to seek.
It takes one to know one.

He that ill bodes ill betides.
We often get out of life what we expect.

He that ill does never gude weens.
Those who do wrong themselves, always think badly of others.

He that invented the maiden first hanselled her.
The 'maiden' was an early form of guillotine and was supposedly so-called because many men had lain with her but none had got the better of her. There is some doubt to the truth of the foundations of the above proverb, but it was reputed that James, Earl of Morton, who introduced the maiden to Scotland was also the first person to suffer by it. A proverb which perhaps owes more to poetic justice than historical truth.

He that isna handsome at twenty, strong at thirty, wise at forty, rich at fifty, will never become handsome, strong, wise or rich.

He that keeks through a keyhole may see what will vex him.
A warning not to spy on others lest you find out something that displeases you.

He that keeps the cat's dish keeps her aye crying.

He that kens what will be cheap or dear needs be a merchant but for half a year.

He that kisses his wife at the market cross will hae mony to teach him.
A warning to do certain things in private unless you are quite happy to hear everyone's view on the matter.

He that lacks my mare may buy my mare.
Said when someone talks disparagingly of an article they themselves want.

He that laughs alane will mak sport in company.

He that laughs at his ain jokes spoils the sport o' them.

He that lends his pot may see his kail in his loof.
A warning not to lend goods unless you are prepared to accept that you may never see them again.

He that lends money to a friend has a double loss.
In doing so he loses both his money and hence his friend.

He that lends you hinders you to buy.
i.e. because they feel they have the right to have a say about what their money is spent on.

He that lippens to chance lippens his back to a slap.

He that lippens to lent ploughs his land will lang lie lea.
The person who relies upon the favours of others is open to being greatly disappointed.

He that lives longest sees maist ferlies.

He that lives on hope has a slim diet.

He that liveth well liveth long.

He that lo'es law will soon get his fill o't.

He that looks not ere he loup will fa' ere he wat.
Look before you leap.

He that looks to freits, freits will follow him.
A warning to those who believe in superstitions, that things will happen to them accordingly.

He that looks wi' ae ee, and winks wi' anither,
I wouldna believe him, though he was my brither.
A childish rhyme said to people who wink – but also a general exhortation not to trust those who affect a charming manner.

He that maks friends fear'd o' his wit should be fear'd o' their memories.
Do as you would be done by.

He that marries a beggar gets a louse for a tocher.

He that marries a daw eats muckle dirt.
i.e. has many troubles to put up with. Both of the above proverbs are said as a warning to those about to marry to check the background/character of their chosen spouse beforehand. The suggestion is that if they do not, they will have troubles to face that they would rather not.

He that marries a widow and twa dochters has three back doors to his house.
Another warning against marrying a widow, this time suggesting that if she already has children the new husband will also end up providing for them as well.

He that marries a widow will have a dead man's head often thrown in his dish.
A warning to those marrying a widow, that they will have the memory of the first husband to live up to.

He that marries before he's wise will die ere he thrive.

He that meddles wi' tulzies may come in for the redding stroke.
Anyone willing to meddle with quarrelsome people is likely to come off worst.

He that never eats flesh thinks harrigals a feast.
'Harrigals' are the heart, liver etc. of a sheep.

He that never rode never fell.
The person who does not try anything will never gain anything.

He that never thinks will ne'er be wise.

He that oppresses honesty ne'er had ony.

He that pays his debts begins to mak a stock.

He that pays last ne'er pays twice.

He that pities anither minds himsel'.

He that plants trees lo'es ithers beside himsel'.
A tree planter must be partially altruistic, as a tree will probably not reach maturity in his lifetime.

He that plays mair than he sees, forfeits his eyes.
'An excuse for over-looking an advantage at game' – Kelly.

He that plays wi' fools and bairns maun e'en play at the chucks.
When a man mixes with individuals less intelligent than himself he must adapt his behaviour accordingly.

He that pleads his ain case has a fool for a client.

He that puts on the public gown maun aff the private person.
Those who stand for public office must expect their whole lives to be examined.

He that puts the cat in the pock kens best how to tak' her oot.

He that refuses a groat for a crack, a horse for a start, or a wife for a fart, will ne'er be weel monied, weel horsed, or weel wived.
Spoken to people who are too choosy.

He that rides ahint anither doesna saddle when he pleases.
Those who depend upon others are not always at liberty to do things when they would choose.

He that rides or he be ready wants aye some o' his graith.

He that's angry opens his mouth and steeks his een.
Angry people tend to speak in haste and damage their own cause.

He that's aught the cow gangs nearest the tail.
The owner of something should be willing to risk more for it than anyone else.

He that says what he likes will hear what he doesna like.

He that's born to a plack'll ne'er get a pound.

He that's born to be hanged will ne'er be drowned.
You will get out of life what you deserve/is predetermined.

He that's born under a thripenny planet will never be worth a groat.

He that's crabbit without cause should mease without amends.

He that seeks alms for Godsake begs for twa.

He that seeks motes gets motes.
Those who seek trouble will generally find it.

He that seeks trouble 'twere a pity he should miss it.

He that sells his wares for words maun live by the loss.

He that serves maunna be slack,
Neither for weather nor yet for wrack.

He that's far frae his gear is near his skaith.
A warning to people to keep a weather eye on their own property.

He that's fear'd o' a fart, should ne'er hear thunder.

He that's first up's no aye first ser'd.

He that shames let him be shent.
'An old Scottish proverb not now used, scarcely understood: a wish that he who exposes his neighbour may come to shame himself.' – Kelly.

He that's hanged in May will eat no flames [pancakes] at Midsummer.
From Sir Walter Scott's The Abbot.

He that's hated o' his subjects canna be a King.

He that shows his purse tempts the thief.
A warning not to lead others into temptation.

He that's ill o' his harboury is gude at the way-kenning.
An unwilling host is likely to be able to tell the unwanted guest the times of the next trains home!

He that's ill to himsel' will be gude to naebody.
He who cannot respect himself will not be able to respect others.

He that sits upon a stane is twice fain.
He is glad to sit down through tiredness but glad again to rise because the stone is hard and uncomfortable.

He that slays shall be slain.
A warning that those who live by the sword will die by the sword.

He that sleeps wi' dogs maun rise wi' fleas.
Those who keep bad company cannot expect to remain unaffected.

He that's mann'd wi' boys and hors'd wi' colts will hae his meat eaten and his wark ill done.
According to Hislop this phrase was used as 'A sarcastic allusion to those who entrust matters of importance to youthful or inexperienced persons'.

He that's no my friend at a pinch, is no my friend at a'.

He that's no used to a sword, leaves't where he shites.
According to Kelly this phrase is 'spoken when people, advanced above their former condition, forget something proper to their station', i.e. when people get above themselves.

He that spares to speak spares to speed.
The person who is reticent to speak about his own talents when an opportunity arises for advancement does himself harm.

He that speaks the thing he shouldna will hear the thing he wouldna.

He that speaks to himsel', speaks to a fool.

He that speaks wi' a draunt, an' sells wi' a cant, is right like a snake in the skin o' a saunt.
A humorous warning not to trust those speaking in drawling, canting terms.

He that speers a' gets wit but o' pairt.

He that speers a' opinions comes ill speed.
The preceding two proverbs suggest that those who ask the opinions of everyone are likely to end up misinformed.

He that spends before he thrives will beg before he thinks.

He that spends his gear before he gets 'twill hae but little gude o't.

He that spends his gear upon a whore, both shame and skaith, he maun endure.

He that spits against the wind spits in his ain face.
A warning not to try and go against the views of the majority.

He that's poor when he's married shall be rich when he's buried.

He that's rede for windlestraes should ne'er sleep on leas.
Kelly gives a slightly cruder version thus: 'He that's redd for windlestraws, should not pish in lays.' The phrase is spoken to those who exhibit fears of anxiety with regard to small and far-off dangers.

He that's scant o' wind shouldna meddle wi' the chanter.
A saying applied to those who take on a task which is greater than they can cope with.

He that's shor'd to death, should have a fart for his dead bell.
Spoken by the bold when they want to show that they are not afraid of others' threats.

He that steals a preen will steal a better thing.

He that steals can hide too.

He that's too modest must go to the wall.

He that strikes my dog would strike myself, if he daured.
Said about/to someone who has committed a cowardly act.

He that stumbles twice at ae stane deserves to break his shin bane.
The person who does not learn by their mistakes deserves everything that happens to them.

He that theiks his house with turds, will find more teachers than reachers.
If you are engaged in something difficult or unpleasant, you will find more people ready to lend advice than lend a hand.

He that thinks in his bed has a day without a night.

He that tholes, overcomes.

He that tigs wi' a stranger pays the smart.

He that tigs wi' the tailor gets a button in his sleeve.

He that tines his siller is thought to hae tint his wit.
Meaning that a person who willingly loses or risks losing money must have lost all sense.

He that wants content canna sit easy in his chair.

He that wants to strike a dog ne'er wants a stick.
Those determined to do something will always find the means.

He that wears black maun wear a brush on his back.
Said as a joke to anyone wearing black, as if they were a chimney sweep.

He that will be angry for onything will be angry for naething.

He that will to Cupar maun to Cupar.
A reflection upon obstinate people. Another line is sometimes added 'Aye better gang than be ta'en', or 'Sae gang tae Cupar an' be damned!'

He that winna bear mitherhead, maun bear stepmitherhead.

He that winna be ruled by the rudder maun be ruled by the rock.

He that winna be counselled canna be helped.

He that winna lout and lift preen will ne'er be worth a great.
The person who refuses to bother with the small things will never be wealthy, i.e. look after the pennies and the pounds will look after themselves.

He that winna thole maun flit mony a hole.

He that winna use the means maun dree the moans.

He that winna when he may, shanna when he wad.
Spoken of somebody who doesn't want a thing until he can no longer have it.

He that woos a maiden maun come seldom in her sight; he that woos a widow maun ply her day and night.

He that would climb the tree maun tak care o' his grip.

He that would eat the fruit maun climb the tree.
There is no gain without pain.

He that would eat the kernel maun crack the nut.

He that would pu' the rose maun sometimes be scarted wi' the thorns.

He that wrestles wi' a turd, fall he undermost, or uppermost, he'll be sure to be bedirten.
Meddle with bad things and you are sure to be tainted.

He thinks himsel nae page's peer.
He thinks nobody compares with himself.

He thinks himsel' nae sheepshank.
Spoken of conceited persons who think themselves to be of great importance.

He thinks himsel' worth mickle mice dirt.
Same as above.

He thinks his breeks a burden.
He will be heartily weary of such a thing – Kelly.

He thinks nae sma' drink o' himsel'.
A phrase applied to conceited individuals.

He tines bottles gathering straes.
He loses greater benefits by wasting time on trifles.

Het kail cauld, nine days auld, spell ye that in four letters.
A well known children's riddle, the key to which is the four letter word 'that'.

Het love, hasty vengeance.

He took the bog aslent [diagonally].
He ran off.

Het sup, het swallow.

He vapours like a tyke in a tedder.
According to Kelly, this is a ridicule upon a conceited swaggering young fellow.

He wadna len' the deil a knife, e'en tae cut his ain throat.
He is an extremely mean fellow.

He wad rake Hell for a bodle.
Said of a miser. A bodle was an odd copper coin worth two pence Scots or a sixth of an English penny.

He wags a wand in the water.
He does no good.

He wants to get a blackfit.
When said of a young man it means he is a bashful/shy lover. A 'blackfoot' was a person who acted as an intermediary between a lover and his mistress.

He warstled up the brae.
i.e. persevered and succeeded.

He was eerie and unco.

He was fain and fey.
Both of the above suggest that the person thus spoken of is strange in his manner.

He was just between the tining and the winning.
i.e. at a critical stage.

He was kep'd in a board-cloth; he has hap to his meat, but none to his wives.

He was like to fire the house.
Spoken of someone who is in a great rage

He was mair fleyed than hurt.

He was miss'd by the water, but caught by the widdie.
He escaped drowning only to be hanged, i.e. what is predestined cannot be changed.

He wasna the inventor o' gunpowder.
Spoken about someone who is very timid or cowardly.

He was ne'er a gude aiver that flung at the brod.
Said to those who spurn reproof/correction.

He was scant o' grey cloth that soled his hose wi' dockens.
According to Kelly, this is the reply given by a haughty maiden to those who tell her of an unworthy suitor.

He was scant o' news that said his faither was hanged.

He wastes a penny candle looking for a bawbee.
Said of someone who makes false economies.

He was wrapp'd in his mither's sark tail.
The Scots used to practice an old custom whereby if a male child was born it was received into the world in its mother's shift. The belief was that this would make the male child well beloved among women.

He watsna whilk end o' him's upmost.
Said of someone who is unsure if they are on their head or their heels, i.e. they are in a turmoil.

He wats not whether he bears the earth, or the earth him.
A phrase applied to excessively proud people.

He wears Langton's coat o' mail.
'Once in a skirmish with the English, the Laird of Langton, being unarmed, turned his coat inside out, to make his opponents believe he had on a coat of mail, and so rushed on to the fray. By "Langton's coat of mail", is meant a presumptuous but brave man' – G. Henderson.

He wears twa faces aneath ae cowl.
He is two-faced.

He wha mair than he's worth doth spend, aiblins a rape his life will end.

He wha marries a maiden marries a pockfu' o' pleasure;
He wha marries a widow marries a pockfu' o' pleas – sure.
Yet more proverbial marriage guidance, warning of the dangers of marrying a widow.

He wha marries for love without money, hath merry nights and sorry days.

He wha swims in sin will sink in sorrow.

He wha tells his wife a' is but newly married.

He wha wishes nae ill to his enemies, will ne'er do wrang by his friends.

He will neither haup nor wind.
A phrase spoken of someone who is very stubborn, i.e. he will neither turn to the right nor the left. The phrase is taken from the cry of hinds to their horses.

He winna send you awa' wi' a sair heart.
He will promise you anything, though he has no intention of keeping to his word.

He woos for cake and pudding.
Well, they do say the way to a man's heart is through his stomach!

He would fain be forward if he wist how.

He would fain have a fool, that makes a fool o' himsel'

He would fain rip up auld sairs.
Spoken of someone who is always looking for a quarrel.

He would gang a mile to flit a sow.
According to Kelly, this phrase was 'spoken of sauntering persons who would take any pretence to go from their proper business'.

He would gar you trow the mune's made o' green cheese, or that the cat took the herring.
He wants to convince you of something which is simply not true.

He wouldna lend his gully – no! to the deil to stick himsel.
Said of those who decline to oblige borrowers in all circumstances.

He would need to be twice sheeled and ance grund that deals wi' you.
It would take a very shrewd person to deal with you.

He would neither mess nor mell.
He would neither be friendly nor fight. A phrase spoken of people who do neither one thing nor the other.

He would not sup kail with him, unless he broke the dish on his head.
'A disdainful answer to them who compare our friend to some unworthy inferior fellow' – Kelly.

He would set a parish by the lugs.
Said of a mischief maker.

He would skin a louse for the tallow o't.
Applied to anyone who is extremely miserly.

He would tine his lugs if they were not tacked to him.
Spoken of the forgetful.

Highlanders – shoulder to shoulder.

Highest in the court, nearest the widdie.

High trees show mair leaves than fruit.
A disparaging remark sometimes made to tall people.

His absence is good company but his backside is a cordial.

His arse makes buttons.
A rather graphic description of someone who has had a terrible fright.

His auld brass will buy her a new pan.
Said of young women who marry older men, suggesting that when their husbands die, they will use his money to attract a younger one.

His bark's waur nor his bite.

His boat is kittle to trim.
He is difficult to manage.

His corn's a' caff.

His e'ening sang and his morning sang are no baith alike.

His een's greedier than his guts.

His eggs hae a' twa yolks.
See below.

His geese are a' swans.
He tells tall tales.

His head's in a creel.

His head will ne'er fill his faither's bannet.
An expression of doubt that the son will live up to the abilities of his father.

His heart's in his hose.

His horse got a bite for a cauld bridle.
i.e. got neither hay nor oats.

His life, but not his honour, feal'd.
Spoken of those who die bravely for a cause.

His meal's a' daigh.

His purse and his palate are ill met.
The first is light, the second is less so.

His room's better than his company.

His siller gangs like snaw aff a dyke.
He is reckless with money.

His tongue's nae slander.
Spoken of somebody who is so little respected that what they say is not taken seriously anyway.

His wame thinks his wizen's cut.
Said when someone is exceedingly hungry.

His wit gat wings and would hae flown, but pinchin' poortith pu'd him down.

Honest is no pride.

Honest men marry soon, wise men never.

Honesty hauds lang the gate.
To 'haud the gate' is to 'maintain the even tenor of your way' – Hislop.

Honesty may be dear bought, but can ne'er be an ill pennyworth.

Honesty's the best policy.
Sometimes the phrase 'I've tried baith' is added at the end.

Honours change manners.

Hooly and fairly gangs far in a day.
Working constantly though slowly will get a great deal of work done.

Hooly and fairly men ride far journeys.

Hope hauds up the head.

Hope is sawin' while death is mawin'.

Hopers go to hell.
The road to hell is paved with good intentions.

Hope weel an' hae weel.

Horns an' grey hair dinna aye come o' years.

Horses are gude o' a' hues.

Hotch, and help yourself to get your bairns.
'A senseless answer to them that bids us help them' – Kelly.

Hotter war sooner peace.

How by yoursel', burn'd be the mark.

How came you and I to be so great?
Spoken as a rebuke when our inferiors are too familiar with us.

Humble worth and honest pride gar presumption stand aside.

Hunger has sharp een.

Hunger is hard in a hale maw.
Hunger is hard to a healthy stomach.

Hunger me, and I'll harry thee.

Hunger ne'er fails a gude cook.

Hunger's gude kitchen to a cauld potato, but a wet divot to the lowe o' love.
Hunger makes any food acceptable, but it is a damper on one's love life.

Hunger waits only eight days.
After which time a starving person will do anything.

Hunger will break through stone wa's.

Hungry dogs are blythe o' bursten puddins.
To the starving anything tastes good.

Hungry folk are soon angry.

Hungry stewards wear mony shoon.

Hunting and hawking and paramours,
For one joy, hath a hundred displeasures.
According to Kelly 'It signifies the mischief of unseasonable recreations, and unlawful pleasures'.

I

I ance gied a dog his hansel, an' he was hang'd ere night.
An excuse for not giving someone a gratuity, lest it lead to harm in some way.

I bake nae bread by your shins.
I am under no obligation to you.

I brought him aff the moor for God's sake, and he begins to bite the bairns.
Said of someone who repays a favour with a disservice.

I canna afford ye baith tale and lugs.
Said as a rebuke to an inattentive person who has asked for a story to be repeated.

I canna baith spin an' rin.

I canna sell the cow an' sup the milk.
The equivalent of not being able to have one's cake and eat it.

I canna sit, and run, and pish, and gather spails.
Said when we are asked to do many things at once.

I can neither mak' buff nor stye o't.
i.e. neither heads nor tails; one thing or another.

I can scarce believe ye, ye speak sae fair.

I can see as far into a millstane as he that pick'd it.

I carena whether the fire gae about the roast, or the roast gae about the fire, if the meat be ready *or*
I carena whether the tod worry the goose or the goose worry the tod.
Spoken by someone who does not care how a thing is done, so long as the desired end is reached.

I could hae done that mysel', but no sae weel.
Spoken when people do a thing amiss, like knocking over a glass of wine etc.

I deny that wi' baith hands and a' my teeth.
I emphatically deny that.

I dinna care a tinkler's curse.
An expression of extreme indifference.

Idle dogs worry sheep.
A warning that lack of industry can bring about trouble.

Idleness is the devil's langsettle. *or*
Idleset and wastry are near friends.

Idleset is the mither o' mickle ill.

Idleset seldom heeds aboot being clean.

Idle young, needy auld.

I draw it frae you, like a fart frae a dead mear.
'Spoken of them who will not do, or say, a thing but with force, and constraint'
– Kelly.

If a' be weel, I'll be wyteless.
According to Kelly, this proverb was 'spoken with a suspicion that all will not be well, and if so, I had no hand in it'.

If a' bowls row right.
If all goes well.

If ae sheep loup the dyke a' the rest will follow.

If a gude man thrives, a' thrive wi' him.
Because he is generous and shares his good fortune.

If a' heights hitt.
If all promises are kept.

If a lee could hae chokit you, ye wad hae been dead langsyne.
A humorous way of suggesting that you suspect someone of telling a falsehood.

If a louse misses its foot on his coat, it'll be sure to break its neck.
A phrase signifying that the coat in question is very threadbare.

If a man be ance doun, doun wi' him.

If a man's gaun down the brae ilka ane gies him a jundie.
Beware! People can be very cruel to those who have fallen upon hard times.

'If' an' 'an' spoil mony a gude charter.

If ane winna anither will; sae are maidens married,
If ane winna anither will – the morn's the market day.

If any man speer at you, you may say you wat not.
A sharp answer to a curious asker.

If a' thing's true that's nae lee.
A saying denoting disbelief in some unlikely story.

If a' things were to be done twice ilka ane wad be wise.
Practice makes perfect, as we learn by our mistakes.

If a' your hums and haws were hams and haggises, the parish needna fear a dearth.
A warning against indecision and procrastination.

If better were within, better wad come out.
A comment upon another's behaviour and how it relates to their underlying character.

If Candlemas is fair and clear,
There'll be twa winters in the year;
and

If Candlemas day be dry and fair,
The half o' winter's to come and mair;
If Candlemas day be wet and foul;
The half o' winter's gane at Yule.
Candlemas day is 2 February.

If e'er I be rich and ye puir, I ken what ye'll get.
A promise – Kelly.

If e'er you mak a lucky puddin' I'll eat the prick.
'That is, I am much mistaken if ever you do good' – Kelly.

If ever I find his cart tumbling I'se gie a pull.
If I ever find him at a disadvantage I will take my revenge.

If grass grows green in Janaveer
It will be the waur for't a' the year.

If he be na a souter he's a gude shoe clouter.

If he be old, he has the mair wit.
An apology for marrying an old man.

If he binds his pock, she'll sit down on't.
Said when a mean man has an even meaner wife.

If he gies a duck he expects a goose.
Spoken of people who expect more in return than they are willing to give.

If he had spew'd as oft as he has rued, he would hae a clean stomach.
'Intimating that he has often repented the doing that thing, saying that word, or undertaking that project' – Kelly.

If he has one, buy him;
If he has two, try him;
If he has three, look about him;
If he has four, come without him.
A horse with one white foot was generally thought to be a good animal whereas the reverse was thought of one with four white feet.

If he's biggit in the moss, he maun gang into the mire.
You must accept what you have only yourself to blame for.

If I can get his cart to water, I shall lend it a put.

If I canna do't by might I can do't wi' slight.

If I canna keep my tongue I can keep my siller.

If I canna kep geese, I can kep gaislins.
If I cannot reap revenge upon a person, I will do so upon his offspring.

If I canna sew I can yerk.

If I come I maun bring my stool wi' me.
As I have not been invited, I had better bring my own seat.

If 'ifs' an' 'buts' were kettles an' pans, there would be nae use for tinklers.
If it were not for the 'ifs' and 'buts' in this world, we would all soon be rich.

If I had a dog as daft as you I would shoot him.
Said as a warning to people to stop fooling around.

If I had you at Maggy Mill's house I would get word about wi' ye.
Used when, in an argument, a person has not had a proper chance to make a defence.

If I hae done amiss I'll mak' amends.

If I live anither year, I'll ca' this fern-year.

If I live anither year I'll call this tarn [last] year.
'That is to say I will change my way of life' – Kelly.

If I'm no kind I'm no cumbersome.

If it be a faut it's nae ferlie.
It is no wonder, as no other result should have been expected.

If it be ill it's as ill rused.
Said of those who disparage what we have.

If it can be nae better it's weel it's nae waur.

If it get you wi' bairn, I'll faither it.
According to Kelly this phrase was 'spoken to urge a modest girl to take a glass of wine'.

If it had been a wolf, it would hae worried you.
'Spoken when one hath, to no purpose, sought a thing, that was afterwards found hard by them' – Kelly.

If it sair me to wear it, it may sair you to look at.
A rebuke to people who criticise others' dress.

If it werena for hope the heart would break.

If it werena for the belly the back wad wear gowd.
Spoken of someone who likes his/her food a little too much.

If it winna be a gude shoe we'll mak a bauchel o't.
A bauchel is an old shoe. Hence, if a thing won't do for one purpose, we'll put it to some inferior use.

If it winna sell it winna sour.
Said of good things – that they are worth keeping.

If I was at my ain bairn foot.
'I am now among strangers, but if I was at home among my friends, I would not suffer myself to be insulted.' – Kelly.

If marriages are made in heaven you twa hae few friends there.
Spoken of couples who are always fighting.

If my tale's ower lang cut a bit aff.

If naebody but wise folk were to marry, the warld wad be ill peopled.

If New Year's eve night wind blows South,
It betokeneth warmth and growth;
If west, much milk, and fish in the sea;
If north, much cold and storms there will be;
If east, the trees will bear much fruit;
If north-east, flee it man and brute.

If onybody speir at ye, say ye dinna ken.
A phrase used when we are unwilling to part with information.

If she was my wife, I would mak a Queen o' her.
i.e. leave her the kingdom to herself – desert her.

If Skidaw hath a cap, Scruffel wots full weet o' that.
Disraeli says in regard to this proverb: 'There are two hills, one in Scotland and one in England, so near that what happens to the one will not be long ere it reach the other . . . the natural sympathies of the two nations were hence deduced in a copious dissertation by Oswald Dyke on what was called "The Union Proverb". This was a favourite proverb with the Hanoverian party at the time of the French expedition to Scotland in the interests of the Stuarts.'

If strokes be gude to gie they'll be gude to tak.
A saying used when punishing bullies.

If that God gie, the Deil daurna reive.

If that had been the first lie you had told, I could hae charm'd you.

If the auld wife hadna been in the oven hersel, she ne'er wad hae thought o' looking for her dochter there.
Unless a person has already been guilty of some crime themselves, it is unlikely that they would suspect another of it.

If the badger leaves his hole the tod will creep in.
A warning to be ever vigilant when in bad company.

If the day be foul
That the bride gangs hame,
Alack and alace
But she'd lived her lane!
If the day be fair
That the bride gangs hame,
Baith pleasure and peace
Afore her are gane.

If the Deil be laird ye'll be tenant.
Spoken of someone who we think is bad.

If the deil find ye idle he'll set ye to wark.
A warning of the evils of laziness.

If the Deil's mill has ceased to grind, and the Rumbling Brig rumbles no more, there will be sorrow in the Vale of Devon.

If the deil were dead, fowk wad dae little for God's sake.

If the Doctor cures the sun sees it, but if he kills the earth hides it.

If the lad gaes to the well against his will,
Either the can will break, or the water will spill.
'Spoken when people mismanage a business, that they were forc'd to go about against their mind' – Kelly.

If the laird slight the leddy sae will the stable laddie.

If the lift fa' the laverocks will be smoored.
Said as a rejoinder when someone mentions some highly improbable turn of events.

If the mare has a bald face the filly will hae a blaze.
If the mother is of one complexion the daughter will be the opposite.

If the oak's before the ash, then you'll only get a splash;
If the ash precedes the oak, then you may expect a soak.

If there's rain in the Mass, 'twill rain through the week either mair or less.
A local Fife saying meaning that the weather on a Sunday will largely determine the weather for the rest of the week.

If the right had been maintained King George had not in London reigned.
A Jacobite saying.

If they wad drink nettles in March, and eat muggins in May,
Sae mony braw maidens wadna gang to the clay.
According to Cheviot, 'Nettles and Southernwood, or muggins, are held to be good for the cure of consumption. This rhyme, it is said, was uttered by a mermaid who

rose out of the Clyde, near Port Glasgow, and addressed the party attending the
funeral of a young woman in those admonitory words'.

If this be a feast I hae been at mony.
Said by a person to imply that they are not impressed by the treatment they are
receiving.

If we canna preach in the kirk we can sing mass in the quire.

If we haena the warld's wealth we hae the warld's ease.
A suggestion that owning property brings with it certain responsibilities and
burdens.

If wishes were horses beggars wad ride, and a' the warld be
drowned in pride.
This proverb is thought to date from before 1628 and is recorded in Carmichaell's
Proverbs in Scots *as 'An wishes were horses pure men wald ryde'.*

If woolly fleeces strew the heavenly way.
Be sure no rain disturbs the summer's day.

If ye be angry, sit laigh and mease you.

If ye be na gall'd ye needna fling.
If the cap fits wear it.

If ye can spend much, put the more to the fore.
If you have a great income, spend accordingly.

If ye dinna haud him he'll do't a'.
Said sarcastically of a lazy person.

If ye dinna like the sermon, ye'll no like the pireliecue.
i.e. If you don't like the first part of the story you will not wish the subject to be
further dwelt upon.

If ye dinna like what I gie ye, tak what ye brought wi' ye.
Uttered to guests who complain about what they are given.

If ye dinna mend yer pace ye'll come short at meal times.
A threatening exhortation to work harder or there will be less to eat.

If ye dinna see the bottom, dinna wade.
Do not undertake anything until you can clearly see what you're getting yourself
into.

If ye do nae ill, dinna be ill like; if ye steal my kail, break na my
dike.

If ye follow the deil ye'll gang to the deil.

If ye gang a year wi' a cripple ye'll limp at the end o't.
You will assimilate the behaviours of those with whom you associate. Therefore, be
careful who you mix with.

If ye had as little money as ye hae manners ye would be the poorest man o' a' your kin.
Said as a reprimand to someone who behaves in a rude manner.

If ye had a' the wit in the warld, fools wad sell ye.

If ye had been anither I would hae denied you the first word.
The person thus addressed is granted more indulgence than another would be.

If ye had gi'en a sixpence for that word, ye wadna hae spoken it.

If ye had stuck a knife in my heart it wadna hae bled.
Spoken by someone who is shocked/surprised at some information.

If ye hae little gear ye hae less care.
In this proverb those with nothing are presumed to have nothing to worry about.

If ye laugh at your ain sport the company will laugh at you.

If ye like the nut, crack it.
If you like something, do not be restrained in showing it.

If ye'll blaw yer ain whustle ye maun uphaud the win'.

If ye lo'e me let it kythe.
If you love me, let it show.

If ye're an unce, ye're twenty stone quarry wecht, and a'body kens that's no scrimpit.

If ye're nae better, ye're snoder like, quo' the wife, when she cut off the doggie's lugs.

If yer errand comes my gate, ye shall be as weel served.

If yer tale was as ready as yer tongue, ye wad shame a' yer ain/kin.
A reprimand to gossips.

If ye sell your purse to your wife, gie her your breeks to the bargain.
A saying used in the days when men were principal wage earners of the family, and were seen as being 'head of the household'. It suggests that if a man gives up financial control to his wife she will become head of the family.

If ye spend muckle, put mair to the fore.

If ye tak' my fair daughter, tak' her foul tail.
You must be prepared to take the bad that goes along with the good.

If ye wanted me, and yer meat, ye would want one gude friend.

If ye want yer business weel done, do't yersel'.

If ye was as skitterful as ye're scornful, ye would file the whole house.

If ye will hae the hen's egg, ye must bear her cackling.
There is no gain without pain.

If ye will tell your secret to your servant, ye hae med him your maister.

If ye winna stand it, ye may sit it.
If you don't like it you can lump it.

If you be angry, claw your wame, an' cool i' the skin ye het in.
Spoken to people whose anger we do not value.

If your errand come my gate, you shall be as weel ser'd.
This can be used as a promise or a threat.

If you wad live for ever, wash the milk from your liver.

If you win at that you'll lose at naething.
A phrase applied to those who are doing something wrong which will inevitably be to their disadvantage.

'If you winna come you'll bide,' quo' Rory to his bride.
Said when we are perfectly indifferent whether someone comes or stays.

If you would be a merchant fine, beware o' auld horses, herring, and wine.
Proverbially speaking the first will die, the second will stink, and the third sour.

If you would be haly, healthy, an' wealthy, rise soon i' the morning.

I gaed through the bear-land wi' him.
A phrase used by a person who has gone though all the particulars of a quarrel with another.

I gied him a bonny blue nocht wi' a whistle on the end o't.
I gave him nothing of any worth.

I gied his birn a hitch.
I helped him out of trouble.

I had but little butter, an' that I coost on the coals.
Even the little I had, I squandered.

I had nae mind that I was married, my bride was sae feckless.
Hislop gives the meaning as: 'The circumstance was of so little importance that no notice was taken of it.'

I hae a cauld coal to blaw at.
Said after suffering a great loss.

I hae a good bow, but it's i' the castle.
Said of those who are always claiming that they could perform heroic deeds, if only they had remembered to bring some necessary article with them which they know is not near at hand.

I hae a heid an' so has a stair.

I hae a lang clue to wind.
I have much to accomplish.

I hae an auld craw to pluck wi' him, and a pock to put the feathers in.
I have an old dispute to settle with him, and I have come prepared.

I hae anither tow on my rock.

I hae a Scotch tongue in my head – if they speak I'se answer.

I hae askit grace at a graceless face.
The words reported to have been uttered by John Armstrong, the border reiver, after having pleaded in vain for his life from King James V in 1529.

I hae a workman's eye in my head.
Said when we notice that something has been done imperfectly.

I hae baith my meat and my mense.
A phrase used when we offer food, or anything else, to someone who refuses it.

I hae brought an ill comb to my ain head.
I have got myself into trouble.

I hae gi'en a stick to break my ain head.
I have undertaken something which is to my own disadvantage.

I hae gotten an ill kame for my ain hair.

I hae had better kail in my cog, and ne'er gae them a keytch.
An answer given by a girl teased about a suitor she dislikes. The phrase refers to the old farming practice of busy reapers throwing their broth up in the air to cool it, which they could do without spilling a drop.

I hae his cods in a cleft stick.
I have him at a disadvantage.

I hae ither fish to fry *or*
I hae ither grist to grind *or*
I hae ither tow on my rock *or*
I have other matters to attend to.

I hae licked mysel' clean.
'I have come well out of a transaction from which I anticipated loss' – Kelly.

I hae mair dogs than I hae banes for.
I have bitten off more than I can chew.

I hae mair to do than a dish to wash.
I have important work to do.

I hae muckle to do, and few to do for me.
I am a very busy person.

I hae seen as fu' a haggis toom'd on the midden.
A disparaging remark about an article, i.e. I have seen as good an article thrown away.

I hae seen mair snaw on ae dike, than now on seven.
The situation is not as severe as I have faced before.

I hae seen mair than I hae eaten, else ye wadna be here.
Spoken as a sharp rebuke to someone who doubts a satement of which the speaker has been an eye witness.

I hae seen mony a smaller madam.
'Either in bulk or station, used in former times by ordinary women to those who call them mistress' – Kelly.

I hae ta'en the sheaf frae the mare.
I have faced up to a difficulty. Kelly gives an alternative meaning – 'That is, I have stop'd my intended journey. A man going a journey, gave his mare a sheaf of oats, that she might perform the better: but altering his mind, he ordered his sheaf to be taken from her.'

I hae the Bible, an' there's no a better book in a' your aught.

I hae the wrang sow by the lug.
I have misunderstood, or, got the wrong end of the stick.

I hae tint the staff I herded wi'.
I have lost the support I relied upon.

I hae twa holes in my head, an' as mony windows.
I am neither deaf nor blind.

I haud blench of him.
'An allusion to the different tenures by which lairds hold their lands, some ward, some black ward, some blench. This last pays no service' – Kelly.

I hope ye're nane the waur o' yer early rising.
Spoken facetiously to those who enjoy a lie-in.

I ken a spune frae a stot's horn.

I ken by my cog how my cow's milk'd.
I can judge how a thing has been done by its very appearance.

I ken by your half-tale what your hale tale means.
I am quite capable of reading between the lines to get the full story.

I ken he'll come, by his lang tarrying.

I ken him as weel as if I had gane through him wi' a lighted candle.
I can see through his character.

I ken how the warld wags: he's honoured maist has moniest bags.
To he that has comes more.

I ken it as weel as fill Bayer [a cow's name] kens her stake.

I ken your meaning by your mumping.

Ilka bean has its black.

Ilka bird maun hatch his ain egg.

Ilka blade o' grass keeps its ain drap o' dew.
Everyone has their own business to attend to. According to Murison this is 'from the refrain of James Ballantyne's song "Confide ye aye in Providence" c.1850, based on a remark made by a poor woman'.

Ilka corn has its shool.

Ilka craw thinks its ain bird whitest.

Ilka dog has his day.

Ilka doorstep has its ain slippery stane.
Every thing has its own problems.

Ilka land has its ain land-law.

Ilka land has its ain leid.
'Leid' means language.

Ilka man as he likes – I'm for the cook.
Each man must choose the partner who suits him best. This suitor obviously values his stomach greatly.

Ilka man buckles his belt to his ain gate.
Everyone does what suits them best.

Ilka man thinks his ain craw blackest.

Ill-less, gude-less, like the priest's holy water.

Ill bairns are aye best heard at hame.

I'll be Daddy's bairn and Minnie's bairn.
Spoken by them who refuse to enter into a dispute/argument.

Ill beef/flesh ne'er made gude broo.
You can only get out what you put in to begin with.

I'll big nae sandy mills wi' you.
Literally, I will not build any sandcastles with you, i.e. I will not join you in any project.

I'll break yer back and send ye tae the skinner's trade.
I'll kill you.

I'll bring him doun on his marrow bones.
I will make him submit. I will bring him to his knees.

I'll bring the screw to the neb o' the mire snipe.
I will bring matters to a crisis.

I'll bring Yule belt to the Beltane bore.
I will cut back on my diet. At one time meat was plentiful at Christmas and scarce in May.

Ill comes upon waur's back.
One bad fortune tends to follow another. This is a condensed version of Henryson's original: 'Off evill cummis war, off war cummis werst of all.'

Ill counsel will gar a man stick his ain mear.
A person who has gained a bad name, is half way to being hanged.

Ill deem'd, hauf hang'd.
A person who has gained a bad name, is half way to being hanged.

I'll dee't in course, as Carrie gaed through the glen.
The 'Carrie' referred to is Alexander Scorgies 'caravan' which was an early nineteenth-century public conveyance between Aberdeen and Keith.

I'll do as McKissoch's coo did, I'll think mair than I'll say.
It sometimes pays to listen rather than to speak.

I'll do as the man did when he sell't his land.
This means that the person will not do it again, for selling one's land or assets is something one rarely does twice.

Ill doers are aye ill dreaders.
People expect to be treated in the same manner that they treat others.

Ill fortune ever follows them that are married in May.
A Scottish superstition thought to have arisen from the fact that Queen Mary married Bothwell in that month.

I'll gae as peaceably on you as on the house floor.
A phrase used as a threat.

I'll gar him draw his belt to his ribs.
I will make him defend himself.

I'll gar him plew the floor wi' his nose.
I will knock him down to the ground.

I'll gar his ain garters tie up his ain hose.
I will no longer support him.

I'll gar ye blirt with baith yer een.
Another threat.

I'll gar ye claw where its no yeucky.

I'll gar ye ken the dog frae the door bar.
I will make you keep your distance.

I'll gar ye laugh water.
I will make you cry/weep.

I'll gar ye mak twa o' that.
I will make you eat your words.

I'll gar yer harns gape.
I will make your brains clatter, i.e. I will give you a beating around the head.

I'll gar ye run like a sheep frae the shears.

I'll gar ye sing Port yowl.
I'll make you cry.

I'll get a better fore-speaker than you for nought.
I don't have to bribe people to agree with me.

I'll gie ye a bane to pike that will haud your teeth gaun.
I will give you work to do that will keep you busy for a long while.

I'll gie ye a flue-on the cheek blade till the fire flee frae yer een holes.
I will give you a severe beating around the head.

I'll gie ye a gob slake.
I will give you a punch in the mouth.

I'll gie ye a meeting, as Mortimer gave his mither.
Another phrase used as a threat.

I'll gie ye a sark fu' o' sair bones.
I'll give you a beating.

I'll gie ye let-a-bee for let-a-bee, like the bairns o' Kelty.
The speaker will give as good as he gets. 'Let-a-bee for let-a-bee' generally signifies mutual forbearance, but the addition of the phrase 'like the bairns of Kelty' reverses the usual meaning.

I'll gie ye one and lend ye another.
A threat of violence.

I'll gie ye on the one cheek, and key you on the other.
A threat.

I'll gie ye the back o' the door to keep.
I will throw you out of the house.

I'll gie ye the thing that winna mool in yer pouch.
I will give you a promise.

I'll gie ye the thing that ye'r seeking.
A threat of violence.

Ill got gear ne'er prospered.
Be sure your sins will find you out.

I'll hae nae simmering or wintering about it.
I will have no delay.

I'll hae neither hand nor foot in't.
I will have nothing to do with it.

I'll haud the grip I've got.

Ill hearing maks wrang rehearsing.

Ill herds mak fat tods.
Beware, careless/lazy people let others take advantage easily.

I'll kame your wig for you.
I will give you a good talking to.

I'll keep my mind to mysel' and tell my tale to the wind.
I will keep things to myself.

I'll ken him, by a black sheep hereafter.
'Spoken with indignation, of one that has deceived me, and whom I will not trust again' – Kelly.

I'll kiss ye behind the lug, and that winna break the blood in yer face.

I'll kiss ye when ye're sleeping and that'll hinder ye to dream o' me when you're deid.

Ill laying up maks mony thieves.
An answer given by people accused of breach of confidence.

I'll learn you to lick, for suppin' is dear.

I'll mak a raip o' draff hold you.
'Signifying that he has no great mind to go away' – Kelly.

I'll mak a shift, as Macwhid did wi' the preachin'.
'Macwhid was a knowing countryman, and a great stickler for the King and the church. At the Restoration, clergymen being scarce, he was asked if he thought he could preach; he answered that he could make a shift; upon which he was ordained and got a living.' – Kelly.

I'll mak the mantle meet for the man.
I will pay according to how well you treat me.

I'll mak your lungs ring like a Culross girdle.
I will make you scream.

I'll ne'er brew drink to treat drinkers.
According to Hislop this saying was 'applied to those who are slow to partake of anything which is offered to them and signifying that although the article is good, still, if unwilling, they will not be "treated", i.e urged or forced to take it'.

I'll ne'er buy a blind bargain, or a pig in a pock.
I will never buy something without having seen that it is to my satisfaction first.

I'll ne'er cast off me, before I go lie.
I will not give my goods away before I die.

I'll ne'er dirty the bannet I'm gaun to put on.

I'll ne'er keep a cow when I can get milk sae cheap.
I will not put myself to any trouble whilst it is easier to put others to trouble.

I'll ne'er keep a dog and bark mysel'.
I will never have subordinates and do their work for them.

I'll ne'er live poor to die rich.

I'll ne'er lout sae laigh, an' lift sae little.
I will never stoop so low for so little reward.

I'll ne'er put the rogue aboon the gentleman.
I will never upset the status quo.

I'll neither mak nor mar, as the young cock said when he saw the auld cock's neck thrawn.

Ill news are aft ower true.

Ill news travels fast.

I'll no mak stepbairns o' them.
I will treat them all alike.

I'll no slip my dog afore the game's afoot.

I'll no tell a lee for scant o' news.
I will not make up stories for want of news.

Ill payers are aye gude cravers.

I'll pay you, and put naething in your pouch.
A warning that the speaker plans on giving the listener a beating.

I'll put daur ahint the door, and do't.
I will carry out my threats.

I'll rather strive wi' the lang rigg than the ill neighbour.
I would rather do all the work myself than be troubled with a quarrelsome partner.

I'll ride my ain horse wi' my ain ha' ding.
I will do business in my own way. From Galt's Sir Andrew Wylie.

I'll say naething, but I'll yerk at the thinking.
I will not tell of your wrongdoing, though it pains me to do so.

I'll see the stars gang withershins first.
I will never let such a thing occur.

I'll sell my lad, quo' Livistone; I'll buy't quo' Balmaghie.
'If a man have a good pennyworth to sell, he will still find a buyer' – Kelly.

I'll serve ye when ye hae least to do.

I'll serve you a' wi' ae vessel.
'I will serve you all alike, or give nothing to any of you' – Kelly.

Ill's the gout, an' waurs the gravel, but want o' gold maks mony a travel.

I'll tak a rung and rizle yer rigging wi't.
A threat.

I'll tak nae mair o' your counsel than I think fit.

I'll tak the best first, as the priest did o' the plooms.

I'll tell the bourd, but no the body.
A saying denoting discretion, i.e. I will tell the joke or story, but not reveal the person involved.

Ill today and waur tomorrow.

Ill to tak and eith to tire.
A phrase applied to horses that are difficult to catch.

I'll wad [wager] a turd against your tongue; I care not whether I win or lose.
'A sarcastical answer to him who impertinently offers to lay wagers' – Kelly.

Ill weeds wax weel.

Ill will ne'er spak weel.

Ill won gear winna enrich the third heir.

Ill won, ill wair'd.

Ill workers are aye gude onlookers.

I'm as auld as your auncient.
I am as wise as you think yourself, i.e I will outwit you.

I'm as far North as you're South.
I'm as clever as you. You will not get the better of me.

I maun do as the beggars do; when my wame's fu', gang awa.
A phrase used in jest when someone who has been sharing a meal with you gets up to leave.

I may come tae brak an egg i' your pouch.

'I'm but beginning yet,' quo' the wife when she run wud.
An answer to those who ask if we have finished.

I met a man who speered at me,
Grow these berries in the sea?
I answered him by speerin again
Is there skate on Clocknaben?
A reply to overly inquisitive persons. Clocknaben is a mountain.

I'm flytin' free wi' you.
I am on very familiar terms with you.

I'm forejidged, forefoughten, and forejeskit.
An alliterative expression denoting extreme fatigue.

I'm going the errand you could not go for me.

I micht bring a better speaker frae hame than you.

I'm like the dogs o' Rawburn, I hae my back tae the wa', an if I dinna slip I'll no fa'.

I'm like the piper's cow, gie me a pickle pea-strae and sell your wind for siller.
From John Galt's Sir Andrew Wylie. *A small gift is worth more than many promises. A bird in the hand etc.*

I'm neither sma' drink thirsty, nor grey bread hungry.
Said when a person is offended by not receiving the hospitality that they had expected.

I'm no every man's dog that whistles on me.
I am independent. I am not at everyone's beck and call.

I'm no obliged to simmer and winter it to you.

I'm no sae blind as I'm bleer-e'ed.
I am not so much blind as unwilling to see.

I'm no sae green as I'm cabbage lookin.

I'm no sae scant o' clean pipes as to blaw wi' a brunt cutty.
Spoken by a woman signifying that she is not so hard up that she has to take a widower when she can attract a bachelor.

I'm no that fu' but I'm gayly yet.
I am not completely full, but I very nearly am.

I'm ower auld a dog to learn new tricks.

I'm speaking o' hay and you o' horse corn.
We are speaking about different things.

I'm wae for your skaith, there's so little o't.
'A mock condolence' – Kelly.

In a frost a nail is worth the horse.
Because it will give the horse some grip and hence may save it from falling and killing itself. Hence a small thing of no great importance may, at an opportune moment, be of great service.

In a gude time I say it, in a better I leave it.

In a post a nail is worth a horse.
Little things can sometimes be very important.

In a thousand pounds o' law there's no an ounce o' love.

Industry makes a braw man and breaks ill fortune.

I ne'er cast off before I lie doun.
I will not give away my goods before my death.

I ne'er lo'ed 'bout gates, quo' the gude wife when she harl'd the gude man o'er the fire.
i.e. I always loved plain dealing.

I ne'er lo'ed meat that craw'd in my crappie.
I have no wish to interfere with matters that might cause me harm.

I ne'er lo'ed water in my shoon, and my wame's made o' better leather.
Said by someone when he is offered a glass of water, but craves something a little stronger!

I ne'er sat on your coat-tail.
Meaning, I never impeded you in any way.

I ne'er saw a foul thing cleanly.
'Spoken when they who used to be dirty enough, pretend to cleanliness' – Kelly.

I neither got stock nor hoch.
i.e. neither money nor interest.

In harvest time lairds are labourers.
'Spoken to urge them to work in harvest, who perhaps think it below them' – Kelly.

In ower muckle clavering truth is tint.

In summer time be cheerful, chaste, and early out of bed;
In winter be well capped, well shod, and well on porridge fed.
A health maxim attributed to Dr John Beaton of Mull who died in 1657.

Inverugie by the sea, Lordless shall try thy lands be,
And underneath thy hearthstane
The tod shall bring her birds hame
Attributed to Thomas the Rhymer.

I pricked nae louse since I darned your hose, and then I might hae pricked a thousand.
'An answer of a tailor to him that calls him pricklouse' – Kelly.

Ireland will be your hinder end.
'Foreboding that he will steal, and go to Ireland to escape justice' – Kelly.

I sat upon my houtie croutie [hams],
I lookit owre my rumple toutie [haunch],
And I saw John Heezlum Peezlum
Playing on Jerusalem pipes.
This old saying refers to the man in the moon.

I scorn to mak my mou' my arse.
Said in indignation to those who would have us deny what we have just said.

I sought nae gude and to nane, like Michael Scott's man.
A phrase applied when people are refused what they don't ask for. The phrase comes from the story of Michael Scott's man in Sir Walter Scott's The Antiquary.

I spoke but ane word, gie me but ane knock.
'Spoken by those who being reprimanded for offering their opinion in a business, excuse themselves, by saying that they will proceed no farther' – Kelly.

Is there ony mice in your arse?
A rude retort to those who speak of themselves in the plural.

It begins to wark like soap on a sow's arse.
According to Kelly this phrase is 'spoken tauntingly when a business grows more involv'd, intricate, and troublesome'.

It canna be worse that's no worth a tinker's curse.

It comes to the hand like the bowl o' a pintstoup.
It comes naturally.

It doesna become your faither's son to speak in that manner to his faither's son.
A caution against low company.

It doesna set a sow to wear a saddle.
It does not suit vulgar people to wear fine clothes.

It gangs as muckle intae my heart as my heel.

It gangs in at ae end, and oot o' the ither.
Said when someone has paid no attention to what has been said.

It has nae other faither but you.
'Spoken when people commend what they are selling' – Kelly.

It has neither arse nor elbow.
It is without shape.

Ither folk are weel faur'd, but ye're no sae vera.
Said in jest meaning that the person so addressed is no oil painting in the beauty stakes. To be 'weel faur'd' is to be good looking.

I think mair o' the sight than the ferlie.
I am more pleased that I had my eyes to see than in what I saw.

I think mair o' your kindness than it's a' worth.
Spoken with resentment, to those who have neglected your business.

'I think we will a' be chapmen', quo' the gudewife when she got a turd on her back.
Kelly says this is 'a reprimand to those who perk up with their superiors, pretend to equal them in cloaths, etc.'.

I think you hae ta'en the grumple-face.
Applied to those who always express displeasure.

It is better to travel hopefully than to arrive.
From Virginibus Puerisque *(1881), by Robert Louis Stevenson.*

It keeps his nose at the grundstane.

It maun e'en be ower shoon ower boots wi' me now.
Said by a person who has gone so far in a matter that they must go through with it come what may.

It may be that swine may flee, but it's no an ilka day's bird.
An extreme expression of incredulity at an improbable or extraordinary statement.

It may be true what some men say; it maun be true what a' men say.

It may come in an hour what winna gang in seven years.

It rains Jeddart staffs.
It rains cats and dogs, or torrentially.

It's a bare moor that ye gang through an' no get a heather cow.
A 'heather cow' is a twig or piece of heath.

It's a bauch brewing that's no gude in the newing.

It's a cauld stamach that naething hets on.

It's a dry tale that disna end in a drink.

It's a far cry to Loch Awe.
Said when a person considers it safe to behave unlawfully because they are so far away from the seat of authority. This saying possibly originates from a renegade member of the Clan Campbell, whose seat of power was at Loch Awe. However Murison says it 'is a translation of the Gaelic "Is fad an eigh o Loch Odha", which is said to have originated in the battle of Glenlivet in 1594 when the Earl of Argyll, far from reinforcements from his own castle of Inveraray on Loch Awe, was severely defeated by the Gordons. So the moral is "Don't stick out your neck too far".'

It's a feeble hand that canna do gude when the heart is willing.

It's a fine place, for a' the folk there are jist like mysel'.
A saying particular to Greenock.

It's a friend that ruses you.

It's a gude enough world if it haud.
A humorous reply given to those who complain that it is a 'weary' world.

It's a gude game that fills the wame.

It's a gude goose but it has an ill gansel.
A gansel could be either a honk, or a harsh sauce made with garlic. The phrase was traditionally applied to a woman suggesting that although she was well-favoured there was more to her than met the eye – namely a harsh tongue.

It's a gude goose that draps aye.
It is a good friend that is always giving.

It's a gude maut that comes wi' will.
A drink is all the better for being given cheerfully.

It's a gude poor man's blade; it will bend ere it break.

It's a gude tongue that says nae ill, but a better heart that thinks nane.

It's a gude tree that will neither knap nor gaw.
It's a good thing that is without fault.

It's a gude warld, but it's ill divided.

It's a gude wood that hath ne'er a withered branch in it.

It's a gude world, but they're ill that are in't.

It's a hard task to be poor and leal.

It's a lamb at the up-takin', but an auld sheep or ye get it aff.
A warning to those starting any habit which is addictive – it's easy to start but very difficult to stop later on.

It's a lean collop that's ta'en aff a chicken.

It's a mean mouse that has but ae hole.

It's an auld tout on a new horn.
It is the same old story dressed up in different words.

It's an awfu' sign o' rain when ye hear it amang the cabbage.

It's an ill bargain where nane wins.

It's an ill bird that files its ain nest.
It takes a truly bad person to harm his own kith and kin.

It's an ill cause that none dare speak in.

It's an ill cause that the lawyer thinks shame o'.

It's an ill fecht where he that wins has the warst o't.

It's an ill kitchen that keeps the bread awa',
Or an ill master that starves his servants.

It's an ill pack that's no worth the custom.

It's an ill servant's nae worth's meat.

It's an ill thow that comes frae the North.

It's an ill turn than patience winna owercome.

It's an ill wind that blaws naebody gude.

It's an ugly lass that's never kissed, and a silly body that's never missed.

It's a' outs an' ins like Willie Wood's wife's wame.
Said of something with an undulating appearance.

It's a pity fair weather should e'er do harm.

It's a poor kin, that has neither whore nor thief in it.

It's a poor tongue that canna tell its ain name.
From Walter Scott's St Ronan's Well.

It's a puir moose that has but ae hole.

It's a puir warld that winna gie a bit and a brat.

It's a rare thing for siller to lack a maister.
Money rarely lies unclaimed.

It's a sair dung bairn that mayna greet.

It's a sair field where a's slain.

It's a sair time when the mouse looks out o' the meal barrel wi' a saut tear in its e'e.
Things are in a very sorry state when even the mice cannot find enough to eat.

It's a sairy brewing that's no gude in newing.
Spoken when people are greatly taken by new projects.

It's a sairy collop that's ta'en aff a chicken.

It's a sairy/silly flock where the ewie bears the bell.
A misogynistic remark that it is a sad household where the wife is in control.

It's a sairy hen that canna scrape for ae bird.
i.e. a sorry parent that cannot provide for one child.

It's a sairy wood, that has ne'er a withered bough in it.

It's as easy to get siller frae a lawyer as butter frae a black dog's hause [throat].
i.e. both are proverbially impossible.

It's a shame to eat the cow an' worry on the tail.
Try not to overlook large faults and then pick on small ones.

It's a silly pack that may not pay the customs.

It's a sin to lee on the deil.
It is wrong to call bad people worse than they are.

It's a sin to put foul hands on it.

It's a sma' sheil that gies nae shelter.

It's a sour reek when the gudewife dings the gudeman.
This proverb originates from a country tale of husband battering. A man seen coming out of his house with tears on his cheeks initially said that they were caused by smoke in the house, but on further enquiry admitted that his wife had beaten him.

It's a south dream that's seen waking.
It's easy to guess what appears to be evident.

It's as plain as a pike staff.
This phrase appears in Scott's Rob Roy, *chap. 26 as: 'It's as plain as Peter Pasley's pike staff.'*

It's a staunch house that there's ne'er a drap in.

It's as true as Biglam's cat crew, and the cock rock'd the cradle.
The statement alluded to is completely untrue.

It's a thrawn-fac'd wean that's gotten against the faither's will.
According to Kelly, 'Kindness extorted comes always with a bad grace'.

"It's aye gude to be ceevil," quo' the auld wife when she beckit to the deevil.

It's a true dream, that is seen making.
It is easy to guess what is evident.

It's best to let saut water tak its ain gate, luck never came o' crossing it.
This saying comes from an old superstition that it was unlucky to save a drowning man.

It's best to sit next the chumley when the lum reeks.
Sometimes what appears to be the most dangerous position is in fact the safest.

It's best travelling wi' a horse in your hand.
It is better to travel on horseback than on foot.

It's better nae to slip ae knot till anither be tied.
It's best to keep what you have until you can see something better.

It's better sheltering under an auld hedge than under a new planted wood.
Sometimes old things are better than new ones.

It's better to drag soon than draw late.
It is better to use strong measures at the appropriate time.

It's better to flyte than to fret.

It's better to hear the laverock sing than the mouse cheep.
According to Murison this is 'a motto for guerillas to keep as much as possible in the open, ascribed by Scott to the Douglases in the War of Independence'.

It's better to sup wi' a cutty than want a spoon.

It's but a year sooner to the begging.
A phrase used facetiously when we come across something which is more expensive than we had anticipated.

It's but kindly that the pock savour of the herring.
It is but natural that the bag should bear traces of what it has contained. Often used to speak about the influence of parents on their children's character.

It's by the mouth o' the cow that the milk comes.
You only get out what you put in to begin with.

It's clean about the wren's door when there's nought within.
Said about messy people.

It's come to mickle, but it's nae come to that.

It's dear cost honey that's licked aff a thorn.

It's drappin' suit.
A phrase used to subtly warn when the subject of conversation should be changed.

It's drink will you, but no drink shall you.
A criticism of a person's hospitality, when they politely ask if you would like a drink, but press the matter no further.

It's easier to big lums than keep them reeking.
The difficult tasks in life require perseverance.

It's easier to forgie than to forget.

It's either a tod or a fern bush.
Used when the speaker cannot be bothered to be precise.

It serves naething to strive wi' cripples.

It sets a haggis to be roasted, for burning o' the bag.

It sets not a haggis to be roasted, for burning of the bag.
'High stations become not mean persons, for they will misbehave in them' – Kelly.

It sets ye not to speak o' him, till ye wash yer mouth with wine, and wipe it with a lawn towel.
'A haughty vindication of a friend when we hear him badly spoken of by mean persons' – Kelly.

It sets you weel to gab wi' your bannet on.
According to G. Henderson this phrase is one of a series of 'expressions of contempt applied to a presumptuous person'.

It sets you weel to slaver, you let sic gaadys fall.

It's fair in hall, where beards wag all.
'Spoken when we give a share of what is going to everybody, that all may eat alike' – Kelly.

It's far to seek an' ill to find.

It's far to seek and ill to find like Meg's maidenhead.

It's folly to live poor to die rich.
Meaning you cannot take your wealth with you when you die.

It's gane awa' like a handfu' o' ingan peelins on a windy day.

It's God that feeds the craws, that neither till, harrow nor saw.

It's gowd that glistens in the lasses' een.
Girls are attracted by wealthy men.

It's growing to the grund, like a stirk's tail.
Meaning that something is not progressing in the desired direction.

It's gude baking beside the meal.
People can do well when they have something nearby to supply/support them.

It's gude fighting under a buckler.
Both of the above indicate that it is easy to do something when every assistance is easily to hand.

It's gude fishing in drumly waters.

It's gude fish when it's gripped.

It's gude game that fills the wame.

It's gude gear that pleases the merchant.

It's gude sleeping in a hale skin.

It's gude to begin weel, but better to end weel.

It's gude to be in your time, ye kenna how long it might last.
It's best to seize things while you have the opportunity.

'It's gude to be merry and wise,' quo' the miller when he mouter'd twice.

To 'mouter' is to take the fees for something. Hence the naughty miller in the saying has taken advantage of his customers by taking his fees twice over.

It's gude to be out o' harm's gate.

It's gude to be sib to siller.
It is good to be related to wealthy persons.

It's gude to dread the warst, the best will be the welcomer.
If one prepares for the worst, anything less seems like good news.

It's gude to hae friends baith in heaven and in hell.
It's best to have friends from all sorts of backgrounds.

It's gude to hae twa strings to yer bow.

It's gude to hae your cog out when it rains kail.
Make the most of your opportunities.

It's gude to nip the briar in the bud.
It's best to tackle thorny problems when they are small and easily dealt with.

It shall not be for your ease and honour both.
'Spoken when we threaten to make a thing done to us, either uneasy or disgraceful to the authors' – Kelly.

It's hard baith to hae and want.

It's hard/ill baith to pray and pay.

It's hard for a greedy ee to hae a leal heart.
It is hard for a covetous person to be loyal and honest.

It's hard to be poor and leal.

It's hard to gar an auld mare leave aff flinging.

It's hard to keep the flax frae the lowe.

It's hard to please a'body.

It's hard to sit in Rome and strive wi' the Pope.
It is hard to fight with those who are in authority over us.

It's idle to spur a ham shackled horse.

It's ill ale that's sour when it's new.

It's ill bringing but what's no ben.
[A 'but an' ben' is a simple house containing two rooms.]
We should produce only what we don't already possess.

It's ill coming atween a fasting man and his meat.

It's ill gieing the fox the geese to keep.

It's ill limping before cripples.

It's ill makin' a silk purse frae a soo's lug.
In his collection Ramsay adds the following phrase: 'or a toutin horn o a tod's tail'. See below for a similar version.

It's ill making a blawing horn out o' a tod's tail.
One cannot make a fine object out of inferior materials.

It's ill making a deadly enemy out of a gude friend.

It's ill meddling between the bark and the rind.
It's better not to interfere between husband and wife, or close relations.

It's ill praising green barley.
It is not wise to praise things when we are not sure how they will turn out.

It's ill speaking between a fu' man and a fasting.
A hungry man and a well-fed man are not usually on good terms with each other. This saying is sometimes used to encourage a guest to have something to eat. It was first recorded by Fergusson in his Scottish Proverbs *as 'Thair is nothing betuix a bursten body and a hungered'.*

It's ill taking corn frae geese.

It's ill to be ca'd a thief , and aye found picking.
It is not helpful to be found in suspicious circumstances if one already has a bad name.

It's ill to belittle what comes frae the bounteous hand o' providence.

It's ill to despair when there's ony out-gate.

It's ill to ken whaur a blister may licht.

It's ill to mak an unlawful oath, but waur to keep it.

It's ill to put a blythe face on a black heart.
It is wrong to act pleasantly whilst thinking otherwise, i.e. don't be two-faced.

It's ill to say it's wrang when my lord says it's right.
It is dangerous to speak against the views of those who are in positions of authority.

It's ill to tak the breeks aff a Hielandman.
Highlanders proper were not in the habit of wearing anything under their kilts. Hence it is difficult to take from someone what they do not possess! Kelly gives another version thus: "'It's ill to take breeks off a bare arse.'

It's ill waur'd that maisters want gear.

It's ill waur'd that wasters want.

It's kindly the poke sa're o' the herring.
It is common for children to take after their parents.

It's kittle for the cheeks when the hurlbarrow gaes over the brig o' the nose.

It's kittle shooting at corbies and clergy.

It's kittle to wauken sleeping dogs.

It's lang ere ye saddle a foal.

It's lang or four bare legs gather heat in a bed.
This saying is applied to young people who get married before they have everything necessary to support a successful marriage, thinking that love will be enough.

It's lang or ye need cry 'schew!' to an egg.
There is no hurry, it will be some time before the egg is a chicken.

It's lang to Lammas.
'Spoken in jest when we forget to lay down bread at the table, as if we had done it designedly because it will be long ere new bread come' – Kelly.

It's like the bairn o' Blythe, it's in the hoose amang ye.
Said when there is an unavoidable truth to be faced up to. Blythe is an isolated Lammermuir farmhouse where a pregnant young woman rounded on the assembled young men, all of whom were denying paternity, with the fact that wouldn't go away – 'It's here in the house among you'.

It's like Truffy's courtship, short but pithy.

It's little o' God's might that makes a poor man a knight.

It's muckle gars tailors laugh, but souters girn aye.
This saying suggests that tailors tend to be serious, whereas shoemakers are the reverse.

It's nae better than it's ca'ed.
Spoken when in necessity we take what we have use for.

It's nae everyman that feels the stink o' his ain fart.
Not everyone is sensible to his own defects.

It's nae laughing to girn in a widdy.
It's no joke to be put in a difficult/dangerous position.

It's nae mair pity to see a woman greet than to see a goose go barefit.
A rather ungallant suggestion alluding to the facility with which women can avail themselves of tears to carry a point.

It's nae play when ane laughs and anither greets.

It's nae shift to want.

It's nae sin to see wasters want.

It's nae sin to tak a gude price, but in gieing ill measure.

It's nae time to lout quhen the heid is aff.
An old saying from the days when battle-axes were used.

It's nae use putting thatch on an empty barn.

It's nae use to be put about for the death ye'll never dee.

It's nae wonder wasters want and lathrons lag behint.

It's natural for a duck tae soom.

It's needless pouring water on a drowned mouse.

It's needless to gar a wud man run.
Said when people urge us to hurry when we are already going as fast as we can.

It's neither a far road nor a foul gate.

It's neither by Civil Law, nor by Canon Law, but by Duns Law, that the Bishops were expelled from Scotland.
i.e. they were expelled by force – namely the covenanting army assembled at Duns Law with General Leslie.

It's neither here nor there, nor yet, ayont the water.

It's neither rhyme nor reason.

It's no 'What is she?' but 'What has she?'

It's no aye gude i' the maw what's sweet i' the mouth.
Looks can be deceptive. Don't always go on first impressions.

It's no aye the fattest foddering that maks the fu'est aumry.

It's no easy to straucht in the aik the crook that grew in the saplin.
Simple childcare advice – start as you mean to go on, or it will be difficult to change later on. It's not always easy to sort out problems when they have been allowed to continue for some time unchecked.

It's no for nocht the gled whistles.
There is a good reason behind most things.

It's no lang since louse bore langett, no wonder she fell and broke her neck.
'Langett' is a rope or chain used to bind a horse's forefoot to his hind one. According to Kelly this phrase was 'spoken when one has suddenly started up to a high station, and behaves himself saucily in it'.

It's no safe wadin' in unco waters.

It's no sonsie to meet a bare fit i' the mornin.

It's no the burden but the owerburden that kills the beast.
A warning not to overload anything with too much work or it will be rendered useless to complete its normal duties.

It's no the cowl that maks the friar.

It's no the gear to traike.

It's no the rumblin' cart that fa's first ower the brae.
It is not always the oldest or most infirm person who dies first.

It's no the way to grip a bird, to cast your bonnet at her.
Kelly calls this 'A vile, malicious proverb, persuading to conceal your resentment, till a proper time of revenge offer, lest your enemies, being appriz'd of your design, arm against you'.

It's no tint, a friend gets.
We all benefit when a friend gets something.

It's no tint that comes at last.

It's not the pick o' the swine that the beggar gets.

It's no what we hae, but what we do wi' what wi' hae, that counts in heaven.

It's ower far between the kitchen an' the ha'.

It's ower late to lout when the head's got a clout.
A warning not to leave things too late.

It's ower late to lock the stable when the naig's awa'.

It's ower late to spare when the back's bare.

It's ower weel hoarded that canna be found.

It's past jokin' when the heid's aff.
See above 'it's nae time to lout etc.'

It spreads like muirburn.
Said of ill news.

It's sair tae haud drink frae drouth.

It's some strong o' the apple.
A common Aberdeenshire expression for beer which is rather tart or sharp.

It's stinking praise comes out o' ane's ain mouth.
Self praise is no praise at all.

It starts like a threid and ends up like a cart-raip.
A saying applied to a rumour which magnifies in the telling.

It's the barley pickle breaks the naig's back.

It's the best feather in yer wing.
It is your greatest strength.

It's the best spoke in your wheel.

It's the laird's commands, an' the loon maun loup.
Spoken of orders from those in authority which must be obeyed no matter how unreasonable or ludicrous they seem.

It's the life o' an auld bannet to be weel set-up.

It's the life o' an auld hat to be weel cocket.
It renews life in the old if they are admired or complimented on their looks.

It's the loose spoke in the wheel that rattles most.

It's the mou' that maks the coo.

It's the poor man's office to look, and the rich man cannot forbear it.
Spoken in reply to those who ask what we are looking at.

It's the wanton steed that scaurs at the windlestrae.

It's the waur o' the wear.

It's time enough tae skreigh when ye're strucken.

It's time enough to mak my bed when I'm gawn to lie down.

It's time to rise, if you be clean under you.
'That is if you have not beshit the bed; for in that case you would be ashamed to rise' – Kelly.

It's tint that is done to old men and bairns.
The old men will die and the children forget.

It's too late to spare, when the bottom is bare.
A plea not to be wasteful.

It stoors in an oor.
A Lanarkshire farming expression to describe the dryness of the soil, i.e. it turns to dust quickly.

It's weak i' the wow, like Barr's cat.
'Wow' means a howl.

It's weel that our fauts are no written in our face.

It's weel won that's aff the wame.
It is well saved that is won from the stomach.

It was but their claes that cast oot.
'That is, the quarrel was not real, but only with design, in order to accomplish some end' – Kelly.

It was nae for naething that the cat lickit the stane.

It was ne'er a gude aiver that flung at the broose.
More words of warning to those contemplating marriage. If there is trouble at the outset, things are unlikely to go smoothly thereafter. The 'broose' was a race held at country weddings.

It was ne'er for naething the gled whistled.
'People who officiously offer their service, may be suspected to have some selfish end in it' – Kelly.

It were a pity tae refuse ye, ye seek sae little.

It were a pity to put a foul hand on't.

It were telling your kin, your craig were broken, that you was like me.
'Spoken with indignation to them that disparage your friend' – Kelly.

It will aye be a dirty dub between them.
It will always be a point of contention between them.

It will be a dirten pingle.
Spoken when two cowards are going to fight.

It will be a feather in your cap.
Such an act will add to your reputation.

It will be a feather out o' your wing.
Opposite of the above.

It will be a gude fire when it burns, quo' the tod when he pish'd on the ice.
'Nothing but a ridicule upon a bad fire' – Kelly.

It will be a het day gars you startle.

It will be an ill web to bleach.

It will be lang ere ye wear to the knee lids.
A phrase suggesting the person thus spoken of is not overly industrious.

It will be the last word o' his testament.
He will delay from doing a thing for as long as possible.

It will come out yet, like the hommel corn.
'Hommel corn' is grain that has no beard. Hence the proverb means that a certain result can be expected given enough time.

It will haud out an honest man, but naething'll haud out a rogue.

It will mak a braw show in a landward kirk.
Said by somebody when their opinion is asked of something which they consider vulgar or gaudy.

It would be a hard task to follow a black dockit sow through a burnt muir this night.
It's pitch black.

It would be a pity to hae spoilt twa houses wi' them.
Spoken when two disagreeable people get married to each other.

It would do a blind man gude to see't.

I've made a vow, and I'll keep it true,
That I'll ne'er stang man through good sheep's woo'.
This phrase is known as the Adder's Aith. These snakes were not supposed to be able to bite through woollen cloth.

I've seen wiser eating grass.
Said about an idiot.

I will add a stane to his cairn.
I will testify to the virtues of the departed.

I will be your servant when you have least to do and most to spend.

I Willie Wastle,
Stand firm in my castle,
And a' the dogs in your toun
Canna ding Willie Wastle doon.
A childhood rhyme used in the game I'm King of the Castle. This rhyme was said to have been sent by John Cockburn, Governor of Hume Castle, as an answer to a summons of surrender by Colonel George Fenwick in 1650.

I will ne'er drite in my bonnet, and set it on my head.
'I will never make a whore of a woman that I resolve to marry, or marry the woman I have made a whore of' – Kelly.

I will put a nick in my stick.
i.e. I will note it, remember it. This phrase originates from the practice adopted by bakers who used nick sticks as a form of tally in settling with their customers. Each family had its own nick stick and each time a loaf of bread was delivered a nick was put in the stick as a counter.

I will sooner walk to the grave o' Sir Patrick Spence and the Scottish Lords, wha lie between Leith and Aberdeen.
I would rather kill myself than do what you wish.

'I winna mak a toil o' a pleasure,' quo' the man when he buried his wife.

I winna creep in his arse, for a week o' his fair weather.
I will not suck up to this person.

I winna lie in my ain dish.
i.e. say I have got food when I have not.

I winna mak fish o' ane an' flesh o' anither.
I will show no favours, but treat all alike.

I wish he and I had a peck o' gold to deal, there should be scarted
backs o' hands, and hinging by the wicks o' the mouth.
*'Spoken when one is said to be stronger than us, intimating that upon a good
occasion we would not yield to him' – Kelly.*

I wish I could put my finger where you can put your whole hand.

I wish I had a string in his lug.

I wish it may be the first sight ye'll see.
*An answer given to someone who tells you they are expecting something good
which you are dubious they will actually get.*

I wish you had brose to lay the hair o' your beard.
A disdainful answer of a girl to her sweetheart.

I wish you had drunk water when you drank that soup drink.
*Spoken to someone who is being indiscreet, suggesting that he would have been
more sensible if he'd been sober.*

I wish you had wist what you said.

I wish you hae as muckle Scotch as tak you to your bed.
*'Spoken when our companions, beginning to take with the drink, begin to speak
Latin . . . believing that by and by they will be at that pass that they will be able
to speak no language' – Kelly.*

I wish you may lamb in your lair, as many a gude ewe has done.
Said to those who lie long in bed.

I wish you readier meat than a rinnin' hare.

I wish you the gude o't that dogs get o' grass.

I wish you was neither adest her nor ayont her.
'Spoken to them who jeer you with some woman you have an aversion to' – Kelly.

I wish you were able, e'en though ye didna do't.

I wish you were laird o' yer word.

I would as soon see your nose cheese, and the cat get the first bite
o't.
A disdainful answer of a girl to her sweetheart.

I would be very loth, and scant o' cloth, to sole my hose wi'
dockans.

I would gie a plack and a bawbee for that.
It is something of value. The phrase is used in Galt's Sir Andrew Wylie.

I would hae my ee fu'.

I would hae something to look at on Sunday.
The reply given by a man who is asked what use a wife would be to him.

I wouldna be deaved wi' your keckling for a' your eggs.
Your bad points outweigh your good ones.

I wouldna ca' the king my cousin.
An expression of extreme contentment.

I wouldna fodder you for a' your muck *or*
I wouldna fodder you for a' your wark.
On balance your bad points outweigh your good ones.

I wouldna hae kent ye if I had met ye in my parritch.
I wouldn't recognise you even if we came face to face.

I wouldna tak a bite o' his bed straw for the love o' his person.
A saucy answer given by a girl when told of a sweetheart she pretends not to like.

I wouldna that my fit war in your shoon.
I would not like to be in your position.

I would rather be your Bible than your horse.
A humorous allusion to the fact that the subject neglects the former and overworks the latter.

I would rather gae by his door than ower his grave.
A wish that a sick friend recovers soon.

I would rather hae a groat than a grip o' your coat.
'A courtship ritual spoken by young fellows when girls run away from them, as if they were careless' – Kelly.

I would rather my bannock burn than that you should turn't.
I would rather suffer than be indebted to you in any way.

'I would rather see then hear tell o't,' as blind Pete said.
It is better to actually have something than to merely hear about it.

I would sooner see ye fleipeyed, like a French cat.
'A disdainful rejection of an unworthy proposal' – Kelly.

J

Jeddart justice – first hang a man and syne try him.
'According to Crawford, in his memoirs, the phrase Jeddart Justice took its rise in 1574, on the occasion of the Regent Morton there and then trying and condemning, with cruel precipitation, a vast number of people who had offended against the laws, or against the supreme cause of his lordship's faction. A different origin is assigned by the people. Upon the occasion, say they, of nearly twenty criminals being tried for one offence, the jury were equally divided in opinion as to a verdict, when one who had been asleep during the whole trial suddenly awoke, and, being interrogated for his vote, vociferated, "Hang them a'!" – Robert Chambers.

Jock's a mislear'd imp, but ye're a rum-deil.
Jock may be mischievious but he's well-behaved by your standards.

'John, John, pit your neck in the nick to please the laird.'
According to tradition a wife is supposed to have said this to her husband who was resisting the laird's efforts to hang him. The phrase is applied to anyone who is unduly complaisant to the wishes of their superiors.

Joke at leisure; you kenna wha may jibe yoursel'.

Jouk, and let the jaw gang by.
Literally, duck and let the deluge pass by, i.e. it is better to yield to the inevitable and wait until it has passed.

'Just as it fa's', quo the wooer to the maid.
Legend has it that when a courtier went to woo a maid she was preparing the meal and had a drop at the end of her nose. When she asked him if he was going to stay the night he replied as above, meaning that if the drop fell into his meat he would leave, and if not he would stay.

Just be fair gude e'en, and fair gude day.
i.e. treat them as you did before. Used in Galt's Entail.

Just enough and nae mair, like Janet Howie's shearer's meat.
Spoken when people have eaten all that is before them.

Just, father, just; three half-crowns mak five shillings; gie me the money and I'll pay the man.

Justice wrangs nae man.

K

Kae me, and I'll kae you.
Here 'kae' means to invite.

Kail hains bread.

Kame sindle, kame sair.
Literally, if the hair is seldom combed it becomes tangled and hence painful to comb, i.e. if we don't carry out routine chores, we are storing up trouble for the future.

Kamesters are aye creeshy.
People are always like their work.

Katie Sweerock, frae where she sat, cried, 'Reik me this, and reik me that.'
A saying applied to lazy people who get others to carry out chores they should be doing themselves.

Keek in my kail pat, glower in my aumrie.
'Spoken to them who officiously pry into our actions' – Kelly.

Keek in the stoup, was ne'er a gude fellow.
Said of one who looks into the pot to see if the drink is nearly finished rather than drinking up and ordering more when his glass is empty.

Keep a calm sough.
Keep your own counsel on certain delicate matters.

Keep aff and gie fair words.
Promise much, but do little.

Keep a thing seven years and ye'll find a use for't.
The hoarder's motto.

Keep gude company and ye'll be counted ane o' them.
You will be judged by the company you keep.

Keep hame and hame will keep you.

Keep as mickle of your Scots tongue as will buy your dog a loaf.
'A reprimand to conceited fellows who affectedly speak English, or, as they say, begin to knap' – Kelly.

Keep hame, an' hame will keep ye.

Keep Mormond Hill a handspike high,
And Rattray Briggs ye'll no come nigh.
A Northeast sailors' warning. Mormond Hill is a few miles from Fraserburgh and Rattray Briggs is a reef of dangerous rocks on the coast between Fraserburgh and Peterhead.

Keep out o' his company that cracks o' his cheatery.
Do not become associated with a person who boasts of his cunning.

Keep something for a sair fit.
Keep something for a rainy day.

Keep that at hame wi' you.
'Spoken when people unawares upbraid us with what some of their own near relations are guilty of' – Kelly.

Keep the feast till the feast day.
'Advice to maidens, not to dispose of their viginity till they be married' – Kelly.

Keep the head and feet warm, and the rest will tak nae harm.

Keep the staff in your ain hand.

Keep woo', and it will be dirt, keep lint, and it will be silk.
Lint improves with keeping, but wool deteriorates.

Keep your ain fish guts to your ain sea-maws.
Keep any extras which you may accrue for your own kith and kin rather than for others. Charity begins at home.

Keep your ain grease for your ain cart wheels.
Similar to the preceding proverb.

Keep your ain side o' the wa'.
Keep your place.

Keep your breath to cool your parritch.
Said of people who have let off steam in a moment of anger.

Keep your foot out o' the fire, an' I'll keep that frae you.
'Spoken to them who expect a thing, that they are not likely to get' – Kelly.

Keep your gab steekit when ye kenna your company.
Be silent when you are in the company of strangers.

Keep your halter fu' and ride in the middle.
'Advice to young women to have as many strings to their bow as possible, and to keep their admirers well in hand' – Cheviot.

Keep your kiln-dried taunts for your mouldy hair'd maidens.
'A disdainful return to those who are too liberal with their taunts' – Kelly.

Keep your mocks till ye're married.

Keep your mouth shut and your een open.

Keep your thoomb on that.
i.e. cover it up discreetly.

Keep your tongue a prisoner and your body will go free.

Keep your tongue within your teeth.
Stay quiet.

Ken'd folk's nae company.

Ken when to spend and when to spare, and ye needna be busy, and ye'll ne'er be bare.
Advice on how to live happily within one's means.

Ken yoursel', and your neighbour winna misken you.

Kill the cock the laird's coming; well I wot he's welcome.
'A senseless bauble, spoken by servants, when they see the laird a coming' – Kelly.

Kindle a candle at baith ends and it'll soon be done.

Kindness canna stand aye on ae side.

Kindness comes o' will; it canna be cost.

Kindness is like cress-seed; it grows fast.

Kindness is like cress-seed – it multiplies by bein' sawn.

Kindness lies not aye in ae side o' the house.

Kindness will creep where it canna gang.

Kings and bears aft worry their keepers.
'Witness the tragic end of many courtiers' – Kelly.

Kings are kittle cattle to shoe behint.
Kings are not to be trusted.

Kings are oot o' play.
Kings should not be made fun of.

King's cauff's better than ither men's corn.
Even the little perquisites which attend the King's service are worth more than most men's wages. This saying was recorded in Carmichael's Proverbs in Scots *around 1628, and is quoted in the writings of both Burns and Scott.*

King's cheese gaes half away in parings.
A large part of a King's income is absorbed in the expense of collecting it.

Kings hae lang hands.
i.e. their power reaches far and wide.

Kiss and be kind, the fiddler is blind.
When the fiddler gives the signal, take the hint and ignore his presence. It was traditional at one time when at a Scottish dance for the fiddler to make his instruments emit a squeak like a kiss and for the gentlemen to take the opportunity to kiss his partner.

Kiss a sclate stane, and that winna slaver you.

Kissing gaes by favour.

Kissing is cried doun since the shaking o' hands.
In 1721 the Church made a proclamation forbidding all kissing by the mouth. Hand-shaking however was allowed. This saying was spoken by women who were asked for a kiss but who were unwilling to allow it.

Kiss my arse Kilmarnock, I'm as little in your common, as you are in mine.
To be in one's common is to be obliged to someone.

Kiss my foot, there's mair flesh on't.
A reply to those who try to ingratiate themselves by asking permission to kiss the hand.

Kiss ye her all but the mouth and then ye will not miss her arse.
'A surlish return to them that jeer you with being too familiar with such a woman' – Kelly.

Kiss ye me till I be white, an' that will be an ill web to bleach.

Kiss yer luckie, she lives in Leith.
'A phrase used when one thinks it not worth giving a direct answer or when one thinks oneself foolishly accused' – Allan Ramsay.

Kitchin well is come to the town.
'Spoken by mothers to their children, when they would have them spare what they give them to their bread; for they have no more to give them' – Kelly.

Knock a carle, and ding a carle, and that's the way to win a carle; Kiss a carle, and clap a carle, and that's the way to tine a carle.
'People of mean breeding are rather to be won by harsh treatment than civil' – Kelly.

Knowledge is eith borne about.

Kythe in your ain colours, that folk may ken ye.

Kiss my niry-nary, that's my arse in English.
Kelly says this was used as 'a ridiculous taunting bauble'.

Kiss the hare's foot.
According to Kelly this is 'spoken to them who come late to dinner', but he does not know the origins of the saying.

L

Lacking breeds laziness, but praise breeds pith.
Positive comment will spur somebody on, negative comment the reverse.

Laddedie, Radernie, Lathockar, and Lanthone,
Ye may saw wi' gloves off, and sheer wi' gloves on.
This saying denotes several high-lying farms in Fife where planting can be so late that it runs into summer, and harvest can be so late that winter is setting in.

Lads will be men.

Lady, Lady Landers, Lady, Lady Landers,
Take up your coats about your head, and fly away to **Flanders.**
A child's rhyme recited on seeing a ladybird.

Laith to bed and laith to rise.

Laith to drink, laith frae't.
Although some people are slow to take to something, once started it can be difficult to get them to stop.

Lang and sma', gude for naething ava.
A cheeky remark about tall thin people.

Lang beards heartless,
Painted hoods witless,
Gay coats graceless,
Mak England thriftless.
A taunting rhyme of the fourteenth century used against the English.

Lang ere the deil dee by the dyke-side.
Said when the improbable death of an ill disposed but powerful person is talked of.

Langest at the fire soonest finds cauld.

Lang fasting gathers wind.

Lang fasting hains nae meat.

Lang leal, lang poor.
An unusual proverb suggesting being selfish is the best policy rather than loyalty or honesty.

Lang lean maks hamald cattle.
According to Hislop, 'That is, poorly kept cattle makes homely, domestic, or common meat.'

Lang look'd for, come at last.
Another version of the watched pot never boils.

Lang may yer lum reek.
An expression wishing the recipient a long and healthy life.

Lang mint, little dint.
Much ado about nothing.

Lang noses are aye takin' till them.

Lang or you cut Falkland wood wi' a penknife.
A phrase used when people enter into large undertakings without sufficient means or preparations.

Lang sick, soon weel.

Lang sport turns aft to earnest.

Lang standing and little offering maks a poor priest.

'Lang straes are nae motes,' quo' the wife when she haul'd the cat out o' the kirn.

Lang tarrowing taks a' the thanks awa'.
He who promises should be quick to act or he will lose the gratitude of the person promised.

Lang-tongued wives gang lang wi' bairn.
Said of people who broadcast their plans long before they are sure they will be completed.

Lasses and glasses are bruckle were.

Lassies are like lamb legs, they'll neither saut nor keep.
Enjoy yourself while you're young.

Lassies now-a-days ort nae God's creatures.
The proverbial reflection of older women, that younger women are by no means nice in their choice of husbands.

Last to bed, best heard.

Lauch and lay't doun again.

Lauch at leisure, ye may greet ere night.

Lauch at your ain toom pouches.
From Scott's St Ronan's Well.

Law licks up a'.

Law-makers shouldna be law-breakers.
Those laying down the rules cannot afford to set a bad example.

Law's a deadly distemper amang friends.

Law's costly; tak' a pint and gree.
Going to the law to settle a matter is expensive – far better to settle it over a drink.

Lay a thing by and it'll come o' use.

Lay by the book.
Spoken when we believe someone, i.e. it is not necessary for them to pick up the Bible and take oath.

Lay me doun as I was before
Lift me up and I'll tell you more.

Lay the head o' the sow to the tail o' the grice.
Place the profit against the loss.

Lay the sweet side o' yer tongue till't.

Lay up like a laird and seek like a lad.
'Be as penurious as a rich man, and as dilligent as a poor one' – Cheviot.

Lay your wame to your winning.
Make sure you balance your consumption with your earnings.

Laziness is muckle worth, when it's weel guided.

Lazy youth maks lousy age.

Leaches kill with license.
'An argument dissuading people, of no skill, from quacking: for if any that they administer to die, they will be blam'd: but if any die under the hands of a physician, no notice is taken of it' – Kelly.

Leal folk ne'er wanted gear.
The loyal are always looked after, loyalty is repaid.

Leal heart ne'er leed.

Lean liberty is better than fat slavery.

Lean on the brose ye got in the morning.
Said facetiously to a person who leans heavily upon others.

Leap year was ne'er gude sheep year.

Learn the cat the road o' the kirn, and she'll aye be lickin'.

Learn young, learn fair; learn auld, learn mair.

Learn your gudewife to mak milk kail.
The equivalent of 'teach your grandmother to suck eggs'.

Learn you an ill habit and ye'll ca't custom.
Said to people one suspects of taking advantage.

Least said, soonest mended.
This appears in Fergusson's 1641 collection as 'Little said, soon mendit'.

Leave aff while the play's gude.
Quit while the going is good.

Leave a jest where it pleases you best.

Leave the court ere the court leave you.

Leave welcome aye behint you.
Don't outstay your welcome.

Leears should hae gude memories.
If they don't want to be caught out!

Lee for him and he'll swear for you.

Leein' rides on debt's back.
A warning of the troubles debt will get you into.

Leese me that bonny mouth that never told a fool tale.
'Leese me' means 'blessings on'.

Lend your money and lose your friend.

Les Ecossais sont lions dans la bataille, et agneux dans la maison.
'The Scots are lions on the battlefield and lambs in the house.' This proverbial compliment was applied by the people of Brussels to the Highland soldiers at the time of Waterloo.

Less o' your jaw and mair o' your legs.
Don't be so cheeky and be off with you. Scott's Redgauntlet *chap. 15.*

Less o' your jaw and mair o' your siller.
I prefer payment to promises.

Less wadna serve him.

Let-a-be for let-a-be.
A phrase promoting tolerance.

Let ae deil dang anither.
An expression of indifference uttered when two bad individuals are found arguing or fighting.

Let a friend go with a foe.

Let alane mak's mony lurden.
Want of correction makes a bad fellow, i.e. spare the rod and spoil the child.

Let a horse drink what he will, but no when he will.

'Let a' trades live,' quo' the wife when she burnt her besom.

Let aye the bell'd wether break the snaw.
A 'bell'd wether' is the oldest and most experienced ram in the flock which wears a bell round its neck. Hence, when undertaking a difficult or dangerous task, one should let the most experienced go first.

Let byganes be byganes.
From Scott's The Black Dwarf.

Let death spare the green corn and take the ripe.
Let the old die rather than the young. Scott's The Antiquary, *chap. 7.*

Let every man be content wi' his ain kevel.
'Kevel' means 'lot'.

Let folk bode weel, and do their best.

Let him cool and come to himsel'.
Let him alone to recover his temper at leisure. Sometimes a second phrase is added 'like McGibbon's crowdie when he set it out at the window bole.'

Let him cool in the skin he het in.
As above.

Let him drink as he has brewen.
Let him do as he pleases with what is his own.

Let him haud the bairn that's aught the bairn.

Let him ride his ain horse wi' his ain hauding.
Let him do as he pleases with his own things.

Let him tak' a spring on his ain fiddle.
Said of a foolish or an unreasonable person, as if to say 'For the present we will allow him to have his own way'. Bailie Nicol Jarvie quotes the proverb with great bitterness when he warns his opponent that his triumph will come before long: 'A weel aweel, sir, you're welcome to a tune on your ain fiddle; but see if I dinna gar ye dance till't afore it's dune.'

Let him tak his fling and he'll find oot his ain weight.

Let him that did the deed yield the remeid.
One should always be prepared to sort out the consequences of one's own actions.

Let him that's cauld blaw the ingle.
Let those that complain do something constructive to sort the matter.

Let him that pays the lawin' choose the lodging.
He that pays the piper has the right to call the tune.

Let his ain wand ding him.

Let ilka ane ruse the ford as they find it.
Let every one speak of a thing as they find it.

Let ilka ane soop before their ain door.

Let ilka cock fight his ain battle.
Scott's Rob Roy *chap. 27.*

Let ilka head wear its ain bannet.
Scott's Rob Roy *chap. 32.*

Let ilka herring hing by its ain tail *or*
Let ilka herring hing by its ain head.

Let ilka man soop the ice wi' his ain besom.
Besoms are used to sweep the ice in the game of curling.

Let ilka man stand on his ain bottom.
Rob Roy, *chap. 32.*

Let ilka sheep hang by its ain shank.

Let na the cobbler go beyond his last.

Let na the plough stand to kill a mouse.
Do not neglect important duties for the sake of smaller matters.

Let ne'er sorrow come sae near your heart, except for sin.
'Spoken heartily when we have made our friend drunk' – Kelly

Let ne'er your gear owergang ye.
Never let wealth make you forget your old friends.

Let sleeping dogs lie.

Let spades and schools do what they may,
Dryse shall take Drysedale Kirk away.
One from Thomas the Rhymer – here betting on a certainty that the Dryse water would sweep away the kirk when in spate one day.

Let that flee stick to the wa'; when it's dry the dirt will rub oot.
Don't worry about that for the present, and we'll forget about it later. This saying appears in Scott's Rob Roy.

Let the eird bear the dike.
Important undertakings should have a solid foundation.

Let the horns gang wi' the hide.
Throw in the extras free of charge to the purchaser.

Let the kirk stand i' the kirk yard.
Let everything be in its proper place.

Let them care that come behint.
Scott's Bride of Lammermoor, *chap. 7.*

Let the morn come, and the meat wi't.

Let them that aught the mare, shoe the mare.

Let them that scorn the tartan fear the kirk.
Scott's The Antiquary, *chap. 33.*

Let the muckle horse get the muckle windlin.
Let the largest horse take the heaviest burden.

Let the saw sink to the sair.
Saw means ointment.

Let the tail follow the skin.

Let the tow gang wi' the bucket.

Let the warld shogg.
'Shogg' means to shake from one side to the other. Kelly says this proverb is 'spoken by them who have a mind to do as they have resolved'.

Let us take the Pettie step to it.
Petty (or Pettie) is a parish on the Nairn Coast. It was the local custom at funerals to run as fast as possible with the coffin so that people often fell in carrying the body to the grave.

Let wha likes be king, I'll be subject.
It doesn't matter who is in overall authority, my life will change little. A common sentiment at budget time.

Let your meat dit your mouth.

Liar, liar lickspit; in behind the candlestick!
What's gude for liars? Brimstone and fires.

Libertons' Luck.
A saying from The Ettrick Shepherd. The luck of an uninvited guest to go away as hungry as he came.

Licht suppers mak lang days.

Lick and lay down.
Means that a man can pay his way.

Lick your loof and lay't in mine, dry leather jigs aye.
'This signifies no more but kiss your hand and give it. Spoken facetiously upon some good fortune unexpected' – Kelly.

Lie in your bed and lippen to that.

Life's life ony gate.
Scott's Old Mortality, *chap. 8.*

Life's too short to be spent in playing mumchance.
Scott's The Abbot, *chap. 15.*

Lift me up and I'll tell you more,
Lay me down as I was before.
The first part of the rhyme is sometimes carved into a stone, tempting the reader to lift it. It is only upon doing so they can read the second line on the reverse which tells them the whole exercise is a joke.

Light burdens break nae bones.

Light lades mak willing horses.

Lightly come, lightly gang.
Easy come, easy go.

Light maidens mak langing lads.

Light meals procure light slumbers.
Scott's Bride of Lammermoor, *chap. 9.*

'Light's heartsome,' quo' the thief to the Lammas mune.
Before battery torches, robbers used to go thieving by moonlight.

Light suppers mak lang days.

Lightsome sangs mak merry gate.

Like a beggar at a bridal.
'At penny weddings certain of the guests gave nothing but good advice; so those who are sparing of their gifts, taking all and giving nothing, are said to be "like beggars at a bridal" ' – Cheviot.

Like a borrowed body.
i.e. one who is unwelcome.

Like a cried fair.
'Anything notoriously public was said to be "Like a cried fair", from the custom, common in the last century of announcing fairs outside the church doors after service on Sunday, with a comprehensive summary of the more important articles that were to be exposed to sale' – Cheviot.

Like a dog's turd broken, and look in both ends of it.
Spoken when two persons, equally vile and base, are compared.

Like a flood through a broken dyke.

Like a magistrate among beggars.
Spoken of those who make a big noise about the little authority they have.

Like a light bung in a gutter.

Like a sandbed.
A saying used to describe someone capable of soaking up large quantities of alcohol without showing signs of being drunk.

Like a sow playing on a trump.
'Trump' is a Jew's harp. Therefore the phrase is used to denote a situation of extreme awkwardness.

Like a wight oot o' anither world.
Used to describe someone who looks pale and delicate.

Like an auld trogger who has missed his market at Bell's day fair.
Used to describe someone who is restless or ill at ease.

Like Bauldy's wedding, there's nae meat but muckle mirth.

Like blood, like gude, like age, mak the happy marriage.

Like butter in the black dog's hause.
i.e. in a dangerous position.

Like Cranshaw's Kirk – There's as mony dogs as folk, and neither room for reel nor rock.
'In a remote pastoral region . . . it is or was usual for shepherds' dogs to accompany their masters to the church; and in times of severe stormy weather, few people except the shepherds, who are accustomed to be out in all weathers, could attend divine service; and in such circumstances, it may have occurred that the dogs may have equalled in number the rational bearers of the word. We have heard the saying applied by bustling servant girls to a scene where three or four dogs were lounging about the kitches hearth, and impeding the work."
– G. Henderson.

Like draws aye to like, like an auld horse to a fell dyke.

Liked gear is half-bought.
Once you have set your heart on something it is difficult not to purchase it.

Like hens, ye rin aye to the heap.
A humorous tease spoken to those who help themsleves to what there is most of on the table.

Like Hilton Kirk, baith narrow and mirk, and can only haud its ain parish folk.
Hilton Kirk was a very small and dimly lit church in Berwickshire. According to G. Henderson, 'the saying is used when many persons assemble in a small house, and there is little room to stir about'.

Like Laird Hacket, that bann't a' the oik an' del't dockens on Sunday.
Laird Charles Hacket acquired the estate of Inveramsay in Aberdeenshire by marriage. Although he was a shrewd and enterprising farmer he was also very well-known for swearing throughout the week and digging dockens on Sunday.

Like Lamington's mare, ye break brawly aff, but sune set up.

Like lips, like lettuce.

Likely lies i' the mire, and unlikely gets ower.
Meaning that many promising undertakings fail, whereas those which at first look less promising are successfully carried through.

Like maister, like men; like priest, like offering.

Like March gowans – rare but rich.

Like Moses' breeks – neither shape, form nor fashion.
Sometimes the word 'hielandman' is substituted for 'Moses'.

Like Orkney butter, neither gude to eat nor creesh woo.
Said of something which has no use whatsoever.

Like Paddy's ghaist, twa steps ahint.

Like Royal Charlie, lang o' comin'.
Spoken of someone who is late in appearing.

Like's an ill mark amang ither folks' sheep.
A saying attributed to King James VI. According to Cheviot:
'One day while walking about the grounds of Falkland Palace, the King observed
Alexander Ruthven brother of Lord Gowrie, asleep on one of the grassy banks,
and looking at the lad closely noticed in his bosom a knot of ribbons of a peculiar
sort which James recognised as his own gift to Queen Anne. The King, who
suspected his wife, immediately rushed off to tax her with falsehood, but
fortunately one of the pages, guessing his intention, managed to restore her the
tell-tale ribbon before his arrival. Accordingly, when James demanded that his gift
should be produced, she immediately complied with his request. At this, the King
scratched his head and his face expanded into a broad grin of satisfaction. "Eh!"
said he, "like's an ill mark". And so the proverb has come down to us with all the
authority of the Scottish Solomon.'

Like the bairns o' Falkirk, they'll end or they mend.

Like the cat, fain fish wad ye eat, but ye are laith to weet your feet.
Said of those who want all the gains without any of the pains.

Like the cowts o' Bearbughty, ye're cowts till ye're best's by.

Like the cur in the crub, he'll neither do nor let do.
A Scottish version of 'dog in a manger'.

Like the dam o' Devon, lang gathered and soon gane.

Like the drinkers o' Sisterpath Mill.
Spoken of people who sit down to have a drink and are clearly there for the
duration.

Like the fiddler o' Chirnside's breakfast, it's a' pennyworth's thegither.
A saying applied to those who buy very small quantities of any article.

Like the gudeman o' Kilpapet, ye're ower simple for this warld, and hae nae broo o' the next.

Like the Hielandman's gun that needed a new lock, a new stick, and a new barrel.

Like the Laird of MacFarlane's geese, they liked their play better than their meat.
The story behind this saying appears in Scott's The Monastery, chap. 13. King
James VI was much amused by the sight of a flock of geese chasing each other up
and down Loch Lomond, whilst he was the guest of the chief of the MacFarlanes
on Inch Tavoe. However when he was later served one of the geese at dinner, and
it proved to be tough and ill fed, the King observed that 'MacFarlane's geese liked
their play better than their meat'.

Like the Laird o' Castemilk's foals – born beauties.

Like the lassies of Bayordie, ye learn by the lug.

Like the links o' the cruik.
Spoken of someone who looks emaciated.

Like the man o' Amperly's coo, she's come hame routin', but no very fu', wi' the tow about her horns.
'The rhyme is applied to a young woman who comes home from a fair or market without a sweetheart' – G. Henderson.

Like the man who met the devil, if they have nothing to say to me, I have nothing to say to them.

Like the man wi' the sair guts, nae getting quat o't.

Like the man's horse, very ill to catch and no worth a penny when caught.

Like the Smith's dog, sleep at the sound o' the hammer and wauk at the crunching o' teeth.

Like the tod's whalps, aye the aulder the waur.

Like the wabster, stealing through the warld.
A reply to an enquiry as to how one is getting on. Another insult to the weaving profession.

Like the wife's tongue, aften better meant than timed.

Like the wife that ne'er cries for the ladle till the pat rins o'er.
i.e. never asks until it is too late.

Like the wife wi' the mony dochters, the best's aye hindmost.

Like the witches o' Auchencrow, ye get mair for your ill than your gude.
'That is, people sometimes grant an individual a favour through fear or malevolence, or to get rid of his importunity' – G. Henderson.

Like to like.

Like to like, a scabbed horse to an auld dike.

Like to like, quoth the devil to the collier.

Like water aff a deuk's back.

Like water to leather – the langer the tougher.

Lippen to me, but look to yoursel.

Lips gae, laps gae, drink and pay.
If you put a drink to your lips be prepared to put your hand to your lap to take out your purse.

Listen at a hole and ye'll hear ill news o' yourself.

List to meat's gude kitchen.

Listen to the wind upon the hill till the waters abate.

Lithgow for wells, Glasgow for Bells, an' Falkirk for beans and peas.

Little and aften fills the purse.

Little can a lang tongue hide.

Little does the poor gude, an' as little get they.

Little dogs hae lang tails.

Little folk are soon angry.
A frequent addition to this phrase provides the supposed reason – 'for their heart gets soon to their mouth.'

Little gear, little care.

Little intermittin' maks gude friends.

Little kent, the less cared for.

Little may an auld horse do if he maunna nicker.

Little meddling maks fair parting.

Little odds between a feast and fu' wame.

Little said is soon mended, and little gear is soon spended.

Little strokes fell muckle oaks.

Little to fear when traitors are true.

Little troubles the ee, but less the soul.

Little's the light will be seen far in a mirk night.
Scott's Bride of Lammermoor, *chap. 26.*

Little wats the ill-willy wife what a dinner may haud in.
Although privately a wife may be annoyed with her husband, in public she should still be cautious for Kelly says 'that a handsome treat may secure good friends and great interest'.

Little winning maks a light purse.

Little wit in the pow that lights the candle at the low.

Little Jock gets the little dish, and that hauds him lang little.
The poorest get the least, which ensures they remain the poorest.

Little kens the auld wife, as she sits by the fire,
what the wind is doing on Hurley-Burley-Swire.
A warning to armchair critics that they cannot possibly know the trouble faced by others. The 'Hurley Burley Swire' is a passage through a ridge of mountains that separate Nithsdale from Tweedale and Clydesdale, and there is a perpetual wind forced through this gap.

Little mense o' the cheeks to bite aff the nose.
It is silly for a person to injure another on whom they depend in some way.

Little wit in the head maks muckle travel to the feet.
People not blessed with much sense are apt to be sent on fool's errands.

Live in measure, and laugh at the mediciners.
To remain healthy, take everything in moderation.

Live upon love, as laverocks do on leeks.

Living, and life thinking.
'An answer to the question, How are you?' – Kelly.

Living at heck and manger.
i.e. living sumptuously.

Loch Eleven.
A popular name for Loch Leven – for it's said to be eleven miles round, be surrounded by eleven hills, be fed or drained by eleven burns, has eleven islands, be lived in by eleven kinds of fish, and Mary Queen of Scots was held prisoner in the castle for eleven months.

Lochtie, Lothrie, Leven and Ore,
Rin a' through Cameron Brig bore.
Four rivers in Fife.

Lock your door, that you may keep your neighbours honest.
Do not lead others into temptation.

Lo'e me little an' lo'e me lang.

Long and small, like the cat's elbow.
A disparaging reflection upon slender people.

Long e'er the King of France get wot of that.
'Spoken when people make a great talk of some little accident' – Kelly.

Long may you pish and fart.
'A ridiculous, dirty way of wishing people long life' – Kelly.

Look before ye loup, ye'll ken the better how to light.
Look before ye leap or think before you act. An early version of this is found in Montgomerie's 'The Cherrie and the Slae':
'Luke quhair thou licht befoir thou lowp,
And slip na certainty for howp,
Quha gyds thee but begess.'

Look to the heart within a breast and not to the coat that covers it.
Do not act upon surface impressions.

'Loose and living, and bound to no man.
An answer to the question, How are you?' – Kelly.

Lordships change manners.

Lorntie, Lorntie,
Were it na your man,
I had gart your heart bluid,
Shirk in my pan.
'The young laird of Lorntie in Forfarshire, on returning home one evening heard the shrieks of an apparently drowning woman proceeding form a pond in an adjacent wood. As he was about to pull her out of the water by her golden tresses, he was prevented by his servant, who warned him that the damsel in distress was a mermaid. Upon perceiving the failure of her snare, she sang the above lines.'
– Cheviot.

Loud coos the doo when the hawk's no whistling, loud cheeps the mouse when the cat's no rustling.
When the cat's away, the mice will play.

Loud i' the loan was ne'er a gude milk cow.
According to Kelly this saying was used as a reprimand to noisy girls, i.e. empty vessels make the loudest noise.

Love and jealousy are sindle sindry.

Love and lairdship's like nae marrows.
'Marrow' means an equal, match or antagonist.

Love and light winna hide.

Love and raw pease are two ill things, one breaks the heart, the other bursts the belly.

Love and raw pease will mak a man speak at baith ends.

Love gangs where it is sent.

Love has nae lack, be the dame e'er sae black.

Love has nae law.

Love has nae suspicions, and whaur there are suspicions there is nae love.

Love maks clever lands.

Love maist, least thought of.

Love ower het soon cools.

Love owerlooks mony faults.

Love thinks nae ill; envy speaks nae gude.

Love your friend and look to yoursel.

Love's darts cleave hearts through mail shirts.

Love is as warm amang cottars as courtiers.

Luck can maist in the melee.
Chance regulated the battle. Scott's Waverley *chap. 46.*

Luck never came of a half droun'd man or a half hang'd one either.

M

MacFarlane's act.
*Their celebrated pibroch of Hoggil nam Bo, which is the name of their gathering
tune, intimates their night-time practices.*

> We are bound to drive the bullocks,
> All by hollows, hirsts and hillocks,
> Through the sleet, and through the rain,
> When the moon is beaming low,
> On frozen lake and hills of snow,
> Bold and heartily we go;
> And all for little gain.

MacFarlane's lantern.
*A proverbial expression for the moon which led the way for the MacFarlanes on
their wild night-time excursions.*

MacGregor as the rock.
MacDonald as the heather.

Maidens' bairns are weel guided.
It is easy for those without experience to give advice.

**Maidens should be mild and meek, quick to hear, and slow to
speak.**

**Maidens should be mim till they're married, and then they may
burn the kirks.**
Anything goes, but only once you're married.

Maidens' tochers and ministers' stipends are aye less than ca'd.

Maidens want naething but a man, and then they want a'thing.
Clearly this saying was conceived before the women's movement existed.

Mair are drooned in drink than in water.

Mair by luck than gude guiding.
A person's good fortune is due to luck rather than personal merit.

Mair hamely than welcome.

'Mair haste, the waur speed'
Quo' the wee tailor to the lang threid.

Mair in a mair dish.
*A 'mair dish' is a bigger dish. This answer is given in fun when asked if you
would like some more.*

Mair nice than wise.

Mair pride than pith.

Mair show than substance.

Mair than enough is ower muckle.

Mair than the deil wear a black manteel.

'Mair whistle than woo,' quo' the souter when he sheared the sow.

Maister's will is gude wark.
The reason for this is that the master is sure to be pleased with it.

Maistry maws the meadows doun.
Scott's Heart of Midlothian, *chap. 45. Maistry in this context means force or energy.*

Maist things hae a sma beginnin'.

Mak ae pair o' legs worth twa pair o' hands.
From Scott's Rob Roy.

Mak ae wrang step and doun ye gae.

Mak a kiln o't, and creep in at the logie.
According to Hislop, 'We surmise that this is intended as an advice to a person who has become possessed of an article, and does not know what to do with it', i.e. make what you will of it. A 'killogie' is, says Jamieson, 'a vacuity before the fireplace in a kiln for drawing air'.

Mak a kirk or a mill o't.
Make what you please of it.

Mak fair weather wi' him.
Make friends with him/come to terms with him.

Mak friends o' fremit folk.

Mak him pay the kane.
'Kane' was duty paid by a farmer to his landlord in kind. The phrase is used to suggest 'make him pay smartly'.

Making a rope of sand.
According to tradition, this was the task imposed by Michael Scott on his familiar spirit, the result of which is still to be seen on the sands between Leith and Portobello. The other tasks prescribed to the spirit were to build a dam across the Tweed at Kelso, and to split the Eildons into three parts. These he performed, but failed to make ropes of sand. It is said that the fairies imposed the task of making sand ropes upon Sir Duncan Campbell of Glenorchy – Black Duncan of the Coul.

Mak nae bauks in gude bere-land.
To 'bauk' is to leave small pieces of ground unploughed. Kelly says this proverb is 'spoken when it's proposed to marry the youngest daughter before the eldest'.

Mak nae orts o' gude hay.
Don't waste good resources.

Mak nae toom ruse.
Don't give empty praise.

Mak not muckle o' little.
Don't make an issue out of nothing.

Mak not twa mews o' ae daughter.
A 'mew' is a son-in-law.

Mak the best o' an ill bargain/market.

Mak twa pairs o' legs worth ae pair o' hands.
Ride away for discretion is the better part of valour in some circumstances.

Mak yer hay while the sun shines.

Mak yer wife a gowdspink, and she'll turn a water wagtail.
If you indulge a person freely they will take advantage and exceed the limits.

Malice is aye mindfu'.

Malisons, malisons, mair than ten,
Wha harries the Queen of Heaven's wren.

Man's twal is no sae gude as the deil's dizzen.
'Man's twal' is only twelve whereas the deil's dizzen is thirteen.

Many men speak o' my meikle drink, but few o' my sair thirst.
One can never tell the exact motivation for an act from only looking at a situation in one particular way. There are two sides to every story. You can look for the good and bad in everything. Burns sublimates this in:

    'What's done we partly may compute
    We ken not what's resisted'.

March comes like a lion, and gangs like a lamb.

March comes wi' adders' heads and gangs wi' peacocks' tails.

March dust, an' March wun,
Bleach as weel as summer's sun – *Clydesdale.*

March dust, an' May sun.
Mak corn white and maidens dun – *Perthshire.*

March water and May sun
Mak claes clean and maidens dun – *Mearns.*

March water's worth May soap.

March whisquer was ne'er a gude fisher.
A windy March was thought to be a sign of a bad year for fishing.

Marriage and hanging gae by destiny.

Marriage is a creel where ye can catch an adder or an eel.
Appears in John Galt's Entail.

Marriage wad tame the sea, if a match could be got for her.

Married folk are like rats in a trap – fain to get ithers in, but fain
to get out themsels.

Marry a beggar an' get a louse for a tocher.

Marry abune your match, and get a maister.
Marry someone from a higher social standing and they will lord it over you.

Marry for love an' wark for siller.

Marrying by meal.
*'In 1867 two persons left Dalkeith for Galashiels to be married, which they legally
accomplished in the following manner. They knelt down, facing each other, each
with a handful of meal, and with a basin between them. They placed their hands
full of meal in the basin and mixed it in token that they would not sever till death
did them part. After swearing on a bible to this effect, they rose up from their
kneeling position and declared themselves man and wife. This was one of the old
methods of contracting marriage in Scotland.' – Cheviot.*

Marry, maidens, marry, maidens;
Marry, maidens, now;
For sticket is your Cardinal,
And sauted like a sow.
*A local Fifeshire rhyme referring to Cardinal Beaton. The meaning is plain. 'The
body of the Cardinal was preserved in salt by the conspirators during the time they
held St Andrew's Castle against the Government forces' – Chambers.*

Marry your son when you will, but your dochter when you can.

Maun dae is a fell fallow.
Necessity is a hard master.

Maybe's a big book.

May-bes are no aye honey-bees.
An answer to those who say 'maybe this will happen'.

May-bes flee no at this time o' the year.

Maybe your pat may need my clips.
*Perhaps you will be glad of my assistance some day, even if you do not welcome
it now.*

May birds are aye cheeping.
*This proverb relates to the proverb that it is unlucky to marry in May, as the
offspring of such marriages are said to die.*

May he that turns the clod ne'er want a bannock.
May the hard working never go hungry.

May I ne'er chew cheese again.

May the mouse ne'er come oot o' the meal girnel wi' the tear in its e'e.
If it does then everyone's in trouble as food is scarce.

May the open hand be filled the fullest.

May you have a cairn for your burial place.

May your heels keep the spur o' your head.
i.e. a wish that you be able to carry out all your projects.

Meal Monday.
'The second Monday in February, which is a holiday in the University of Edinburgh, is called "Meal Monday", because the day was originally held as a holiday, in order to allow the students to go to their country homes, to procure a supply of oatmeal to last them until the end of the session' – Cheviot.

Mealy mou'd maidens stand lang at the mill.

Measure twice, cut but ance.
If you prepare things properly you will only have to do them once.

Meat and mass never hindered man.

Meat and measure mak a' men wise.

Meat feeds, claith cleeds, but breeding maks the man.

Meat is gude, but mense is better.

Meddle wi' your match.
Pick on someone your own size.

Meer's milk, and deer's milk,
And every beast that bears' milk,
Between St Johnston and Dundee
Come a' to me, come a' to me.
It was said that witches have special powers for procuring milk. If they obtain a small quantity of hair from the tail of a cow and tie a knot in it they can milk the cow simply by tugging at the hair.

Men are no to be met by inches.

Mends is worth misdeeds.

Men fight best in a narrow ring.
Presumably because they can't help themselves.

Men loup the dike where its laighest.

Mennans are better than nae fish.
Something, no matter how small, is better than nothing.

Men's no mice.
'An encouragement to act bravely' – Kelly

Men speak o' the fair as things went there.
People speak as they find.

Merrily well if my mouth was wet.
An answer to the question 'How are you?' suggesting that the speaker would be even better if given a drink.

Messengers should neither be headed nor hang'd.
An excuse given for carrying an unpleasant message.

Mettle's kittle in a blind mear.

Michaelmas mune rises nine nights alike sune.

Micht owercomes richt, by a time.

Mickle fails that fools think.

Mills and wives are aye wanting.

Mind me to a' that ask for me, but blad me in naebody's teeth.

Mind thysel', the world will mind the lave.

Minnows are better than nae fish.

Mint before you strike.
Give warning before you strike.

Minting gets nae bairns.
Offering to do something accomplishes nothing.

Mischief's mither's but like midge's wing.

Mister maks a man o' craft.

Mist in May and heat in June mak the hairst right soon.

Mist on the hills, weather spills;
Mist i' the howes, weather growes.
A Fife weather-forecasting rhyme.

Mistress before folk, gudewife behint backs: whaur lies the dishclout?
A saying applied in jest to those who are very particular in their manner of speaking.

Mocking's catching.

Money is aye welcome, were it even in a dirty clout.

Money is flat and meant to be piled up.
The saver's motto!

Money is better than my lord's letter.

Money is like the muck midden, it does nae gude till it be spread.

Money maks a man free ilka where.

Money maks and money mars.

Money maks the mear to go whether she has legs or no.

Money wared on naething travels a bad road.

Money will make the pot play, if the deil'l pish in the fire.

Money would be gotten, if there was money to get it wi'.
Polite request.

Mony a dog has dee'd sin' ye were whelped.

Mony a dog will dee ere you fa' heir.

Mony a fair thing's fu' false.

Mony a frost, and mony a thowe,
Soon maks mony a rotten yowe.

Mony a gude tale is spoilt in the telling.

Mony a pickle maks a mickle.
Lots of little things can make a great thing. Often erroneously said as 'Mony a mickle maks a muckle'. 'Muckle' is merely a variant of the word 'mickle', both meaning a large quantity or amount.

Mony ane brings the rake, but few the shovel.
Many seek, but few give.

Mony ane for land taks a fool by the hand.
Many only marry for material wealth.

Mony ane kens the gude fellow that disna ken the gudewife.
The reason for this is that some men are only 'gudefellows' when they escape their domestic environments for the company of the local hostelry.

Mony ane kisses the bairn for love o' the nurse.
Many show kindness to the friends and relations of those upon whom they have designs in the hope of attracting their good opinion.

Mony ane lacks what they would fain hae in their pack.

Mony ane maks an errand to the ha' to bid my leddy good day.
Many occupy their lives with trifles.

Mony ane opens his pack and sells nae wares.

Mony ane's coat, saves their doublet.
Some people are saved from trouble by their social position.

Mony ane's deen ill wi vreet.
A Buchan saying belittling literacy on the grounds that many a person has committed crime with the aid of writing.

Mony ane ser's a thankless maister.

Mone ane's gear is mony ane's death.

Mony ane's gotten an amshach at the spar.
Many have ended up falling as a consequence of being thrown by the millstone they were trying to guide by the spar.

Mony ane speaks o' Robin Hood that ne'er shot wi' his bow.

Mony ane speers the gate they ken fu' weel.

Mony ane tines the half-merk whinger for the ha'-penny whang.
This saying literally means 'a sixpenny dagger is often lost for the sake of a halfpenny thong'. 'Spoken', says Kelly, 'when people lose a considerable thing for not being at an inconsiderable expense'.

Mony ane wad blush to hear what he wadna blush to dae.

Mony ane wad hae been waur had their estates been better.

Mony an honest man needs help that hasna the face to seek it.

Mony a thing's made for the pennie.
Many contrivances are thought of to get money.

Mony a thing's made for the penny, as the auld wife said, when she saw the plack man.

Mony a true tale's tauld in jest.
This saying is recorded in Carmichael's Proverbs in Scots *as 'Manie suith word said in bourding'.*

Mony aunts, mony emes, mony kin, but few friends.
A person may have many relations, but few friends among them.

Mony a wise man sits in a fool's seat, and many a fool in a wise man's.

Mony care for meal that hae baked bread enough.
Some people will still complain even when they have enough to eat themselves.

Mony cooks ne'er made gude kail.
Too many cooks spoil the broth.

Mony excuses pishes the bed.

Mony fair promises at the marriage-making, but few at the tocher-paying.
Many promise the earth to secure a bargain but are less forthcoming when the deal has been struck.

Mony gude-nights is laith away.
The person who doesn't want to leave will take time saying goodbye.

Mony hands mak slight work.

Mony haws, mony snaws.
A piece of long-range weather forecasting connecting a large harvest of berries with a bad winter to follow.

Mony heads are better than ane.

Mony hounds may soon worry ae hare.

Mony irons i' the fire, some maun cool.

Mony kinsfolk but few friends.

Mony'll sup wi' little din, that wadna gree at moolin in.

'Mony masters,' quo' the puddock to the harrow, when every tine gave her a tig *or*
'Ower mony maisters,' quo' the puddock to the harrow, when ilka tooth gie her a tug.

Mony paiks mak healthy weans.

Mony purses haud friends lang thegither.

Mony rains, mony rowans, mony rowans, mony yewns.
A good crop of rowans usually followed a wet season, and was held to be significant of a defective harvest.

Mony say 'weel' when it ne'er was waur.
'Spoken to them that say "well" by way of resentment' – Kelly.

Mony think mair o' wha says a thing than o' what the thing's that is said.

Mony time I have got a wipe wi' a towel, but ne'er a daub wi' a dishclout before.
Spoken when the speaker feels they have been harshly dealt with by someone who has no right to judge them.

Mony ways to kill a dog forbye chokin' him wi' butter.

Mony ways to kill a dog though ye dinna hang him.

Mony words dinna fill the firlot.
A 'firlot' is a fourth part of a boll, dry measure.

Mony words mickle drouth *or*
Mony words wad hae muckle drink.

Mony wyte their wife for their ain thriftless life.
Many people blame others for the consequences of their own actions.

Moray has fifteen days' more summer than its neighbours.
A saying which takes its rise from the mild and genial climate of Morayshire.

More folk than King Duncan change the course of their voyage.

More land is won by the lawyer with the ramskin than by the Andrea Ferrara with his sheepskin handle.
The pen is mightier than the sword.

More plain than pleasant.

Mother Macniven.
The name given to the grandmother witch, the very Hecate of Scottish popular superstition. From Scott's The Abbot *chap. 26.*

Mother yer ain mither, man, till ye're a faither.
Don't try to get round me with soft words.

Mouths are nae measure, unless the throat was stopped.

Mows may come to earnest.
"To mow" is to speak in mockery' – Jamieson.

Moyen does muckle, but money does mair.
Influence does much, but money is even more effective.

Muck bodes luck, dame go drite there benn.
According to Kelly there is a similar English proverb: 'Shitter luck is good luck'.

Muck and money gae thegither.

Muck is the mither o' the meal kist.
A proverbial phrase extolling the virtues of fertiliser.

Muckle but no' manfu'.
'Big but not brave' – Kelly.

Muckle corn, muckle care.

Muckle crack fills nae sack.
Much talk does not keep one from hunger.

Muckle cry an' little woo', as the deil said when he clippit the soo.

'Muckle din about ane,' quo' the deil, when he ran off wi' the collier.

Muckledom is nae virtue.
i.e. size of body, or head.

Muckle fails that fools think.

Muckle gifts mak beggars bauld.

Muckle gude may it do you, and merry go doun, every lump as big as my thoom.
A nasty wish – that every mouthful may choke you.

Muckle has, would aye hae mair *or*
Muckle wad aye hae mair.
Those who have a lot always want more.

Muckle head, little wit.

Muckle maun a gude heart thole.

Muckle may be done by timing ane's turn.

Muckle meat, mony maladies.

Muckle meat tak's muckle weet.
Spoken to one who asks for a drink during mealtime, implying that if you eat less you will not be so thirsty.

Muckle mou'd folk are happy at their meat.

Muckle musing mars the memory.

Muckleness has nae mair, or else a coo could catch a hare.

Muckleness is no manliness.

Muckle pleasure, some pain.

Muckle power maks mony faes.

Muckle skaith comes to the shae, before the heat comes to the tae.

Muckle spoken, part spilt.
A saying applied when so much has been said on a topic that a lot of it has been lost.

Muckle to mak a wark aboot, a deid cat in your parritch.
A sarcastic remark levelled at fuss-pots, or those who are bragging of very little.

Muckle water rins by the miller watsna o' when he sleeps.

Muckle whistlin' for little red lan'.
An Aberdeenshire saying. The saying arose from the farmer whistling to his oxen in order to encourage them.

Muckle wi' thrift may aye be mair.

Musselburgh was a burgh when Edinburgh was nane,
Musselburgh shall be a burgh when Edinburgh's gane.
Chambers gives another version which contains a pun as its solution – see next.

Musselburgh was a brogh,
When Edinburgh was nane,
And Musselburgh'll be a brogh
When Edinburgh is gane.
According to Chambers, 'This is a pun or quibble. Brogh is a term for a musselbed, one of which exists at the mouth of the Esk, and gives name to the burgh.'

'Must' is for the King to say.
Said when someone orders us to do something instead of making a request.

My caup's no aneath his ladle.
I am not indebted to him.

My head was buzzing like a bee's skep.

My market's made, ye may lick a whup-shaft.
According to Hislop, 'The saucy reply given by a woman already betrothed to a would-be suitor'.

My Minnie has the lease o't.
According to Kelly this is spoken jocosely when we don't want to finish a story or song.

My mither gied me butter and bread, my faither gied me claes,
To sit about the fireside and knap folk's taes.
This proverbial rhyme usually accompanies a practical joke.

My next neighbour's skaithe is my perfect peril.

My son's my son till he's got a wife: my dochter's my dochter a' the days of her life.

My tongue's no under your belt.
I am not at your mercy.

N

Naebody can tell what's in the shaup till its shelt.
Used in John Galt's Sir Andrew Wylie, *chap. 25.*

Naebody daur say strae to him.

Naebody is riving your claes to get you.
Nobody is unduly bothered about you.

Naebody said hae ye a mooth.
No-one offered any refreshment.

Naebody should drink but them that can drink.

Naebody's nails can reach the length o' Lunnon.
A saying which arose after the Union of the Scottish and English parliaments in 1707. It means that the powers of bribery and cajolery which had often been used in Edinburgh could not be employed to the same effect on an executive as far away as London.

Naebody speired her price.
Spoken of a woman who never receives a marriage proposal.

Naebody's sweetheart's ugly.

Naebody will come after you that will set a langer term.

Naebody will tak you for a conjurer.

Nae butter will stick to my bread.
I am unlucky.

Nae carrion will kill a craw.

Nae counsellor like the pound in purse.
From Scott's St. Ronan's Well *chap. 28.*

Nae cows, nae care.

Nae curb will tame love.

Nae deaf nuts.
According to Cheviot this phrase refers to 'something substantial'.

Nae equal to you but our dog Sorkie, and he's dead so ye're marrowless.
Said sarcastically to boastful people.

Nae faut; but she set her bannet ower weel.
Her only fault is that she is too goodlooking.

Nae faut that the cat has a clean band, she sets a bannet sae weel.
Said ironically to people who pretend to do, have, or wear something that does not become them.

Nae fleeing frae fate.

Nae fleeing without wings.

Nae fools like auld anes.

Nae friend like a bosom friend, nae enemy like a bosom enemy.

Nae friend like the penny.

Nae gain without pain.
Nothing comes easily.

Nae gairdner ever lichtlied his ain leeks.
No person will speak ill of what they value dearly.

Nae great loss but there's some sma' 'vantage.

Nae haste but of well-fair.

Nae haufs and quarters – hale o' mine ain, and nane o' my neigh-bours.
The exclamation of a Scottish child when he/she finds anything. Used in Scott's The Antiquary, *chap. 23.*

Nae hawk flees sae high but he will fall to some lure.
Everyone has their price.

Nae hurry wi' your corns; nae hurry wi' your harrows;
Snaw lies ahint the dike, mair may come and fill the furrows.
A cautionary rhyme uttered at seed time.

Nae jesting wi' edg'd tools.

Nae langer pipe, nae langer dance.

Nae lass proves thrifty that is married in May.

Nae luck till the second tumbler, and nae peace after the fourth.

Nae mair haste than gude speed.

Nae mair to dae, but ha'se, and go to Gody.
'Ha'se' means to come in arms and Gody is a godmother. The phrase is spoken when people all of a sudden become very friendly. According to Kelly it takes its source from 'the fondling of children by their nurses'.

Nae man can baith sup and blaw at ance.
No one can do two opposing things at once.

Nae man can live langer in peace than his neighbours like.
Good neighbours should be cherished.

Nae man can mak his ain hap.
i.e. plan his own destiny.

Nae man can seek his marrow i' the kirn sae weel as him that has
been in't himsel.
It takes one to know one.

Nae man can thrive unless his wife will let him.

Nae man has a tack o' his life.

Nae man is wise at a' times, nor on a' things.

Nae mills, nae meal.
The end justifies the means, or provides the purpose for the work.

Nae muckle buckit.
Not of much size.

Nae penny, nae paternoster.

Nae plea is the best plea.

Nae profit without pains.
Nothing comes without effort in this life.

Nae reply is best.
Especially to an angry man.

Nae rule sae gude as rule o' thoom, if it hit.
'But it seldom does' according to Kelly.

Nae service nae siller.
You don't get something for nothing.

Nae sooner up than her head's in the aumrie.
*Applied to greedy people, implying that they are no sooner out of bed than they
think of their stomachs and go looking for food in the cupboard.*

Nae swat, nae sweet.

Naething but fill and fetch mair.
Advice to never give up.

Naething comes fairer to light than what has been lang hidden.
*One gets great pleasure from finding something which has been lost for a long
time.*

Naething comes out o' a close hand *but*:
Naething enters into a close hand.

Naething freer than a gift.

Naething is got without pains but an ill name and lang nails.

Naething is ill said if it's no ill ta'en.

Naething is ill to be done when will's at hame.
It is always easier to accomplish tasks in which we are interested.

Naething is sae difficult but we may owercome by perseverance.

Naething like being stark dead.
There is nothing like doing something thoroughly. A malicious proverb said to have been used on hearing of the death of an enemy.

Naething's a bare man.
Kelly says this phrase is 'a jocose answer to children when they say they have gotten nothing'.

Naething sae bauld as a blind mear.
Ignorance can breed confidence.

Naething sae crouse as a new washed louse.
'Spoken of them who have been ragged and dirty, and are proud and fond of new or clean clothes' – Kelly.

Naething's a man's truly, but what he comes by duly.

Naething sooner maks a man auld-like than sitting ill to his meat.
Nothing ages a person faster than being ill-fed.

Naething to be done in haste but gripping fleas.
A cautionary proverb to think things through first.
   Motherwell, in his introduction to Henderson's Collection, *relates an anecdote in connection with this proverb. A collector of 'rusty sayed saws' was in the habit of jotting down any phrase new to him on the back of letters, cards, etc., which he then thrust into his pocket. On one occasion the collector quarrelled with a chance acquaintance, and promptly handed him, as he thought, his card as a challenge to mortal combat. But when the gentleman to whom the card had been given came to examine it he found in place of his adversary's name the words, 'Naething should be done in haste but gripping fleas'. So what might have been a tragedy ended in a comedy after all, for the humour of the situation was so irresistible that a reconciliation was immediately effected.*

Naething to do but draw in your stool and sit down.
Said when all preliminaries have already been taken care of and only the finishing touch is needed. Often applied to a courting man, when all that is left is for him to actually propose.

Naething to do but draw out and loup on.
Applied to those who think a thing's easy when in fact it is difficult.

Naething venture, naething win.

Nae weather's ill an' the wind be still.

Nae wonder tae see wasters want.

Nae wonder ye're auld like, ilka thing fashes you.

Nane are sae weel but they hope to be better.

Nane but a fool is always right.

Nane but fools and knaves lay wagers.
In his collection Henderson uses the word 'poets' for 'fool', possibly as a joke upon some of his friends, several of whom were well-known poets.

Nane can mak a bore but ye'll find a pin for't.
None can criticise you, but you will find an excuse.

Nane can play the fool sae weel as a wise man.

Nane can tell what's i' the shaup till it's shelt.
You can't judge from outward appearances alone.

Nane ferlie mair than fools.
Fools see more wonders than wise men.

Nane kens whaur a blister may light.
No-one knows where trouble might strike next.

Nane o' your fluk-ma-hoys.
None of your nonsense: used in Scott's St Ronan's Well *chap. 28.*

Nane worse sho'd than the souter's wife, and the smith's mear.

Narrow gaithered, widely spent.

Nature has put her tether on him.
Nature has not been lavish in her gifts to him.

Nature hates all sudden changes.

Nature passes nurture.

'Near deid' ne'er filled the kirkyaird *or*
It's lang or like-to-dee fills the kirkyaird.
Spoken of those who are always saying how ill and close to death they are but who nevertheless seem to live as long as everyone else.

Nearer e'en the mair beggars.

Nearer God's blessing than Carlisle fair.
You need but go to your closet for the one, but you must go out of the kingdom for the other' – Kelly.

Nearer the bane the sweater.
Used in Scott's Bride of Lammermoor.

Nearer the rock the sweeter the grass.
At best it appears so. Some things appear more appetising than others because they were more difficult to obtain.

Nearest the heart nearest the mou.
A saying applied when someone meaning to name one person, by mistake names another – perhaps a sweetheart, and hence betrays what is on their mind.

Nearest the king nearest the widdy.
People who support the king should be careful what they say, as they only hold their positions at his pleasure.

Near's my kirtle, but nearer's my sark.

Near's my sark, but nearer's my skin.
Some people are closer to me than others, but at the end of the day I am closest to myself.

Near the kirk, but far frae grace.

Necessity has nae law.

Necessity's the mither o' invention.

Neck or naething, the king lo'es nae cripples.
This saying is a wish that should someone be in an accident, they either break their neck or escape injury completely, because any disability will render them useless.

Need gars naked men run and sorrow gars wabsters spin.
The second clause again casts doubts on the character of the weavers suggesting that they only work when forced to.

Need gars the auld wife trot.
Used in Scott's Old Mortality.

Need maks a man o' craft.

Need maks greed.

Need maks the naked quean spin.

Ne'er a barrel o' better herring.

Ne'er an Englishman loved a dry-lipped bargain.

Ne'er bite unless you make your teeth meet.
Do not threaten an action unless you can carry it through completely.

Ne'er break out o' kind to gar your friends ferlie at you.
Do not act out of character merely to astonish your friends.

Ne'er came a hearty fart out o' a wren's arse.
According to Kelly this is 'Spoken when niggardly people give some insignificant gift'.

Ne'er compare a docken to a tansie.
Galt's The Entail, *chap. 65.*

Ne'er count the lawin' wi' a toom quaich.
A quaich is a shallow drinking cup with two ears.

Ne'er do ill that gude may come o't.
The end does not always justify the means.

Ne'er draw your dirk when a dunt will do.
Don't resort to extreme measures when they are not necessary.

Ne'er fash your beard.
Scott's Bride of Lammermoor *chap. 13.*

Ne'er fash your thoom.
Don't trouble yourself.

Ne'er find faut wi' my shoon, unless you pay my souter.
A rebuke to those who criticise somebody's appearance.

Ne'er friar forgot feud.

Ne'er gang to the deil wi' the dish-clout on your head/in your hand.
Kelly relates the following explanation and anecdote: 'If you will be a knave be not in a trifle, but in something of value. A presbyterian minister had a son who was made Archdeacon of Ossery; when this was told to his father, he said, "If my son will be a knave, I am glad that he will be an archknave".' This has the same sense as 'As good be hang'd for an old sheep as a young lamb'.

Ne'er gie me death in a toom dish.
A joke said by persons who like their food, i.e. if you are going to kill me, please do not do it by starvation.

Ne'er gude, egg nor bird.
Spoken of someone who has always been bad.

Ne'er judge a man by the coat on his back.

Ne'er kiss a man's wife, or dight his knife, for he'll do baith after you.

Ne'er let on, but laugh in your ain sleeve.
Some things are best kept to yourself.

Ne'er let the nose blush for the sins o' the mouth.
A warning not to drink too much.

Ne'er let your feet run faster than your shune.
Don't outstrip your own resources.

Ne'er lippen ower muckle tae a new freen' or an auld enemy.

Ne'er look for a wife until ye hae a house and a fire to put her in.
Humorous marriage guidance.

Ne'er luck when a priest is on board.
This is an old superstition with Scottish sailors – probably originating from the story of Jonah.

Ne'er marry a penniless maiden that's proud o' her pedigree.

Ne'er marry a widow unless her first husband was hanged.
The suggestion here is that otherwise the new husband will never live up to the reputation of the first husband.

Ne'er meet, ne'er pay.
'Spoken when we cheerfully help a friend' – Kelly.

Ne'er misca' a Gordon in the raws o' Strathbogie.
Never speak badly of somebody on their home territory. The Gordons were the ruling clan in Strathbogie.

Ne'er ower auld to learn.

Ne'er pot boiled but the scum was cast uppermost.

Ne'er put a sword in a wudman's hand.

Ne'er put the plough before the owsen.

Ne'er put your arm out farther than ye can draw't easily back again.
Used in Scott's Rob Roy, *chap. 22. Similar to the following proverb.*

Ne'er put your hand farther out than your sleeve will reach.
Don't overstretch your resources.

Ne'er quit certainty for hope.
A bird in the hand etc.

Ne'er rax above your reach.
Don't try to go beyond your abilities/resources/strength.

Ne'er say gae, but gang.
If you want something well done, do it yourself.

Ne'er say 'ill fallow' to him you deal wi'.

Ne'er seek a wife till ye ken what to do wi' her.

Ne'er shew me the meat but the man.

Ne'er shew your teeth unless ye can bite.

Ne'er speak ill o' the deil.

Ne'er speak ill o' them whase breid ye eat.
Don't bite the hand that feeds you, or it might stop doing so.

Ne'er spend gude siller looking for bad.
Used in Roy's Generalship, *part 2.*

Ne'er strive against the stream.
Don't try to go against the majority.

Ne'er tak a stane to brak an egg when ye can dae it wi' the back o'
your knife.
*Do not use excessive force when it is not necessary. Sometimes the alternative
'Ne'er tak a forehammer to break an egg when ye can do it wi' a penknife' is used.*

Ne'er tell your fae when your fit sleeps.

Ne'er throve Convent without woman's counsel.
From Scott's The Abbot, *chap. 14.*

Ne'er throw the bridle of your horse ower a fool's arm.

Ne'er too late to learn.

Ne'er use the tawse when a gloom will do.
Don't resort to extreme measures when they are not necessary.

Ne'er was a wife weel pleased coming frae the mill but ane, and
she brak her neck bane.
*Kelly says this is 'commonly said to wives when they come from the mill, but the
occasion, sense, or meaning I know not'. Hislop however suggests 'Is it not
because they are always dissatisfied with the "mouter" which the miller takes?'*

Ne'er waste a candle to chase a will-o'-the-wisp.

Ne'er waur happen to you than your ain prayer.

Neevie, neevie, neck nack;
Which hand will you tak?
Tak' the right, tak the wrang;
I'll beguile ye if I can.
*A child's nursery rhyme used among boys while whirling the two closed fists round
each other, one containing the prize, the other empty.*

Neither buff nor stye.
Neither one thing nor another.

Neither far away nor foul gate.
Neither a long distance or a bad road.

Neither fair gude e'en nor fair gude day.
He won't say anything one way or the other.

Neither fish, flesh, nor gude red herring.
Used to signify that an article is good for nothing.

Neither sae sinfu' as to sink, nor sae holy as to soom.
Refers to the ancient method of testing a suspected witch. The phrase is used to imply a person is less than perfect but not thoroughly bad.

Never's a lang term.

New lairds hae new laws.

New moon, new moon, tell me if you can,
Gif I have a hair like the hair of my gudeman.
According to Cheviot, 'Girls in Galloway gathered a handful of grass at the new moon, and if a hair was found amongst it, the colour of the hair determined that of her future husband.'

Next to nae wife, a gude wife is the best.
More Caledonian misogyny.

Nineteen nay-says o' a maiden is half-a-grant.

Nipping and scarting's Scotch folk's wooing.

Nobility without ability is like a pudding without suet.

No farlie dirt go dear, when a fart cost five shillings.
'A satirical expression of great folks, when those, of a meaner birth, pretend to education, breeding, or fine cloaths' – Kelly.

No to see daylicht til.
To be blind to someone's faults.

Nought's to be had o' womans' hand unless you gie her all the plea.

Nowadays truth's news.

Now's now, and Yule's in winter.

O

O' a' fish in the sea herring is king.

O' a' flatterers self-love is the greatest.

O' a' ills, nane's best.

O' a' ills the least is best.

O' a' little, tak a little; when there's nought, tak a'.

O' a' meat i' the warld, the drink gaes best doon.

O' ane ill come mony.

O' a' sorrows, a fu' sorrow's the best.
Traditionally said when friends die and leave good legacies.

O' a' the months o' the year, curse a fair Februar.

O' a' wars peace is the end.

O' bairns' gifts ne'er be fain; nae sooner they gie than they tak it again.

Oft coming keeps friends lang thegither.

O' gude advisement comes nae ill.

Oh for a drap o' gentle blude, that I may wear black abune my brow.
According to Kelly 'In Scotland no woman is suffered to wear a silk hood unless she be a gentlewoman, that is, a gentleman's daughter, or married to a gentleman. A rich maid, having the offer of a wealthy yeoman or a bare gentleman, wished for the last, to qualify her to wear a black hood. It is since spoken to such wealthy maidens upon the like occasion.'

O' ill debtors men get aiths.
All you will get from a debtor is a promise rather than the money itself.

Old men will die, and children will soon forget.
This proverb occurs in a ballad by Robert Sempill (1567) called 'Ane Complaint upon Fortoun':

> *But as the proverbe speikis, it plaine appeiris,*
> *Auld men will die, and bairns will sune forget.*

Old Sma' Back.
A cant Scottish expression for death. Used in Scott's Quentin Durward *Chap. 37.*

O' little meddling comes muckle care.

One magpie's joy,
Two's grief,
Three's a marriage,
Four's death.
A popular English version of this rhyme uttered when one sees a magpie is:

> *One for sorrow*
> *Two for mirth*
> *Three for a wedding*
> *Four for a birth.*

In Scotland one magpie was regarded as an omen of joy whereas two brought sorrow – in England it was the other way round.

One, two, three, what a lot o' fishwives I see.
According to Cheviot, when fisherfolk are gathered together they have a particular dislike to being numbered. Hence rude boys would annoy the fishwives by calling this phrase out to them.

On painting and fighting look adreich.
When observing a painting or a fight, it is best to look from a distance. Sound advice.

On the fourteenth of October, was ne'er a souter sober.
St Crispin's day falls on the fourteenth of October, old style. As St Crispin was the patron saint of souters they were usually to be found celebrating that particular day.

On the sea sail, on the land settle.

Onything for ye about an honest man's house but a day's work.

Onything is better than the yell kail.
i.e. broth without meat.

Onything is naething.
A promise to give 'anything' is worthless. Used in Scott's Rob Roy, Chap. 18.

Onything sets a gude face, quo the monkey wi' the mutch on.

Open confession is gude for the soul.
This proverb is recorded in Fergusson's Scottish proverbs, *and hence must pre-date 1641.*

Oppression will mak a wise man wud.

O' the marriages in May, the bairns die o' decay.

O' twa ills, choose the least.

Our ain reek's better than ither folk's fire.

Our sins and debts are aften mair than we think.
A cautionary saying.

Our sowens are ill sour'd, ill seil'd, ill sodden, thin, an' little o'
them. Ye may stay a' night, but ye may gang hame if ye like. It's
weel ken'd your faither's son was ne'er a scambler.
*Kelly says 'This proverb arose from a speech made by a Scotsman to a guest that
she would gladly have shaken off, and is repeated when we think our friend does
not entertain us heartily'.*

Out o' Davy Lindsay into Wallace.
*Said when a person has progressed from one thing to another. David Lindsay and
Wallace were two books formerly used in schools.*

Out o' debt, out o' danger.

Out o' God's blessing into the warm sun.

Out on the high-gate is aye fair play.

Out o' sicht, out o' langour.
Out of sight out of mind.

Out o' the peat pot into the gutter.
A Scottish equivalent of the English 'Out of the frying pan and into the fire'.

Out o' the warld and into Kippen.
*At one time Kippen was considered to be so remote that it was out of this world.
The proverb is used when a person is going to a strange unknown place.*

O, wad some power the giftie gie us
To see oursels as ithers see us!
From Robert Burns' poem 'To a Louse'.

Ower braw a purse to put a plack in.
Said when somebody builds a grand house on a small income.

Ower far north for you.
Too clever for you.

Ower gude for banning and ower bad for blessing.
This proverb was used to refer to Rob Roy's character.

Ower haly was hang'd but rough and sonsie wan awa'.

Ower high, ower laigh, ower het, ower cauld.
Said when someone or thing goes from one extreme to the other.

Ower late to spare, when the bottom is bare.

Ower mony cooks spoil the broth.
Ower mony grieves hinder the wark.

Ower mony irons in the fire, some maun cool.
Said when somebody has so many projects on the go at once, that they are unlikely to make a success of them all.

Ower muckle cook'ry spills the bruise.

Ower muckle cook'ry spoils the brochan.

Ower muckle hameliness spoils gude courtesy.
Familiarity breeds contempt.

Ower muckle loose leather about your chafts.
A somewhat unsubtle, but marvellously expressive way of saying that a person is not looking well, or too thin.

Ower muckle o' ae thing is gude for naething.

Ower narrow counting culyes nae kindness.
Meanness does not cultivate kindness from others.

Ower near neighbours to be gude friends.

Ower reckless may repent.

Ower sicker, ower loose.
A saying applied to someone who is either too strict and hard, or too free and easy.

Ower strong meat for your weak stomach.

Ower sune is easy mended.
Least said, soonest mended.

Owe the mare, owe the bear, let the filly eat there.
'Spoken when we see a man's goods squandered by his own people' – Kelly.

O what a tangled web we weave
When first we practise to deceive.
From Scott's Marmion.

Own debt and crave days.

P

Patch and lang sit, build and soon flit.
A long gradual rise is more likely to be permanent than a rapid one.

Paterson's mare aye goes foremost.

Pay-before-hand's never weel ser'd.
Tradesmen suffer equally from two types of customer – those who never pay, and those who pay before the job is done and hence never stop acting as foremen.

Pay him hame in his ain coin *or*
Pay him in his ain coin.

Pay plack and bawbee.
Pay all that you owe.

Pedlar's drouth.
An expression meaning hunger.

Pennyless souls maun pine in purgatory.

Penny-wheep's gude enough for muslin-kail.
Penny-wheep was the weakest kind of small beer sold for a penny a bottle and muslin kail is a common kind of broth. Hence poor service deserves nothing better than a poor reward.

Penny wise and pound foolish.

Perth is gone, the bridge is down.
A Highland saying uttered on the occasion of a great catastrophe. The Perth bridge was destroyed by the swelling of the Tay on 14 October 1621.

Peter's in, Paul's out.
Said when, after waiting an age for a principal character to arrive, another principal leaves on his arrival.

Pigs may whistle, but thay hae an ill mouth for't.
Said when somebody is trying to perform a task for which they are incompetent.

Pint stoups hae lang lugs.
This saying arises because those who drink a lot often say more than is good for them.

Pish and fart, sound at the heart.

Pishing, and pills wagging, puts the day away.
'Spoken when people trifle away their time, that they should bestow on their necessary business' – Kelly.

Pith's gude at a' play but threading o' needles.

Pittenweem'll sink wi' sin, but neither sword nor pestilence sall enter therein.
A local Fife saying.

Plack aboot's fair play.

Placks and bawbees grow pounds.

Plaister thick and some will stick.

Play carle wi' me again if you daur.
Do not dare to argue with me. Often said by parents to stubborn children.

Play's gude; but daffin' dow not.
Play is good but folly is useless.

Play's gude while it lasts.
Play's gude while it's play.

Play wi' him in his ain coin.

Play wi' your play feers [fellows].
Don't play tricks on your elders.

Pleaing at the law is like fighting through a whin bush – the harder the blows the sairer the scarts.
A comment on the difficult process of law and the state it is likely to leave you in.

Please your kimmer, and ye'll easy guide your gossip.
A 'kimmer' is a gossip, hence the saying suggests that if you encourage a gossip to speak on a certain subject they will run out of things to say.

Please yoursel' an' you'll aye please somebody.

Please yoursel', and you'll no dee o' the pet.

Plenty is nae plague.

Plenty maks dainty.
According to Kelly abundance makes us fastidious.

Poets and painters are aye poor.
This proverb appears in no collection before Henderson's. It is therefore possible that it is a record of his own and his friends' experiences, he being a painter and being friendly with poets such as Motherwell.

Poets and painters hae liberty to lo'e.

Poor be your meal poke, and aye your nieve in the nook o't. Otherways, in the nether end o' it.
'A jocose imprecation to them who call us poor' – Kelly.

Poor folk are fain of little.

Poor folk maun fit their wame to their winning.

Poor folk maun live.

Poor folks are soon pish'd on.

Poor folk seek meat for their stamacks, and rich folk stamacks for their meat.

Poor folks' friends soon misken them.
i.e. forget them because they are poor.

Poorly sits richly warms.
'Spoken when people sit on a low stool by the fire' – Kelly.

Poor men hae nae souls.
'This is an old proverb in the time of popr'y when the poor had no masses, or dirige's said for them' – Kelly.

Poortith cauld.

Poortith pairts gude company.
Poverty leads to arguments about money and hence separates friends.

Poortith's better than pride.

Poortith's pain, but nae disgrace.
Poverty is uncomfortable, but nothing to be ashamed of.

Poortith taks awa pith.
From Scott's Fortunes of Nigel, *chap. 35.*

Poortith wi' patience is less painfu'.

Possession is eleven points o' the law.

Possession's worth an ill charter.

Poverty is a bad back friend, but ill fame is a waur ane.
From Scott's Heart of Midlothian, *chap. 12.*

Poverty is the mither o' a' arts.

Poverty pairts gude company, and is an enemy to virtue.

Powder me weel, and keep me clean,
I'll carry a ball to Peebles green.
This refers to Mons Meg, the famous cannon at Edinburgh Castle.

Praise without profit puts little i' the pat.
Fine words do not put food in one's stomach.

Prayer and practice is gude rhyme.

Pray to God to help you, and put your hand to work.

Preach according to your stipend.
A warning to live within your means/income.

Pretty man, I maun say, tak a peat and sit down.
Kelly says this is 'an ironical expression to a mean boy who would gladly be esteemed'.

Pride and grace ne'er dwell in ae place.

Pride an' sweerdness need muckle uphaudin.

Pride finds nae cauld.
According to Kelly 'Spoken heretofore to young women when, in compliance with the fashion, they went with their breasts and shoulders bare.' The saying still applies to today's fashion victims.

Pride in a poor briest, has mickle dolour to dree.

Pride ne'er leaves its maister till he get a fa'.
A warning to all not to become complacent.

Pride prinks her brow for the deil to pouse.
Pride bedecks herself and the devil despoils.

Pride's an ill horse to ride.

Pride that dines wi' vanity sups wi' contempt.

Pride will hae a fa'.

Pride without profit wears shoon and goes barefit.
'Spoken when people have something fine about them when everything else is shabby' – Kelly.

Provision in season maks a bein house.

Prudence should be winning when thrift is spinning.

Puddings and wort are ready dirt.
A word of contempt when you are displeased with someone or something.

Puddins and paramours should be hetly handled.
Both are not so pleasant when cold!

Put a coward to his metal, and he'll fight the deil.
Once roused, people can find incredible courage.

Put anither man's bairn in your bosom and he'll creep oot at your sleeve.
You cannot expect to be loved, just because you look after someone.

Put a stout heart to a stey brae.

Put canna in your pouch and try.
The reply given to someone who says he can't do something.

Put nae force against the flail.

Put on your spurs and be at your speed.

Put that in your pipe and smoke it.

Put the man to the mear that can manage the mear.

Put the matter to your knee and straight it.
Spoken in anger to fault finders. Used in Galt's Entail, *chap. 50. Devote your resources to worthwhile projects.*

Put the saddle on the right horse.
'Spoken when we are blamed for the miscarriages that were occasioned by others'
– Kelly.

Put twa pennies in a purse an' they'll creep thegither.

Put your finger in the fire, and say it was your fortune.
Said of a person who has knowingly placed himself in difficulties, but who attributes his position to fortune.

Put your hand in the creel, tak' oot an adder or an eel.
Spoken when choosing something is a bit of a lottery.

Put your hand nae further oot than your sleeve will reach.

Put your hand twice to your bannet and ance to your pouch.
A piece of advice hinting that the more polite one is the less often one has to pay.

Put your shanks in your thanks and mak gude gramashes o' them.
Literally this says 'Put your legs in your thanks and make good gaiters of them.'
A rebuke to those who pay in thanks only, when something a bit more substantial is expected.

Put your thoom upon that.
Keep it secret, i.e. conceal it.

Put your tongue in my arse and worry me to death.
According to Kelly this is 'a contemptuous return to him that threatens to beat us'.

Q

Quality without quantity is little thocht o'.

Quarellers do not usually live long.
From Scott's St. Ronan's Well, *chap. 8.*

Quarrels are easier begun than ended.

Quey calves are dear veal.
A quey is a two-year-old cow, and hence too valuable as a cow to be killed as a calf.

Quhare the hearte heavit in het bluid ower hill and howe,
There shall the dinke deer droule for the dowe,
Two fleet-footed maidens shall tread the green,
And the mune and the stars shall flash between.
Quhare the proud high hold and heavy hold beire
Ane fremauch shall feed on ane father's frene's faire,
In dinging at the stars the D shall drop doun,
But the S shall be S when the head S is gone.
A saying from Thomas the Rhymer, meaning that the arms of the Scots shall supersede those of the Douglas. In endeavouring to exalt himself, the Douglas shall fall, but the Scots shall flourish when the Royal Stuarts are no more. It was also said by the Rhymer:

Quhare the wingit horse at his maister sal wince,
Let wise men cheat the chevysance.
Let wise men desert Douglas when he opposes the King. The Scots did this, and prospered exceedingly.

Quhen Skirling shall be captain, the cock shall lose his tail.
According to Birrel's Diary *(1532–1605) when Edinburgh Castle was surrendered to Cockburn of Skirling on behalf of Queen Mary on 21 March 1567, the weather-cock of St Giles Church was blown away – so fulfilling the ancient prophecy.*

Quick at meat, quick at wark.

Quick, for you'll ne'er be cleanly.
Do something quickly, for you will never do it neatly.

Quick returns mak rich merchants.

Quietness is best.
Silence is golden.

R

Rab Gibb's contract – stark love and kindness.
An expression used when we drink to a friend. According to Murison it was 'The answer of Rob Gibb, master of the horse to King James V, when asked why he served him'.

Raggit folk and bonny folk are aye ta'en haud o'.
Said as a joke when somebody catches or tears their clothing on a nail.

Rain, rain, gang to Spain, and never come back again.

Rain, rain, rattlestanes, dinna rain on me,
But rain on Johnnie Groat's house, far owre the sea.
Sung during a hailstorm, according to Chambers.

Rainbow, rainbow,
Rin away hame,
Come again at Martinmas,
When a' the corn's in.

– Chambers.

Rainbow, rainbow, rin away hame,
The cowe's to calf, the yowe's to lamb.

– Chambers.

Rainbow, rainbow, rin awa' hame,
The kye'll be milked afore ye get hame.

– Ayrshire.

Raise nae mair deils than ye are able to lay.
Don't take on more tasks than you can handle.

Rather spoil your joke than tine your friend.
Do not tell jokes if it is at the expense of a friend, as their friendship is worth a lot more than a laugh.

Rattan an' moose
Lea' the poor woman's hoose;
Gang awa ower to the mill,
And there ane and a' ye'll get your fill.
This verse was written on the walls by those whose dwellings were vermin-infested, in the hope of them leaving the premises.

Raw dads mak fat lads *or*
Raw dawds mak fat lads.
Presumably because they are not experienced enough to get work out of them.

Raw leather raxes weel.

Read your lesson without a word.
According to Cheviot, 'without a mistake'.

Ready to eat the nails frae their fingers.
i.e. greatly annoyed.

Reavers shouldna be ruers.
A person should not be a robber if he has a conscience and wants to repent.

Reckless youth maks ruefu' eild.
One cannot escape the past. One can be sure that the past will catch you up.

Reckon money after all your kin.

Reckon up your winning at your bedstock.
Kelly gives another version: 'Reckon on your winning by your bed stock'.

Red brackens bring milk and butter.
The bracken in autumn is associated with rich pasture.

Red fish.
i.e. a salmon. A phrase used by fisherfolk some of whom are superstitious about pronouncing the word salmon.

Red wood maks gude spindles.
'Red wood' is the name given to the dark-coloured wood found in the heart of trees.

Reek comes aye doun again, however high it flees.
What goes up must come down, whether it be a person's fortune or an object.

Refer my coat and lose a sleeve.

'Rejoice bucks,' quo' Brodie, when he shot at the buryin' and thought it was a weddin'.

Remember, man, and keep in mind, a faithfu' friend is hard to find.

Remember me to all that ask for me, but blade me in nobody's teeth.

Remember me to your bedfellow when you lie alane.

Remember shearer's drouth.
'In various parts of Scotland when a gentleman entered the harvest field, he was immediately accosted by a deputation of female shearers and requested to "Remember shearer's drouth". If he refused to pay his footing he was compelled to "ride the stang", i.e. set astride on a pole and carried aloft, or he was thrown up in the air by his stalwart tormentors, and only saved from a heavy fall by being received in their brawny arms, or again he was cast upon the ground and held there, till a gratuity was considered' – Cheviot.

Remove an auld tree an' it'll wither.

Renton is its name, and renit it shall be,
And the auld lairds o' Renton shall rot by the tree.
This rhyme is ascribed to Thomas the Rhymer, and applied to the Homes of Renton, on account of the cruelty of Sir Alexander Home of Renton, who was Sheriff of Berwickshire from 1616 to 1621, and was very harsh in the discharge of his duty. In due course the Rentons lost the estate.

Rice for good luck, and bauchles for bonnie bairns.
This saying refers to the custom of throwing rice and old shoes after newly married couples.

Riches are got wi' pain, kept wi' care, and tint wi' grief.
A proverb pointing out the hardships associated with wealth.

Rich folk hae routh o' friends.
Money attracts many 'friends'.

Rich folk's wit rives poor folk's jaws.

Rich mixture maks gude mortar.

Richt wrangs nae man.

Ride fair and jaup nane.

Right, Roger, sow's gude mutton.
Said when somebody is completely mistaken.

Ringing his clapper.
Using one's tongue freely.

Ringworm! Ringworm red!
Never mayest thou either speed nor spread,
But aye grow less and less,
And die away among the aise [ashes].
'In Shetland a person afflicted with ringworm takes a few ashes between the thumb and forefinger on three successive mornings before breakfast, and applying the ashes to the part affected repeats this rhyme, at the same time throwing some ashes into the fire' – Cheviot.

Ripe fruit is soonest rotten.

Rise, daughter, and go to your daughter,
For your daughter's daughter has had a daughter.
'A rebus on four generations' – Chambers.

Rise when the day daws, bed when the night fa's.

Robin, that herds on the height, can be blythe as Sir Robert the Knight.

Rodden tree and reid threid,
Put the witches to their speed.
Both of these articles were supposed to ward off witches. It was at one time common in Scotland to attach a cross of this wood to the byre door with a red thread, as a security to the cattle against witches.

Rome wasna biggit in ae day.

Round and round the unseen hand
Turns the fate o' mortal man;
A screich at birth, a grane at e'en,
The flesh to earth, the soul to heaven.
An epitome of man's career.

Rot him awa' wi' ham an' eggs.
A humorous suggestion to a young wife on how she might get rid of an old husband.

Royt lads may mak' sober men.
To 'royt' is to go about idly or dissolutely. Hence dissolute youths may turn out well after all.

Rue and thyme grow beith in ae garden.
'Repent and give over an attempt before it is too late, alluding to the sound of the two herbs here named' – Kelly.

Rue in thyme should be a maiden's posie.

Rule youth weel, for eild will rule itsel'.

Ruse the fair day at e'en.
Don't give praise until a thing is complete.

Ruse the ford as ye find it.
Speak as you find.

Rusted wi' eild, a wee piece gate seems lang.
The ravages of time can make a short road seem much longer.

S

Sae mony men, sae mony minds.

Saft beddin's gude for sair bones, quo' Howie, when he streeked himsel' on the midden head.

Saft's yer horn, an' easy blawn.

'Saft's your horn, my friend,' quo' the man, when he took haud o' the cuddy's lug.

Said the trout to the fluke, when did your mou' crook?
My mou' was never even, since I came to John's Haven.
Johnshaven is a fishing village in Kincardineshire. The rhyme refers to the lopsided mouth of the flounder.

'Sail,' quo' the King: 'Haud,' quo' the wind.

Sair back and sair bones
Drivin' the Laird o' Morphies's stanes,
The Laird o' Morphie'll never thrive
As lang as the kelpie is alive.
According to Chambers 'the family of Graham of Morphie, in Mearns, are popularly said to owe their extinction to the action of a water-kelpie, whom one of the lairds bridled with a pair of branks, and compelled to carry stones to build his castle. The kelpie, on being released, uttered the above malediction.'

Sair cravers are aye ill payers.
And vice versa.

Sairs shouldna be sair handled.
One should handle delicate matters gently.

Sair wark and poortith downa weel be joined.

Sairy be your meal-pock, and aye your nieve i' the neuk o't.
An ill wish that someone's meal bag will be empty when they next delve in to get some food.

Sairy man, and then he grat.
'An ironical condolence of some slight misfortune' – Kelly.

Salt water ne'er harmed Zetlander.

Satan reproves sin.

Saturday's change, and Sunday's prime,
Is enough in seven years' time.
A new moon on a Saturday and a Sunday full moon used to be considered unlucky.

Saturday flit, short while sit.

'Saut,' quo the souter, when he had eaten a cow a' but the tail.
These words are used to spur on those who are beginning to tire when they have almost completed a difficult task.

Save yoursel frae the deil and the laird's bairns.
A warning given by poor people in days gone by, to their children. It was well known that if they hurt the laird's children they would be punished, but if it were the other way round, nothing could be done.

Saving the ladies.
This phrase refers to an old Scottish custom. After seeing the ladies home from balls, the gentlemen returned to the supper room and each naming a lady, drained a glass in her honour.

Saw thin, shear thin.

Saw wheat in dirt, and rye in dust.

Saw ye that and shotna at it, and you sae gleg a gunner.
A cheeky remark aimed at a boaster who is claiming to have seen something extraordinary.

Say aye 'No', and ye'll ne'er be married.
A humorous remark made to someone who has just refused some offer.

Saying gaes gude cheap *or*
Saying gangs cheap.

Says the Shochie to the Ordie, where shall we meet?
At the Cross of Perth, when a' men are fast asleep.
These two streams join the Tay about five miles above Perth. The saying refers to a predicted nocturnal flooding of Perth, similar to what occurred in 1210.

Say weel and dae weel, and wi' ae letter; say weel is gude, but dae weel is better.

Say what you will, an ill mind will turn't to ill.

Scant-o'-grace hears lang preachings.

Scanty cheeks mak a lang nose.

Scarting and eating wants but a beginning.

Scart-the-cog wad sup mair.
To 'scart the cog' is to scrape the inside of the dish, hence suggesting that the contents have been so popular, a little more would not go amiss.

Scart ye my arse, and I'll claw your elbow.

Scorn comes commonly wi' skaith.

Scornfu' dogs eat dirty puddins.
From Scott's Redgauntlet, *chap. 11.*

Scorn not the bush that bields ye.
Don't hurt that which protects you.

Scotsmen aye reckon frae an ill hour.

Scotsmen aye tak their mark frae a mischief.
The above proverb and the preceding one are both comments on the less positive side of the Scottish character. It is said that Scotsmen tend to calculate things in relation to the date of some mishap or death. This is the silliest notion I have come across since my last car accident.

Scotsmen tak a' they can get, and a little more if they can.
Quoted as a saying about Scotsmen by Lord Advocate MacDonald in the House of Commons, 6 March 1888.

Scour the duds o' Yetholm.
A Roxburghshire saying – made as a reproach against the dirty habits of the Yetholm gypsies.

Seagull, seagull, sit on the sand,
It's never good weather, when you're on the land.

Second thoughts are best.
A caution against acting upon impulse.

See for love and buy for siller.

Seein's believing a' the warld ower.

Seek muckle, and get something; seek little, and get naething.
It pays to set one's sights high.

Seek never het fire under cauld ice.
i.e. Some things are just as they appear.

Seek till you find, and ye'll never loss your labour.

Seek your sa' where you got your ail, and beg your barm where you buy your ale.
The surly reply of someone who is asked for assistance by another person who previously shunned him.

Seil ne'er comes till sorrow be awa.

Sel, sel, has half-filled hell.
Selfishness has caused grief for many people.

Seldom ride tines his spurs.
If you don't use it, you can lose it.

Seldom seen, soon forgotten.

Self praise comes aye stinking ben.
Self-praise is no recommendation.

Self praise is nae honour.

Send a fool to France, and a fool he'll come back.

Send your gentle blude to the market, and see what it will buy.
Said to those who boast of coming from a high-ranking family, but who possess little else.

Send your son to Ayr; if he do weel here, he'll do weel there.

Send you to the sea, and ye'll no get saut water.
Said when somebody does not live up to your expectations.

Service is no inheritance.
'An argument for servants to seek out for some settlement' – Kelly.

Ser' yoursel' and your friends will think the mair o' ye.
The answer given by those who are asked to do a favour when they would prefer not to.

Ser' yoursel' till your bairns come o' age.

Set a beggar on horseback, he'll ride to the deil.

Set a lass on Tintock tap,
Gin she hae the penny siller,
The wind will blaw a man till her;
But gin she want the penny siller,
There'll ne'er as ane be evened till her.
A Lanarkshire rhyme on marriage.

Set a stout heart to a stey brae.
Face a hard task with courage and determination. This saying is recorded in Alexander Montgomerie's famous poem 'The Cherrie and the Slae', first published in 1597 thus:
    'Sic gettis ay as settis ay stout stomakis to the bray.'

Set a thief to grip a thief.

Set him up and shute him forward.
Spoken of one who is over pretentious. From Scott's St. Ronan's Well.

Set roasted beef and pudding on the opposite side o' the pit o' Tophet, and an Englishman will make a spang [spring] at it.
From Scott's Rob Roy, Chap. 28.

Set that doun on the backside o' your count book.
Take note of my help, and make sure you repay it in the future.

Set us agoing.
A phrase used in olden days when asking a minister to say grace, which conveys the pleasing idea that the blessing is an essential preliminary to the breaking of bread.

Set your fit upon that, an' it winna loup in your face.

Set your knee to it and right it.
Kelly says this phrase is 'Taken from setting bended sticks straight. Spoken in anger, to them who alledge that what we have done is amiss.'

Shake yer lugs and lie doun again.
An expression of contemptuous indifference. From Galt's The Entail.

Shak yer ain mats at yer ain back door.
Attend to your own life and let others attend to theirs.

Shallow waters mak maist din.
Another version of empty vessels making the loudest noise.

'Shame be in my meal' – pock gin I dinna.
May I suffer if I don't do something.

'Shame fa' the couple,' as the cow said to her fore feet.

Shame fa' the dog that, when he hunted you, didna gar you rin faster.

Shame fa' the gear and the bladry/thrumphry o't.
'Tune of an old Scottish song, referring to the marriage of a young girl with an old man' – Kelly.

Shame fa' them that think shame to do themsels a gude turn.

'Shame fa' the ordiner', quo' the cat to the Cordiner.
'An expression of dissatisfaction with an order given' – Kelly.

Shame fa' their souple snouts.
An imprecation on the avaricious, from Scott's Rob Roy, *chap. 22.*

Shame's past the shed o' yer hair.
You have a brass neck.

Shank yersel awa.
Take to your legs. Go away.

Shank's naiggy.
Your own legs are your horse, i.e. you are on foot.

Sharp hunger maks a short grace.

Sharp sauce gie's a gude taste to sweetmeats.

Sharp wit aften mends foul feature.

She brak her elbow at the kirk door.
Said of a woman who becomes lazy when she marries.

She disna aye gang the straight road to the well.

She frisks about like a cat's tail i' the sun.

She has a face like a dish clout.
i.e. pale/terrified.

She has an ill paut wi' her hind foot.
She is stubborn and tricky to deal with. This phrase comes from farming and cows who kick when they are milked.

She has a tongue like a tinkler.

She has a tongue like a trumpet.
She talks loudly.

She has a tongue that wad clip clouts.
She has a sharp tongue.

She has a tongue to deave the miller.

She has gi'en them green stockings.
According to Hislop this was 'Spoken when a young woman marries before her elder sisters.'

She has got a kid in her kilting.
'That is, she has got a bastard about her' – Kelly.

She has pish'd in the tub-hole.
'The tub-hole is a hollow place in the ground, over which the kive (mashing fat) stands, spoken of an ale-wife when she breaks, and turns bankrupt' – Kelly.

She has ta'en her sheep to a silly market.
She has made a poor marriage.

She hauds up her gab like an awmous dish.

She hauds up her head like a hen drinking water.
Both of the above sayings are used on people who behave in an impudent or forward manner.

She hauds up her head like a hundred pound aver.
As above.

She'll be a gude sale whisp.
Admirable as a barmaid, but not considered suitable to marry.

She'll keep her ain side of the house, and gang up and down yours.
A saying used to dissuade a man from marrying a woman who is considered to be too bold and pushy. It is a warning that she will take over everything in his life.

She'll put you under her hough, and feed you with farts.
Another saying with the same meaning as 'She'll keep her ain side etc.'

She'll wear like a horseshoe, aye the langer the cleaner.

She lookit at the moon, but lichtit i' the midden.
An old proverb applied to women who boast before marriage that they will find a 'fine' match, but who afterwards end up marrying ordinary men.

She lookit at the sun, but landit in the gutter.

She looks like a leddy in a landward kirk.
A saying applied to someone who appears highly conspicuous on account of their dress or manner.

She pined awa' like Jenkin's hen.
She died an old maid.

She's a bad sitter that's aye in a flutter.

She's a drap o' my dearest blude.

She's a hussy that wants a hip,
And so may you your underlip.
'A senseless return of a woman to him that hails her a hussy' – Kelly.

She's a maiden as the man left her.
According to Kelly 'Intimating that she is a whore'.

She's an ill whore that's no worth the down laying.

She's as blythe as she's bonny.

She's as ugly as a starless midnicht.

She's a wise wife that wats her ain weird.
She is a clever wife who knows her own destiny.

She's aye playing hum'n my lug.
She is a nagging wife.

She's baith back and breast.
Applied to women whose figures mean that it is hard to tell one side of them from the other. From Scott's Redgauntlet *– Letter 5.*

She's better than she's bonnie.
'A Highlander, in speaking favourably of his wife is reported to have misquoted this saying and characterised her as being "bonnier than she was better".' – Hislop.

She's black, but she has a sweet smack.
Wealthy but not very beautiful – for those who would marry only for money.

She's greeting at the thing she laugh'd at farn year.
'Signifying that she is in labour' – Kelly.

She's grown gatty, that was ance a dawtie.
She has grown ill-tempered, who was once a pet.

She's her mother ower again.
She behaves in a very similar manner to her mother.

She's like Aillie Belchie,
Sinned to the nineteenth degree.
A Berwickshire saying said of those who are flagrant offenders. According to Dr Henderson, Alice Belchie was a hind's daughter at Lintlaw, in the Parish of Buncle, Berwickshire, and it was said she murdered three of her illegitimate children. At her late wake an 'honest man' prayed for mercy on Alice, 'who has sinned to the nineteenth degree'.

She's like Geordie Dean's daughter-in-law, nought but a spindle shankit devil.
From the Ettrick Shepherd's 'The Shepherd's Calendar' – The School of Misfortune.

She's like the man o' Aperley's cow,
She's came hame routin', but no very fu',
Wi' the tow about her horns.
i.e. the cow came home unsold, and the rhyme is applied to a young woman who returns from a local fair/market without a partner.

She's little better than she should be.

She's lost her market.
Similar to above.

She's meat for his maister.
She is far too good for him.

She's no fit to sew his buttons on.
Opposite of above.

She's no to be made a sang about.
'An abatement of a woman's commendation to beauty' – Kelly.

She's spinning clues to the midden, and woe to the wabster.

She's weel enough an she be gude.
A grudging acknowledgement of a woman's beauty. From Galt's Sir Andrew Wylie, *chap. 44.*

She that fa's ower a strae's a tentless taupie.
The person who falls at the smallest of obstacles is a fool.

She that gangs to the well wi' an ill will,
Either the pig breaks or the water will spill.

She that taks a gift, hersel she sells, and she that gies ane does naething else.

She wadna hae the walkers, and the riders gaed by.
According to Dean Ramsay's Reminiscences *this saying was made by the celebrated beauty Becky Monteith as a reply when asked how she had not made a good marriage.*

She was aye as if she had been ta'en oot o' a bandbox.
She was very neat and trim.

She wasna to seek at a clashing.
She is a gossip.

Shod i' the cradle, and barefit i' the stubble.
Applied to people who dress inappropriately.

Shore [threaten] before you strike.

Shored folk live lang, an' so may him ye ken o'.

Short accounts mak lang friends.

Short folk are sune angry.

Short folk's heart is sune at their mouth.

Short rede, gude rede.
Short counsel, good counsel: from Scott's The Fair Maid of Perth.

Short rents mak careless tenants.

Short sheep had short rents.
Cheviot: 'A Border proverb referring to the great increase of the value of land in that district through the introduction of a breed of sheep bearing a longer and more valuable fleece of wool' – The Black Dwarf *chap. 1.*

Shouther to shouther stands steel and pouther.

Show me the guest the house is waur o'.

Show me the man, and I'll show you the law.

Sic a man as thou wad be, draw thee to sic companie.
Birds of a feather flock together.

Sic as a Friday, sic is a Sunday.
A general superstition as to the state of the weather

Sic as ye gie, sic will you get.
You only get out of life what you put in.

Sic faither, sic son.

Sic mannie, sic horsie.
An Aberdeenshire saying.

Sic reek as is therein comes oot o' the lum.

Sic things maun be if we sell ale.
According to Kelly, this was the reply an innkeeper's wife gave when her husband complained that the visiting exciseman was being too familiar with her.

Side for side's neibour like.

Silence and thought hurt nae man.

Silence gies consent.

Silence grips the mouse.

Silks an' satins put out the kitchen fire.

Siller maks a' easy.
From Scott's Heart of Midlothian *chap. 21.*

Silly bairns are eith to lear.
Children who are weakly in their body take easily to their lessons.

Simmer is a seemly time.

Since less winna serve.
A reluctant consent.

Since word is thrall, and thought is free,
Keep well thy tongue I counsel thee.
From Scott's Fair Maid of Perth, *chap. 25.*

Sinning my mercies.
A peculiar Scottish phrase, expressive of ingratitude for the favours of providence. Used in Scott's Redgauntlet, *Letter 1.*

Sins and debts are aye mair than we think them.

Sit down and rest you, and tell us how they drest you, and how you wan awa'.
'A jocular way of asking a person about people whom he has been to see' – Hislop.

Sit on your arse, and call your sorrans.
'Sorrans' are servants. Kelly says 'A reproof to them that would have others do for them, what they ought to do themselves. Spoken ironically.'

Sit on your feat and nane will rise you.

Sit still a little longer, we are all sober enough to get over Deacon Dickson's wall.
According to Cheviot 'This used to be a common expression at jovial parties in Edinburgh, and took its rise from an adventure that happened to a certain Deacon Dickson as he was wending his way up the High Street to his home in the Castle Hill, after partaking rather freely of the corporation liquour. He and a companion took it into their muddled heads that since they had made their way earlier in the evening, a wall had been built across the street between St. Giles and

*the Royal Exchange. Anyway they couldn't make it over the obstacle so made a
circuitous route home. The Deacon told this difficulty to his wife, and the next
morning she and her gossips went to look for the wonderful wall, and so the story
got about.'*

Sittin' like a craw in a mist.
Said of someone who looks forlorn.

Skill is nae burden.

Skin and birn.
*The whole of anything. This phrase comes from sheep farming. It represents the
full account of a sheep, by bringing the skin with the tar mark, and the head with
the brand on the nose.*

Skreigh o' day.
Dawn.

Slander leaves a sair behint *or*
Slander leaves a slur.

Slighted love is sair to bide.

Slipshod's no for a frozen road.

Slip the girths.
*Tumble down – like a pack horse's burden when the girth gives away.
Metaphorically, come to grief: from Scott's* Rob Roy, *chap. 19.*

Slow at meat, slow at wark.

Sma' barrels hae big bungs.

Sma' fish are better than nane.

Sma' is the kin that canna spare to fill baith sack and widdie.

Sma' winnings mak a heavy purse.

Smooth waters rin deep.

Snailie, snailie, shoot oot yer horn,
And tell us if it'll be a bonny day the morn.
*A popular rhyme with country children at one time, eager to forecast the next day's
weather.*

Sober, neighbour! The night's but young yet.
*A phrase used to remonstrate with someone who is doing something too quickly.
It is used to signify that there is plenty of time spare for the purpose in hand. Also
used by one drinker to another as an encouragement to prolong their drinking.*

Sodgers, fire, and water soon mak room for themsels.
One has little control over any of these.

Sok and seil is best.

Solway waters.
A euphemisn for smuggled brandy.

Some ane has tauld her she was bonny.

Some are gey drouthy, but ye're aye moistified.
An insinuation that a person likes their drink.

Some are no sooner weel than they're ill again.
Some people are always complaining.

Some are only daft, but ye're red-wud raving.
i.e. very mad.

Somebody may come to kame your hair wi' a cutty stool.
'Spoken by mothers to stubborn daughters, intimating that they will come under the hands of a stepmother who, it is likely, will not deal too tenderly with them' – Kelly.

Some can stand the sword better than the pint-stoup.

Some folk look up, and ithers look down.

Some fork low, but ye fork ower the mow.
Some people do not work hard enough, but you overdo it.

Some gaed east, and some gaed west,
And some gaed to the craw's nest.
A child's rhyme used to indicate that certain persons or things are scattered in all directions.

Some hae a hantel o' fauts, ye're only a ne'er-do-weel.
Some people, although badly behaved, have some redeeming qualities, the person thus addressed has none.

Some hae hap, and some stick i' the gap.
Meaning that some have and some have not good fortune.

Some hae little sense, but ye're aye havering.

Some hae meat that canna eat,
And some wad eat that want it;
But we hae meat, and we can eat,
For which the Lord be thankit.
This verse is generally known as the Selkirk Grace. Robert Burns may have repeated it when he dined with the Earl of Selkirk at St Mary's Isle, but the probability is that it was current at the time among the peasantry. According to Chambers, these lines were current in the south-west of Scotland before the poet's time, and were always called the Covenanter's Grace.

Some say the deil's deid an buried in Kirkcaldy,
Some say he's risen again and danced the Hieland Laddie.
Said to be an anti-Jacobite rhyme.

Some show a gliff o' the gowk, but ye're aye goavin.
To 'show a gliff o' the gowk' is to behave foolishly. 'Goavin' is staring as a fool does. Hence this phrase means that some people behave foolishly but you are always very foolish.

Some strake the measure o' justice, but ye gie't heapit.

Some tak a', but ye leave naething.

Some that has the least to dree are loudest wi' 'wae's me'.
It is often those who suffer least who complain the most.

'So on and accordingly,' quo' Willie Baird's doggie.

Soon eneuch is weel enough.

Soon eneuch to cry 'chuck' when it's oot o' the shell.

Soon gotten, soon spent.

Soon ripe, soon rotten.

'Soor plooms,' quo' the tod when he couldna climb the tree.

Sorrow and an ill life mak sune an auld wife.

Sorrow an' ill weather come unca'd.
Both are beyond our control.

Sorrow be in their een that first saw him, that did not cast him in the fire, and say sorrow have it they had.
'A malicious answer to them that ask us if we saw such a man, meaning one that had done us harm' – Kelly.

Sorrow be in their hands that held so weel to your head.
According to Kelly, 'spoken to drunken men when they are ill-natured'. Hislop gives another form, as –

Sorrow be on your hands that held sae weel to your head.
An imprecation on a person who has surpassed another in an undertaking.

Sorrow be in your thrapple.
An imprecation on a person who talks too much. From Scott's Guy Mannering, *chap. 1*

Sorrow in them or they get the better o' me.

Sorrow is soon enough when it comes.

Sorrow shake you out o' the wabster's handiwark.
i.e. shake you out of your clothes.

Souters and tailors count hours.
Tradesmen and those involved in commerce are aware of the value of time.

Souters shouldna be sailors, that can neither steer nor row.

Souters shouldna gae ayont their last.

Spare at the spigot and let out at the bunghole.
'Spoken to them who are careful and penurious in some trifling things, but neglective in the main chance' – Kelly.

Spare to speak, spare to speed.

Spare weel and hae weel.

Spare when ye're young and spend when ye're auld.

Speak gude o' pipers, your faither was a fiddler.

Speak o' the deil and he'll appear.
A humorous remark made when the subject of a conversation suddenly appears.

Speak weel o' the Hielands, but dwell in the Laigh.
A piece of advice to those who lived on the Moray Coast to be friendly with their Highland neighbours but still to keep their distance.

Speak when ye're spoken to; do what ye're bidden; come when ye're ca'd, and ye'll no be chidden.
A strong remark used as a rebuke when somebody joins in a conversation without waiting to be invited to do so.

Speak when ye're spoken to,
Drink when ye're drucken to,
Gang to the kirk when the bell rings,
And ye'll aye be sure o' a seat.
A contemptuous answer to unwelcome advice.

Speir at Jock Thief if I be a leal man.
Spoken by rogues, who, when their respectability is called into question, refer to persons equally bad.

Spells may be broken by true men.
From Scott's Fair Maid of Perth, *chap. 6.*

Spend, and God will send; spare, and be bare.

Spilt ale is waur than water.

Spit in your loof and haud fast.
Take a firm hold of a thing.

Spit on a stane, and it will be wet at last.

Spunky, spunky, ye're jumpin' light,
Ye ne'er tak hame the school weans right;
But through the rough moss, and owre the hag pen,
Ye droun the ill anes in your watery den.
According to Chambers this was a child's rhyme in Ayrshire about the Will-of-the-Wisp.

St Andrew's day won't come to us for another year.
A Scottish version of 'Christmas comes but once a year'.

Stable the steed, and put your wife to bed when there's night wark
to do.
From Scott's Redgauntlet, *letter 10.*

Standers-by see mair than gamesters.

Staunin' dubs gather dirt.

Stay and drink o' your ain browst.
Wait and join in the mischief which you have caused.

Stay nae langer in a friend's house than ye're welcome.

Steek your een and open your mou',
And see what the King'll send ye.
A rhyme for kids when an adult goes to put something nice in their mouth.

Step by step climbs the hill.

Stickin' gangsna by strength, but by the right use o' the gullie.
From Scott's The Antiquary, *chap. 21. Use of skill is better than use of force.*

Sticks and stanes may brak my banes,
But names will ne'er hurt me.

Stick weel to the skink an' dinna trust to the castock.
*It used to be customary for hospitable housewives to warn their guests to partake
heartily of the skink – strong broth or soup – and not rely on the second course,
the castock – stems of the cabbage and the joint which accompanied them.*

Stolen waters are sweet.

Stook the stable door when the steed is stol'n.

Stretching and gaunting bodes sleep to be wanting.

Strike a dog with a bane and he'll no yowl.

Strike as ye feed, and that's but soberly.
*According to Kelly this is 'a reproof to them that correct those over whom they have
no power'.*

Strike the iron as lang as it's het.

Stuffing hauds out storms.
Advice to eat well before undertaking a journey in bad weather.

Sturt follows a' extremes.

Sturt pays nae debt.
Said to people who fly into a rage when asked to pay what they are due.

Sudden friendship's sure repentance.

Sudden rise, sudden fa'.

Sue a beggar and gain a louse.

Sunday seldom comes aboon the pass o' Bally-Brough.
This saying implies that in the good old times there was little observance of the Sabbath beyond the Highland line.

Sunday wooin' draws to ruin.

Sune eneuch if weel eneuch.

Supped out wort ne'er made gude ale.
According to Kelly this proverb is 'spoken when one asks us for a drink of our wort, for what is drunk in wort will never be ale, good or bad'.

Suppers kill mair than doctors cure.

Sup wi' yer head, the horner's dead, he's dead that made munns.
'Munns' are spoons without handles. According to Kelly it's 'spoken to children who ask for a spoon. Lap it up, don't sup it'.

Surely he hadst Jamie Keddie's ring.
'A Perthshire expression applied to one who comes and goes without attracting much attention. According to tradition Jamie Keddie found a ring in a cavern of Kinnoul Hill, which possessed magical properties, enabling its owner to become invisible.' – Cheviot.

Surfeits slay mair than swords.
A warning to take all things in moderation.

Swallow, swallow, sail the water,
Ye'll get brose, and ye'll get butter.
'Said by boys throwing stones at swallows skimming over water in search of flies' – Chambers.

Swear by your burnt shins.
Sweet at the on-taking, but soor in the aff-putting.
An allusion to the contracting of debt, or some other liability.

Sweet i' the bed, and sweir up i' the morning, was ne'er a gude housewife.
'A jocose reproof to young maids when they lie lang-a-bed' – Kelly.

Sweet milk, sour milk

Thick milk, thin,
Blased milk, bladded milk
Milk new come in;
Milk milket aff milk
Milk in a pig,
New-calved kye's milk
Sour kirnie whig.
'Different kinds of milk' – Chambers.

T

Tak a drink and gae to bed.
An expression of contempt addressed to boasters. From Scott's Fair Maid of
Perth, *Chap. 33.*

Tak a hair o' the dog that bit you.
A familiar version of the law of Homeopathy (similia similibus curantur),
*which is usually interpreted by drinkers thus – cure your hangover by taking
another glass.*

Tak a lass wi' the teer i' her ee.
*A suggestion that the most favourable time to court a girl who has previously been
unresponsive is when she is upset at having split up with another.*

Tak a piece; your teeth's langer than your beard.
Said to children to encourage them to take an extra titbit when it is offered.

Tak a spring on your ain fiddle; ye'll dance till't afore it's done.
Go to the devil if you like.

Tak a staup oot o' their bicker.

Tak an order o' the auld smith an' ye like.
The meaning is much the same as 'tak a spring'. See above.

Tak as you come.
'A proverb debarring choice' – Kelly.

Tak awa Aberdeen and twal mile round and far are ye?
*Aberdonians tend to think that the North of Scotland would be nothing without
it. I couldn't agree more!*

Tak care o' that man whom God has set his mark upon.
*According to Kelly, 'The Scots generally have an aversion to any that have any
natural defect or redundancy, as thinking them mark'd out for a mischief.'
Hopefully we live in more sensible times now.*

Tak a man by his word and a cow by her horn.

Tak folks on the right side.
Humour people.

Tak help at your elbows.
This is a Scottish version of 'God helps those who help themselves'.

Tak him up on his fine eggs, and ane o' them rotten.

Tak him up there wi' his five eggs, and four o' them rotten.

Tak keltie's mends.
According to Cheviot, '"Kelty" is the fine of a bumper. That is, don't drink fair cup out in order to be fined in a bumper.'

Tak nae mair on your back than ye're able to bear.
Don't take on more than you can comfortably deal with.

Tak pairt o' the pelf when the pack's a-dealing.
Grab what you can when the opportunity presents itself.

Tak some to yersel as ye sell the rest.
Spoken facetiously. 'Take some personal satisfaction from your good' – Kelly.

Tak the bit and the buffet wi't.
Take the blows and jibes if greater advantages come with them.

Tak the head for the washing.

Tak the will for the deed.

Tak time ere time be tint.
This comes from Montgomerie's 'The Cherrie and the Slae':

> *Tak tyme, in tyme, or tyme be tint,*
> *For tyme will not remain.*

Tak up the next you find.
'Spoken jocosely when people say they have lost such a thing' – Kelly.

Tak up the steik in your stocking.
Reform.

Tak us as ye find us.

Tak wit wi' yer anger.

Tak your ain tale hame.
Take your own advice to heart, from Scott's The Antiquary, *chap. 27. Apparently at the time of the Union in 1707 the Chancellor Lord Seafield objected to his brother dealing in cattle. He thought it was derogatory to his rank. His brother is said to have replied 'tak your ain tale hame, my lord, I sell nowt, but ye sell nations'.*

Tak your ain will and ye'll no dee o' the pet.

Tak your ain will o't, as the cat did o' the haggis – first ate it, and then creepit into the bag.
Said to people who persist in carrying out an unreasonable act.

Tak your meal wi' ye an' your brose will be the thicker.
A saying sarcastically applied by those who indulge in a good meal before they go to have one with a friend, signifying that they do not expect to be overly-well fed there.

Tak your pick, and say your pleasure.

Tak your thanks to feed your cat.

Tak your venture, as mony a gude ship has done.

Tak your will, you're wise enough.

Tale for tale is travellers' justice.
Said when it is our turn to speak.

Tam-tell-truth's nae courtier.

Tammie Norrie o' the Bass,
Canna kiss a bonnie lass.
The 'Tammie Norrie' is a puffin which has a peculiar beak. This saying is a rhyme aimed at bashful lovers. Tammie Norrie was also applied to bashful or stupid-looking men.

Tape to tape.
To use sparingly or eek things out.

Tappit hens like cock-crowing.

Tarry lang brings little hame.
A warning about the ill effects of time wasting.

Taste and try before you buy.

Taury breeks pays nae freight.
People who are in the same line of business can usually expect perks from each other.

Tears ready, tail ready.
'A humorous reflection upon a woman who is ready to cry' – Kelly.

Tears drown sorrow.
Those who cry the most often get over their grief soonest.

Tell a tale to a mare, an' she'll let a fart.
'Spoken when heedless blockheads mind not what we say' – Kelly.

Tell me waur the flea may bite,
And I'll tell you whaur love may light.

Tell nae tales out o' the schule.
A warning against being a tell-tale.

Tell the truth and shame the deil.

Tell your auld gly'd giddim that.
'Gly'd' means squinting and 'giddim' grandmother. This phrase is spoken to those who tell us something we do not like.

Thanks winna feed the cat.
Said when we are offered thanks, rather than something more practical.

That auld St Andrews fair,
A' the souters maun be there –
A' the souters and souters' seed;
And a' them that birse the thread;
Souters out o' Mar,
Souters twice as far,
Souters out o' Gorty,
Souters five and forty,
Souters out o' Peterhead,
Wi' deil a tooth in a' their head,
Riving at the auld bend leather.
'Rhyme on St Andrew's fair' – Chambers.

That beats prent.

That bolt came ne'er out o' your bag.
The thing is better done/told than you could do it.

That gied him sagged teeth.
That set his teeth on edge.

That'll be a sair wish to some folk.
From Scott's Guy Mannering, *chap. 26.*

That'll be a sap out o' my bicker.
That is bad news as it will reduce my income.

That'll be when puddocks grow chucky stanes.
i.e. never.

That's abune your thoom.
Said to a person who is about to do something of which he is thought to be incapable.

That's a piece a stepmither never gied.
Said when we give someone a good large piece of something, implying that stepmothers are mean.

That's as ill as the ewes in the yaird and nae dogs to hunt them.
That is quite right.

That's a tale o' twa drinks.
A warning that a story will take a little time to tell.

That's a teed ba'.
Taken from the game of golf, denoting a situation which is cut and dried or already settled.

That's but ae doctor's opinion.

That's equal aqual.
From Scott's Heart of Midlothian, *chap. 8.*

That's felling twa dogs wi' ae stane.

That's for that, as butter's for fish.
Such a thing is exactly what is wanted.

That's for the faither, and no for the son.
Spoken when something is made quickly and is not built to last.

That's Halkerston's cow, a' the ither way.
Halkerston, a lawyer and landed proprietor, gave permission to one of his tenants to graze an ox. The tenant's ox was gored to death by a heifer belonging to the lawyer. The tenant went to Halkerston, and told the story the reverse of what had occurred. 'Why, then,' said the lawyer, 'your ox must go for my heifer – the law provides that.' 'No,' said the man, 'your heifer killed my ox.' 'Oh,' said Halkerston, 'the case alters there,' and forthwith reversed his tactics.

That's hame as weel as true.
i.e. true and convincing. From Scott's Bride of Lammermoor, *chap. 7.*

'That's hard,' quo' the auld wife, when she shit a mill-stane.
A phrase uttered when we think our fortune has been dealt a hard blow.

That's ill paid maut siller.
'Metaphorically, a benefit ill requitted' – Jamieson.

That's Jock's news.
Spoken when people recount news which everyone already knows.

That's like seekin' for a needle in a windlin o' strae.

That's my gude that does me gude.

That's my tale, whaur's yours?
'Spoken by a person who has forestalled another by telling the same news or story which the other was about to do' – Hislop.

That's the best gown that gaes up and doun the house.

That's the piece the step-bairn never got.
'Spoken when we give what is large and thick, or the crown of the cake' – Kelly.

That's the way to marry me if ere you shou'd hap to do it.
'A sharp reply to those who presume to be too familiar' – Hislop. However Kelly gives this alternative meaning 'Spoken when people are going the proper way about a business'.

That's waur and mair o't.

'That's weel awa',' as the husband said when his wife swallowed her tongue.

That's your mak'um fatherless, that has let mony a man die in his bed.
Here 'mak'um' means make him, alluding to the name Malcolm. According to Kelly this phrase was used as 'a jest upon a man when he shows his sword'.

That voyage never lucks quhar ilkane hes ane vote.
A case of too many hands on the tiller! Taken from Montgomerie's 'The Cherrie and the Slae'.

That was langsyne, when geese were swine
And turkeys chewed tobacco,
And sparrows bigget in auld men's beards
And mowdies delved potatoes.
A saying given in response to a tall story.

That will be when the deil's blind, an' he's no bleer-e'ed yet.
That will never happen.

That will ne'er craw in your crap.
You will never smell that.

That winna be a mote in your marriage.

That which God will gie the deil canna reeve.
'Spoken when we have attained our end in spite of opposition' – Kelly.

The aik, the ash, the elm tree
They are hanging a' three.
It was a capital crime to mutilate these trees. Or:

The aik, the ash, the elm tree,
Hang a man for a' three,
And ae branch will set him free.
Or:

Oak, ash, or elm tree,
The laird can hang for a' three;
But fir, saugh, and bitter weed,
The laird may flyte, and make naething by't.
Or:

The oak, the ash, and the ivy tree,
Flourish best at hame in the north countrie.
From Chambers.

The auld horse maun dee in some man's hand.

The auld horse may dee waiting for the new grass.

The ass that's no used to the sunks bites his crupper.
'"Sunks", a sort of saddle made of cloth, and stuffed with straw, on which two persons can sit at once' – Jamieson.

The aucht an' forty dauch.
Was the old popular name of Strathbogie. The district was divided into forty-eight davochs or dauchs. Each davoch contained as much land as four ploughs could till in a year.

The auld eight.
A phrase applied to any body of people who have long monopolised power and place.

The auld fisher's rule – every man for his ain hand.

The auld grey toun.
Dunfermline.

The auld kirk.
Whisky.

The auld round O.
Arbroath.

The back and the belly hauds ilka ane busy.

The back o' anes the face o' twa.
A reply to a man who is chaffed about a sweetheart. Better see their back than their face.

The back o' beyont far the gray mear foaled the fiddler.

The back o' my hand to you.
Away with you.

The bag to the auld stent, and the belt to the Yule hole.
'Said when we eat as heartily as we did at Christmas' – Kelly.

The bairn is eith to busk that is unborn.
A warning that things can appear simpler/more pleasant in theory than they are in practice. This saying appears in Robert Henryson's The Preiching of the Swallow.

The bait maun be gathered when the tide's out.

The banes bear the beef hame.

The banes o' great estate are worth the picking.

The bat, the bee, the butterfly,
The cuckoo, and the swallow.
The heather fleet, and corncraik,
Sleep a' in a little holie.
'Heather fleet' is another name for the snipe.

The baulder, the bonnier.

The best fruits are slowest in ripening.
The best things in life are worth waiting for.

The best is aye best cheap.

The best is aye the cheapest.

The best o' him is buffed.
He is past his best.

The best o' wabs are rough at the roons.
Roons are edges.

The best revenge is the most speedy, and most safe.

The best that can happen to a poor man is that ae bairn dee and the rest follow.
In his collection, Kelly is democratically angry at the questionable sentiment of this proverb. He says 'A cursed distrustful proverb! God is able to maintain the poor man's child as well as young master or young miss, and often in a more healthy and plump condition.'

The best laid schemes o' mice and men gang aft agley.
i.e. often go awry. Taken from Robert Burns, Poems *(1786).*

The better day the better deed.
The humorous answer given by someone who is accused or blamed for doing something on a Sunday.

The better you do weel.
Another answer to the question 'How do you do?'

The bigger the rant, the better the fun.

The biggest horse is no aye the best traveller.

The biggest rogue cries loodest oot.

The bird that can sing, an' winna sing, should be gart sing.

The bird maun flichter that flees with a'e wing.
This proverb is often used to justify having a further treat, especially a drink.

The black ox ne'er trod on his foot.
According to George Vere Irving (Notes and queries, 3rd series, Vol. XII, p. 488) the expression 'is at this day frequently applied in Scotland to an unfeeling person, and means that he has never experienced misfortune'.

A note in Scott's The Antiquary *tells us 'The black ox is said to tramp on one who has lost a near relation by death, or met with some severe calamity.'*

The blind horse is aye the hardiest.
It has to be.

The blind man's peck should be weel measured.

The blind mear's first in the mire.

The book o' maybes is very braid.
A reply given to those who say 'Maybe this will happen', etc.

The breath o' a fause friend's waur than the fuff o' a weasel.
Fuffing is the frightening sound made by a weasel before it attacks, but even this is not considered as awful as the breath of a deceitful friend.

The burn of Breid sall rin fu' reid.
From Thomas the Rhymer – a reference to the bloodshed at Bannockburn? Bannocks were the chief bread of the Scottish people in Thomas the Rhymer's time.

The cadger's dizzen.
i.e. thirteen.

The carles and the cart avers mak' it a', and the carles and cart avers eat it a'.
The ploughman and their horses consume what they produce in the first place.

The cart doesna lose its errand when it comesna hame toom-tail.
To come back toom-tail is to go away full and come back empty. The proverb is applied to those who accomplish more than their errand.

The cat kens whose lips she licks.

The cat's oot o' the pock.
Everything is out in the open now.

The cat would fain fish eat,
But she has no will to wet her feet.
Spoken to those who want something but are not prepared to work for it.

The cause is gude, and the word's 'fa' tae'.
'A profane grace of hungry persons who sit down to a good meal' – Kelly.

The chained dog maun snatch at the nearest bone.

The clartier the cosier.
The dirtier the more comfortable.

The clink o' an ill bell gangs far.
Bad news travels fast and far.

The coo has calved.
An old saying from the days of smuggling. It means the ship has successfully landed her cargo. It is generally applied to any good fortune.

The corbie says unto the craw
'Johnny fling your plaid awa"
The craw says unto the corbie,
'Johnny, draw your plaid aboot ye.'
If the raven calls first in the morning it will be fine, if the crow calls first it will be wet.

The cost owergangs the profit.
It's not worth the trouble.

The cow may dee ere the grass grow.

The cow may want her tail yet.
Said as a warning to people that they might need your kindness later, even though they deny you theirs just now.

The cow that's first up gets the first o' the dew.
Another version of 'It's the early bird that catches the worm'. This saying is used as an incentive to be up and working early.

The craws are eating the beare the year,
We'll no get ony to shear the year.
'Spoken when a number of crows are seen in a field of barley' – Chambers.

The cure may be waur than the disease.

The daft days.
A phrase to denote the festive season of winter, especially Yuletide.

The day has een, the night has lugs.
A warning to be cautious at all times.

The day that you dae weel will be seven moons in the lift, an' ane in the midden.
It would appear highly unlikely that the person so addressed will ever do anything well.

The dead claes need nae pouches.

The death o' ae bairn winna skail a house.

The death o' his first wife made sic a hole in his heart that a' the lave slippit easily through.
'It is supposed that he who has lost the wife of his youth and love will easily bear the loss of a second or third, who are commonly married rather for convenience than love' – Kelly.

The death o' wives, an' the standing o' sheep, is the best thing e'er cam a poor man's gate.

The deil and the dean begin wi' ae letter, when the deil gets the dean the kirk will be better.

The deil aye drives his hogs to an ill market.

The deil bides his time.

The deil gaes ower Jock Wabster.
Appears in Ramsay's Gentle Shepherd *as 'The deil gaes ower Jock Wabster, hame grows hell, and Pate misca's ye mair nor tongue can tell'.*

The deil gaes awa when he finds the door steekit against him.
A warning to resist temptation.

The deil gae wi' him, and peace abide wi' us.

The deil made souters sailors that can neither steer nor row.
This saying is applied to those who undertake work/a task of which they are incapable.

The deil ne'er sen a wind out o' hell but he wad sail wi't.

The deil needs baith a syde cloak and a wary step to hide his cloven feet.
Wrongdoers must be careful to conceal their true character. From Galt's The Entail, *chap. 51.*

The deil rook him.

The deil rules the roast.

The deil's a busy bishop in his ain diocie.
You can be sure that bad people will be active in promoting their own bad ends.

The deil's aye gude to beginners.

The deil's aye gude to his ain.
Originally meant in all seriousness, this saying is now usually used in jest. Originally it was believed that the devil had the power to provide for his followers.

The deil's bairns hae deil's luck.
Spoken enviously when bad people prosper.

The deil's boots don't creak.
Temptations are insidious and creep up on you unawares.

The deil's cow calves twice in ae year.

The deil's dead, and buried in Kirkcaldy.

The deil doesna aye show his cloven cloots.
Evil things and people can come in disguise.

The deil's greedy, but ye're mislear'd.
You are exceedingly greedy.

The deil's greedy, sae are ye.
As above.

The deil's gude when he's pleased.

The deil's journeyman ne'er wants work.

The deil's maist to be feared when he preaches.

The deil's nae sae ill as he's ca'ed.
Most people may be found to have some redeeming feature.

The deil's ower grit wi' you.
'Ower grit' – too familiar.

The deil's pet lambs lo'e Claverse's lads.
A saying dating back to the Covenanters, claiming that the followers of Graham of Claverhouse were on intimate terms with the devil.

The deil was sick, the deil a monk wad be; the deil grew hale, syne deil a monk was he.
A warning that promises that they will change their ways made by those on their sick beds are seldom kept on recovery.

The deil will tak little or he want a'.

The dorty dame may fa' in the dirt.
According to Jamieson 'dorty' is applied to a female who is saucy with her suitors. The phrase implies that she may have to marry a less eligible person than the one refused.

The drucken man gets aye the drucken penny.

The e'ening brings a' hame.
The twilight years and approach of death softens many people's political and religious differences.

The Englishman greets, the Irishman sleeps, but the Scotsman gangs till he gets it.
A saying purporting to give an account of the behaviour of these three nations when they want meat.

The eye may change but the heart never.

The Fair day of Auld Deer
Is the warst day in a' the year.
Aberdeenshire saying. The third Thursday of February.

The fairest apple hangs on the highest bough.

The fairest face, the falsest heart.

The farther ben the welcomer.

The farthest way aboot is aft the nearest way hame.

The fat sow gets a' the draff.

The fat sow's tail's aye creeshed.
Those who already have plenty are always getting additions to their stores.

The feathers carried awa the flesh.
'Spoken to fowlers when they come home empty' – Kelly.

The feet are slow when the head wears snaw.

The fiend laughs when ae thief robs anither.

The first dish is aye best eaten.

The first fuff o' a fat haggis is aye the bauldest.
The first threat of a boaster/coward is always the worst.

The first gryce and the last whalp o' a litter are aye the best.

The first of the nine orders of knaves is he that tells his errand
before he goes it.
*Kelly says 'Whether any jocose author has digested knaves into nine orders I know
not. But this is spoken to a boy who being bid to go an errand, will pretend to tell
how he'll speed before he goes.'*

The first snail going with you, the first lamb meeting you, bodes a
gude year.
An old superstition.

The first thing a bare gentleman calls for in the morning is a
needle and thread.
To sew his rags together.

The fish that sooms in a dub will aye taste o' mud.
You can never change your upbringing.

The fison of your hips is loupen to your lips, you dow not hotch for
hunger.
*According to Kelly this was 'an immodest expression of young girls to young
fellows'.*

The flesh is aye fairest that's farthest frae the bone.

The foot at the cradle and the hand at the reel is a sign that a
woman means tae dae weel.

The foremost hound grips the hare.

The friars of Faill
Gat never owre hard eggs or owre thin kail,
For they made their eggs thin wi' butter,
And their kail thick wi' bread.
And the friars of Faill, they made gude kail
On Fridays when they fasted;
They never wanted gear enough
As lang as their neighbour's lasted.
*Faill was a small monastery near Mauchline in Ayrshire. This rhyme was
frequently applied when a complaint of either hard eggs or thin broth was made
– from Chambers.*

The fu' and the empty gang a' ae gate.

The fu'er my house, the toomer my purse.

The geese is a' on the green, and the gan'er on the gerse.
An answer to one who says 'gie's', i.e. give me.

The goat gies a gude milking, but she ca's ower the cog wi' her feet.
Spoken of useful, but troublesome people.

The goose pan's aboon the roast.

The grace o' a grey bannock is in the baking o't.

The grace o' God is gear enough.

The grandsire buys, the faither bigs, the son sells, and the grandson thigs.
Literally this saying says that the grandfather buys the estate, the father builds upon it, the son sells the property, and forces the grandson in turn to beg. The saying is alluding to the uncertainty of worldly goods, and the fate which can befall family fortunes.

The gravest fish is an oyster;
The gravest bird's an ool;
The gravest beast's an ass;
And the gravest man's a fool.

The gray mear is the better horse.
The wife is master.

The great beast devours the little beast, and the least fends as he can.

The greater the truth the greater the libel.
This proverbial phrase is a misquotation from an epigram by Burns. While staying in Stirling the poet wrote some unfavourable verses about the reigning family as compared with the Stuarts. Upon being admonished, he said 'Oh but I mean to reprove myself for it', and wrote the following lines

Rash mortal, and slanderous poet, thy name
Shall no longer appear in the records of fame,
Dost not know that old Mansfield who writes like the Bible,
Says 'the more 'tis a truth, sir, the more 'tis a libel.'

The greatest burdens are no the maist gainfu'.
Those who work the hardest are not necessarily the best paid.

The greatest clerk's no aye the wisest man.

The greatest tochers mak not the greatest testaments.

The greedy man and the cook are sure friends.

The greedy man and the gileymour [cheat] are soon agreed.

The gude dog doesna aye get the best bane.

The gudeman's mither is aye in the gudewife's gait.

The gude or ill hap o' a gude or ill life is the gude or ill choice o'
a gude or ill wife.
The man who has a good wife can bear any ill fortune, whereas the man who
chooses his wife unwisely can expect no happiness in life.

The gule, the Gordon, and the hoodie craw,
Are the three warst things that Moray ever saw.
A saying which arose at the time of religious persecutions, as the Gordons were
adherents of the old faith, and the men of Moray no less zealous for the new one.
The gule/gool is a sort of weed which infests corn.

The happy climate where gin is a groat a bottle, and where there
is daylight for ever.
A phrase used in olden times by seamen to refer to Shetland.

The happy man canna be harried.
'Spoken when a feared misfortune happened for the best' – Kelly.

The haughty hawk winna stoop to carrion.

The heart o' auld Aberdeen.
The jail.

The height atween Tintock Tap and Coulterfell
Is just three-quarters of an ell.
A Lanarkshire saying which indicates that those two hills are nearly of a height.

The height o' nonsense is supping soor dook wi' a fork.

The height o' nonsense is supping soor milk wi' a brogue.
Another version of 'keeping back the sea with a pitchfork'.

The hen's egg gaes to the ha' to bring the goose's egg awa.
'Spoken when poor people give small gifts to be doubly repaid' – Kelly.

The hen's no far aff when the chicken whistles.

The herring loves the merry moonlight,
The mackerel loves the wind,
But the oyster loves the dredging sang
For they come o' a gentle kind.
From Scott's The Antiquary.

The higher climb the greater fa'.

The higher the hill the laigher the grass.

The higher the tree the sweeter the plooms; the richer the souter,
the blacker his thooms.

The horse that bring's grist to the mill is as useful as the water that
ca's the wheel.

The hurt man writes wi' steel on a marble stane.

Their ain will tae a' men, a' ther will tae women.

Their father's fathers were never fellows.

Their heid's no sair that did that.
They are dead.

The king lies doun, yet the warld rins round.
The world does not stop just because the King lies down, i.e. no one is indispensable.

The king may come in the cadger's gait.
Beware – those you offend may in the future return in a superior position.

The king may come to Kelly yet, and when he comes he'll ride.
'It signifies that the time may come that I may get my revenge upon such people, and then I will do it to purpose' – Kelly.

The kirk's aye greedy.

The kirk is muckle, but ye may say mass in ae end o't.

The laird kens only the ill in the parish, and the minister only the gude.

The laird may be laird and still need the hind's help.

The laird's brither's an ill tenant.

The laird's ha' levels a'.
People of different rank could meet on equal terms in the house of a joint superior.

The lamb where it's tipped, and the ewe where she's clipped.
An old proverbial rule concerning tithes, i.e. 'The lamb pays tithes in the place where the ewe took the ram, and the old sheep where they are shorn' – Kelly.

The langer we live we see the mair ferlies.
'Ferlies' are wonders.

The langer ye tread on a turd, it will be the braider.
'Spoken when people make a great stir, about scandalous words which they are supposed to have deserv'd' – Kelly.

The langest day has an end.

The lass that has ower mony wooers aft wales the warst.
A warning against having too many suitors.

The lass that lightlies may lament.
To 'lightlie' is to despise or treat with contempt. Hence the girl that scorns her lovers may live to regret her actions.

The lasses o' Exmagirdle may very weel be dun,
For frae Michaelmas till Whitsunday they never see the sun.
'Ecclesmagirdle is a small village under the northern slopes of the Ochil Hills, which is in shadow for a great part of the year' – Chambers.

The lasses o' Lauder are mim and meek,
The lasses o' the Fanns smell o' peat reek,
The lasses o' Gordon canna sew a steek,
But weel can they sup their crowdie.
The lasses o' Earlston are bonny and braw,
The lasses o' Greenlaw are black as a craw,
The lasses o' Polwart are the best o' them a',
And gie plenty o' work to the howdie.
'The rhyme characterises the young women of certain villages in Berwickshire'
– G. Henderson.

The last best, like the gude wives' daughters.
'A mother says her unmarried daughter is the best of the family' – Kelly.

The last word has him, speak it wha will.

The lazy lad maks a stark auld man.

The lean dog is a' flees.

The leefu' man is the beggar's brither.
'Leefu' means lending.

The less debt the mair dainties.

The less I lee.
A phrase which implies that the whole truth and nothing but the truth has been spoken regarding a matter.

The less play the better.

The less wit a man has the less he kens the want o't.

The liberal man is the beggar's brither.

The light will mak itsel' seen.
Truth will out.

The Lindsays in green, should ne'er be seen.
The Lindsays fought with the royal forces at Brechin in 1452. They were mainly dressed in green, and as many of them fell in battle that day the colour was thereafter considered as unlucky to the clan.

The lion and the unicorn, fighting for the crown,
Up starts the little dog, and knocked them baith down;
Some gat white bread, and some gat brown,
But the lion beat the unicorn, round about the town.
'A rhyme about the royal coat of arms' – Chambers.

The little gentleman in black velvet.
A Jacobite toast to the mole that made the mound upon which the horse of William of Orange stumbled and fell, thereby causing the king's death.

'The Lord gie us a gude conceit o' oursels,' quo the wife, and gaed whistlin' ben the kirk.

The loudest bummer's no the best bee.

The lower we lie, the mair we are under the wind.

The lucky pennyworth sells soonest.

The mair mischief, the better sport.
See the Introduction for the origin of this phrase.

The mair cost the mair honour.
Spoken to people when they propose an expensive thing, when a cheaper thing would suffice.

The mair dirt the less hurt.

The mair noble, the mair humble.

The mair the merrier; the fewer better cheer.

The mair ye greet, ye'll pish the less.

The mair ye steer the mair ye'll sink.

The maister's ee is better than his hands.

The maister's ee maks the horse fat.
Hislop quotes the story – 'A fat man riding upon a lean horse was asked how it came to pass that he was so fat while the horse was so lean?' 'Because,' said he, 'I feed myself, but my servant feeds the horse.'

The maister's foot's the best fulyie.
'Fulyie' means manure, i.e. the constant supervision of the work ensures that everything is done properly.

The maister's foot's the best measure.

The man may eithly tine a stot that canna count his kine.
The person who does not know what he is doing cannot be expected to look after his own business.

The maut's abune the meal.
The man is drunk.

'The meal cheap and shoon dear,' quo' the souter's wife, 'I'd like to hear.'

The men o' the East
Are pykin their geese,
And sendin' their feathers here-awa there-awa.
An old rhyme said by children when it started to snow.

The men o' the Mearns manna do mair than they may.
Even the men of Kincardineshire can only do their utmost – a proverb intended to be complimentary to the men of that county.

The merle and the blackbird, the laverock and the lark,
The goudy and the gowdspink, how many birds be that?
The laverock and the lark, the bawkie and the bat,
The heather fleet, the mire snipe, how many birds be that?
Answer – three in the first part, and two in the second.

The Michaelmas moon rises ay alike soon.

The miller got never better moulter than he took with his ain hands.
'Moulter', the miller's perquisite for grinding the grain.

The misterfu' maun nae be mensefu'.
The needy must not be modest; they cannot afford to be.

The mither is a matchless beast.

The mither ne'er had a sang but her dochter had a verse o't.
Like mother like daughter.

The mither of mischief is no bigger than a midge's wing.

The mither's breath is aye sweet.

The moudiewart feedsna on midges.

The mouth that lies slays the soul.

Them that canna get a peck maun put up wi' a stimpart.
A 'stimpart' is the fourth part of a peck, i.e. those who cannot obtain luxuries must put up with necessities.

Them that canna ride maun shank it.
Those who cannot ride will have to walk instead. Meaning we must act according to our abilities

Them that herd swine, aye hear them gruntin'.

Them that likesna water brose will scunner at cauld steer.
'Cauld steerie' is sourmilk and meal stirred together in a cold state. The phrase is used as a taunt to those who complain of common food.

Them that's brocht up like beggars are aye warst to please.

Them that sells the gudes guide the purse, them that guide the purse rule the house.

Them that's ill fleyed are seldom sair hurt.

Them that's slack in gude are eydent in ill.

Them that winna wark maun want.

The muckle mischief confound ye.

The muck midden is the mither o' the meal kist.

The muirhen has sworn by her tough skin,
She sal never eat of the carle's win.

The mune ripens corn.

Them wha gae jumpin' awa aft come limpin' back.

Them wha maun be weel cled canna aye be weel fed.

Them wha stand on a knowe's sure to be noticed.
Those who elevate themselves to a public position are sure to be noticed by everyone.

The name o' an honest man's muckle worth
– Cheviot.
The name o' an honest woman's is mickle worth
– Hislop.
The name of an honest woman is mickle worth
– Kelly.
Kelly gives the following meaning for his version: 'A reason given for a woman, who has borne a bastard, for marrying an inferior person.'

The nearer e'en the mair beggars.
A humorous welcome given to people who drop in to visit a friend.

The next time ye dance in the dark ken wha ye tak by the hand.
Make sure you know what/who you are getting involved in/with before undertaking anything.

The nights fair draw in, after the Brig O' Allan Games.
A local saying commenting on the approach of dark winter nights.

The oldest cheeses have most mites.

The peasweep aye cries farthest frae his ain nest.

The peesweep aye cries frae its ain nest.

The people o' the Carse o' Gowrie want water in the summer, fire in the winter, and the grace o' God a' the year round.

The Perth burghers made but a bad bargain in giving six feet o' ground for twa inches.
An ancient joke referring to the tradition that the Earl of Kinnoul gave the North and South Inches to the town in exchange for a burial plot in the Church of St Johns.

The phrase changes though the custom abides.

The piper does not play till he knows who pays him.

The piper wants muckle that wants the nether chaft.
An expression used when some necessary part is found to be wanting.

The poor man is aye put to the warst.

The poor man pays for a'.
He pays for the rich through his labours and he pays for himself with his wages.

The poor man's shilling is but a penny.

The post o' honour is the post o' danger.

The priest christens his ain bairn first.
An apology for serving ouselves before our guests.

The proof o' a pudding's the preein' o't.
The proof of the pudding is in the tasting, i.e. you cannot pass judgement until you have experienced something at first hand.

The proudest nettle grows on a midden.
The proudest of people have often come from very humble origins.

The rain comes scouth when the wind's in the south.
'Scouth' means freely or heavily in this sense.

There are mair knaves in my kin than honest men in yours.

There are mair maidens than maukins.
Used to console a man when he has lost his girlfriend.

There are mair married than gude house hauders.
There are more people who qualify as householders than are competent for the duties of the position.

There are mair married than gude life days.
A phrase used to dissuade people from constant toil.

There are mair wark-days than life-days.

There are mair ways tae the wud than ane.

There are nane sae weel shod but may slip.
No person, no matter their wealth, is immune from mishap.

There are twa eneuchs, an' he has gotten ane o' them.
i.e. big enough and little enough. The phrase is given in answer to people who say they have enough, out of modesty.

There are tricks in ither trades by selling muslins.

There belangs mair to a bed than four bare legs.
More advice for the couple intending to marry, warning them that there are many hidden costs.

There belangs mair to a ploughman than whistling.

There cam' ne'er sic a gliff to a daw's heart.
A phrase spoken when people are suddenly covered in cold water.

The red cock has craw'd.
There has been a case of arson.

The redder's lick is aye the warst o' the battle.
'The redder's lick' is a blow received by someone who is trying to stop a fight.

There lies one who neither feared nor flattered flesh.
The brief but striking and true eulogium pronounced by the Regent Morton over the grave of John Knox. This is the version of the epitaph given in James Melville's Diary, and is most likely the correct form of the expression used by Lord Morton, though frequently another version is given: 'There lies one who never feared the face of man.'

There maun be nae patience when God says haste.

There ne'er came ill frae a gude advice.

There ne'er was as a bad, but there micht be a waur.

There ne'er was a fair word in flyting.

There ne'er was a fire without some reek.

There ne'er was a five pound note but there was a ten pound road for't.
No matter how much money we have it never seems to be enough, as we instantly raise our sights even higher.

There ne'er was a goose without a gander.

There ne'er was a poor man in his kin.

There ne'er was a rebellion in Scotland without either a Campbell or a Dalrymple being at the bottom of it.
'This is a saying of Charles II, and indicates the constant attachment of these two families to the cause of civil and religious liberty.' – From Chambers' collection.

There ne'er was a slut but had a faut, or a daw but had twa.

There's a clue in your arse.
Spoken to restless people.

There's a day coming that'll show wha's blackest.
Beware judgement day.

There's a difference between 'Will you sell?' and 'Will you buy?'

There's a dog in the well.
There is something amiss.

There's a dub at every door, and before some doors there's twa.
Every household has a skeleton in its cupboard, and some more than one.

There's a flee in my hose.
I have something on my mind giving me trouble.

There's ae day o' reckoning and anither day o' payment.

There's a great difference between fen o'er and fair weel.
'Between those who have only enough to keep them alive, and those who have abundance' – Kelly.

There's a gude and bad side to everything, a' the airt is to find it out.

There's a gude shape in the shear's mouth.
Yes, but it requires skill to make it happen.

There's a heap o' killin' in a 'caird'.

There's a het hurry when there's a hen to roast.

There's a measure in a' things, even in kail supping.
There is a reason for everything.

'There's a mote in't,' quo' the man when he swallowed the dish-clout.

There's an act in the Laird o' Grant's court, that no abune eleven speak at ance.
'A jocular remark when too many people speak at once; that it is founded on fact is questionable' – Hislop.

There's a braw time coming.

There's a crook in ilka lot.

There's a day coming that'll shew whose arse is blackest.
The Day of Judgement.

There's a hole in my coat.

There's a hole in the house.
'Said when some unsafe person, before whom it is unwise to speak, is present' – Kelly.

There's Ane abune a'.
A reminder given by those with religious belief to others.

'There's an unco splutter,' quo' the sow i' the gutter.

There's a piece wad please a Brownie.
Spoken to children when you give them something nice to eat.

There's a reason for ye, an' a rag about the foot o't.
Spoken when the reason given for doing something would appear to be a lame one.

There's as gude fish in the sea as ever came out o't.

There's a sliddery stane before the ha' door.
Used in times past to signify the uncertainty of favour from those of a superior social standing.

There's as mony Johnstons as Jardines.
There is an equal chance, or it's six of one and half a dozen of the other. A Dumfriesshire saying.

There's as muckle atween the craig and the wuddy, as there is atween the cup and the lip.

There's a storm in somebody's nose, licht whaur it like.
Said when we see someone getting angry and about to explode with rage.

There's a time to gley and a time to look even.
Sometimes one has to turn a blind eye.

There's a tough sinew in an auld wife's heel.

There's a whaup i' the raip.
There is a curlew in the rope, i.e. there is something amiss.

There's a word in my wame, but it's ower far down.
An expression used by someone who cannot find the appropriate word.

There's aye a glum look where there's cauld crowdy.

There's aye a wimple in a lawyer's clue.

There's aye ill will among cadgers.

There's aye life in a living man.

There's aye some clock i' the broth.
'Clock' means beetle, i.e. nothing is ever perfect.

There's aye some water whaur the stirkie drowns.
There is no trouble without some cause.

There's aye sorrow at somebody's door.

'There's baith meat and music here,' quo the dog when he ate the piper's bag.

There's beild beneath an auld man's beard.

There's but ae gude wife in the warld, and ilka ane thinks he has her.
'The rule admits large exceptions, for some are fully apprized of the contrary'
– Kelly.

There's evil for the house of Bower
When the bride goes round the castle tower.
'This rhyme refers to the house of Bell's tower, Perthshire. It was said when, "the wraith bride o' the peel" appeared, calamity was certainly impending over the family. According to tradition the apparation appeared to a lady of the family, named Isobel, on the night before her marriage; in consequence of which she hanged herself by one of the ropes of the bells in the tower, hence the name of the house. The Bowers were a very ancient family whose principal seat was at Kincaldrum, in Angus.' – Cheviot.

There's fey blood in your head.
You are risking your life.

There's first gude ale, and syne gude ale,
And second ale, and some,
Hink-sink, and ploughman's drink,
And scour-the-gate, and trim.
Different kinds of malt liquor.

There's kail in put's wame.
'Put' is a dog's name. Spoken when we see a youth who is hearty and merry, as if he has a full stomach.

There's life for honest folk in this bad warld yet.
A Jacobite saying used when they thought the prospects of 'honest men', as they called themselves, were improving.

There's life in a mussel as lang as it can cheep.
'We may succeed yet' – Kelly.

There's little for the rake after the shool.
There is not much to be had of a thing once greedy people have been at it. Sometimes the proverb is given as 'There's no muckle to rake after the besom'.

There's little wit in the pow that lichts the candle at the low.
'He has little wit who does a thing in a dangerous or extravagent manner' – Hislop.

There's little sap in a dry pea-shaup.

'There's little to reck,' quo' the knave to his neck.

There's little to sew where the tailor is true.

There's mair gates than one to a stack-yard.

There's mair in his heid than his harns.
He is intoxicated.

There's mair knavery amang kirkmen than honesty amang courtiers.
'If facetious bull upon mentioning of some knavery' – Kelly.

There's mair knavery on sea and land than all the warld beside.
A facetious remark made upon mentioning some knavish action.

There's mair room without than within.
A remark made by a person who thinks that their company is not wanted. Kelly gives a slightly more basic explanation: 'an apology for breaking wind backward.'

There's mair ways o' killing a dog than hanging him.
The same ends can be brought about in many different ways.

There's mair ways than ane o' keeping craws frae the stack.
There is more than one way to tackle a problem.

There's mair whistling wi' you than gude red land.
'Red land' is ground turned over by the plough. Hence the proverb is hinting that there is more play than work.

There's mickle 'tween market days.
Much can happen in a week.

There's mirth among the kin when the howdie [midwife] cries 'A son'.

There's mony a tod hunted that's no killed.
Scott's Heart of Midlothian, *Chap. 20.*

There's mony a true tale tauld in jest.

There's mony chances, baith o' gude and ill, befa' folks in this warld.

There's muckle ado when dominies ride.
When people do something out of their ordinary sphere, there must be some necessity for it.

There's muckle ado when muirland folk ride,
Boots, and spurs, and a' to provide.
A Peebleshire saying meaning that most people will not go out of their ordinary way except under pressure.

There's muckle between the word and the deed.

There's muckle hid meat in a goose's ee.

There's muckle love in bands and bags.

There's my thoom I'll ne'er beguile thee.
It was an old Scottish custom for lovers who plighted their troth to lick the thumbs of each other's right hands. These they then pressed together and vowed their mutual fidelity.

There's nae best ale in Bervie.
Suggesting that it is all bad.

There's nae birds this year in last year's nest.

There's nae breard like midden breard.
*'The grains of corn in a dunghill grow again. Spoken when we see people of mean
birth rise suddenly to wealth and honour' – Kelly.*

There's nae companion like the penny.
A suggestion that money will look after you like nothing else can.

There's nae corn wi'out cauf.

There's nae deils like the sea deils.

There's nae fence against a flail.

There's nae fool like an auld fool.

There's nae general rule wi'out exceptions.

There's nae great loss without some gain.

There's nae gude o' speakin' ill o' the laird within his ain bounds.

There's nae hair sae sma' but has its shadow.
Everything has an effect upon the world no matter how small.

There's nae harm done when there's a good lad gotten.
'An apology for a woman that has borne a bastard' – Kelly.

There's nae hawk flees sae high but he will stoop to some lure.
Every man has his price.

There's nae help for them that will gang wrang.

There's nae iron sae hard but rust will fret it;
there's nae claith sae fine but moths will eat it.
Nothing lasts forever, no matter the quality.

There's nae lack in love.

There's nae law again a man looking after his ain.
Scott's Rob Roy, *Chap. 29.*

There's nae reek but there's some heat.

There's nae remede for fear but cut aff the head.

There's nae sel' sae dear as our ain sel'.

There's nae sic a word in Wallace.
Wallace *is a book of the actions of Sir William Wallace. Said in fun when we
deny something.*

'There's nae sin in a merry mind,' quo' the auld wife as she gaed
whistlin' ben the kirk on Sunday.

There's nae sun sae bright but clouds will owercast it.

There's naething between a poor man and a rich but a piece o' an ill year.
Much can happen in the space of a year to render a rich man poor.

There's naething but 'mends for misdeeds.

There's naething dune on earth but what is seen.

There's naething got by delay but dirt and lang nails.
A warning against procrastination.

There's naething ill said that's no ill ta'en.

There's naething in him but what he puts in wi' the spoon.

There's naething mair precious than time.

There's naething sae gude on this side o' time but it micht hae been better.

There's naething sae like an honest man as an arrant knave.

There's nae woo sae coorse but it'll tak some colour.

There's nane sae blind as them that winna see.
You cannot force people to acknowledge situations they do not want to admit.

There's nane sae busy as him that has least to do.

There's nane sae deaf as them that winna hear.

There's nane sae weel shod but may slip.

There's nane without a fault.

There's ne'er a fire wi'out some reek.

There's ne'er a great feast but some fare ill.

There's neither ruth nor favour to be found wi' him.
Spoken of a miserly mean-spirited person.

There's nocht for it but the twa thoombs.
It's back to basic methods. Taken from the basic method used to kill a louse.

There's nocht sae queer as folk.

There's ower mony nicks in your horn.
You are too cunning for me.

There's ower muckle saut water there.
Said when we suspect that someone's grief is unreal, i.e. crocodile tears.
Scott's Guy Mannering, *Chap. 38.*

There's ower muckle singin' in your head tonight, we'll hae a shower afore bedtime.

There's plenty o' raible when drink's on the table.
To 'raible' is to speak in a careless/loose way.

There's remede for a'thing but stark deid.
This is reputedly the phrase spoken by James Stewart to the Earl of Morton when he accused him of treason, a charge which finally led to his execution in 1581.

There's skill in gruel making.

'There's sma' sorrow at our pairting,' as the auld mear said to the broken cart.
'Spoken when a husband or wife dies who do not love one another, as if the surviving party was not sorry for the loss. They will say on such occasions, "It is not a death but a lousance"' [freedom from bondage] – Kelly.

There's steel in the needle point, though little o't.
Said when something which has been commended for its excellent qualities is found to be lacking in quantity.

There's the chapman's drouth, and his hunger baith.
A phrase applied to one who eats heartily whilst also drinking plenty. The saying arose from the habits of travelling packmen who always took full advantage if they were offered a hearty meal gratis.

There's the end o' an auld sang.
When the Scottish Parliament passed the resolution agreeing to the Union, Lord Belhaven remarked, 'there's the end o' an auld sang'.

There's three o' a' things.

There's tricks in a' trades but honest horse couping.

There's twa enoughs, and ye hae gotten ane o' them.
The two enoughs are big enough and little enough. This saying is used as an answer to those who say that they have enough – meaning that the speaker has little enough.

There's twa things in my mind, and that's the least o' them.
Said when the speaker declines to give a reason for something which he does not wish to do.

There twa fools met.
A phrase used when someone says he has refused a good bargain, i.e. he was a fool to make such an offer, the other a fool to refuse it.

There wad be little parritch in your caup if he had the pourin' o't.

There was anither gotten the night that you was born.

There was a wife that kept her supper for her breakfast, an' she dy'd e'er day.
Spoken when someone suggests we keep something for later.

There was mair lost at Sherramuir, whaur the Hielandman lost his faither, and his mither, and a gude buff belt worth baith o' them.
A remark made in jest when somebody has sustained a trifling loss.

There was ne'er a fair word in flytin'.

There was ne'er a gude toun but there was a dub at the end o't.
Nothing is perfect.

There was ne'er a height but had a howe at the bottom o't.

There was ne'er a silly Jocky but there was as silly a Jenny.
'God makes' em and pairs' em' as the monkey said to his feet. A comment upon couples.

There was ne'er a thrifty wife wi' a clout about her head.

There was ne'er enough when naething was left.
There was an old wife and she had naught,
The thieves came and they stole naught,
The wife went out, and cried naught,
What should she cry? She wanted naught.
'Spoken when people complain of injuries unjustly, when they have lost little, or nothing' – Kelly.

There was little meat and muckle mirth
At little Bauldy's wedding.
A Berwickshire phrase collected by Dr Henderson – 'Spoken at a merry-making where the creature comforts are deficient.'

There was ne'er a cake but had a make.
'Make' means match.

There was ne'er a slut but had a slit, there was ne'er a daw but had twa.
An old phrase which at one time was applied to any woman who was seen with a tear in her clothing.

There will be a hole in the groat today, and the supper to seek.
An old saying used by labourers when they fear a rainy afternoon.

There will be news o' that yet.

The road to the Kirk o'Riven
Where gang mair dead than living
A phrase which refers to the Banffshire village of Rathven.

The robin and the lintie, the laverock and the wren
Them that harries their nests will never thrive again.

The robin redbreast and the wren
Coost out about the parritch pan
And ere the robin got a spune
The wren she had the parritch dune.
A saying used to describe a row between husband and wife.

The sailor's life is a heartsome life.

The scabbit head lo'esna the kame.

The scholar may waur the maister.

The Scots wear short patience and long daggers.

The Scottish race shall flourish free,
Unless false the prophecie;
Where the sacred stone is found,
There shall sovereignty have ground.
Translated from the Gaelic. Hector Boece gave the following version – 'The Scots shall brook that realm as native ground, if weirds fail not, where'er this stone is found.' Translated by Nicolson, the saying refers to the Coronation Stone of Scone, carried to England by Edward I, and deposited in Westminster Abbey, in the coronation chair, where every British sovereign has been crowned ever since. The stone was brought North again as a political gesture in the late 1990s.

The Scot will not fight till he sees his ain bluid.

The scout, the scart, the cattiwake,
The Solan goose sits on the laik, yearly in the spring.
Ray – Refers to birds which frequented the Bass in Ray's time.

The Second City of the Empire.
A name sometimes given to the City of Glasgow.

The secret hid from true love is aften tauld to the king.
What we are scared to tell our loved ones is often exposed when, as prisoners, our life is brought to light.

The shortest follies are the best.

The shortest road's the nearest.

The shortest road's where the company's gude.

The shots o'er gang the auld swine.

The siller penny slays mair souls than the nakit sword slays bodies.

The silliest strake has the loudest hech.
The silliest stroke is accompanied by the loudest cry. Those who pretend to do most perform least.

The simple man's the beggar's brither.

The skirl at the tail o' a guffa.
The name given to the hysterics or crying following on from laughter.

The Sloke, Milnwharcher, and Craigneen,
The Breska and the Sligna;
They are the five best Crocklet hills,
The auld wives ever saw.
An Ayrshire saying regarding five hills near Loch Doon.

The slothfu' man is the beggar's brither.
The lazy man is the beggar's brother. A warning that sloth brings about financial ruin.

The slothfu' man maks a slim fortune.
As above.

The smith has aye a spark in his hause.

The smith is fiery when the iron is hot.
Scott's Fair Maid of Perth *Chap. 33.*

The smith's mear and the souter's wife are aye warst shod.

The snail is as sune at its rest as the swallow.

The sons of the rock.
A saying referring to natives of Stirling.

The sooth bourd is nae bourd.
The true joke is no joke.

The souter gae the sow a kiss, 'grumph,' quo' she, 'it's for a birse.'
A birse was a bristle used to stiffen thread when sewing leather. This phrase is applied when an ulterior motive is suspected for some act.

The stane that lies nae in your gate braks nae your taes.
Spoken as a warning not to interfere in other people's business.

The Starlings of Kirkwall.
An Orkney nickname applied to the residents of that town.

The still sow eats up a' the draff.
Sometimes the quiet ones can get away with murder unsuspected.

The stoutest head bears langest oot.

The stoup that gaes aft to the well comes hame broken at last.
Over-use of a thing takes its toll.

The strong and the hearty get a' thing in this world.

The strongest horse loups the dike.
An old saying used at gaming tables 'meaning that he that throws best will win the game' – Kelly.

The Stuarts the race of Kings, and of tinkers.
Translated from the Gaelic. Stuart was a favourite name with the tinkers.

The subject's love is the king's life guard.

The sun and the moon may go wrong, but the clock o' St Johnston never goes wrong.
A local saying from Perth.

The sun is nae waur for shining on the midden.

The sun will be on our side o' the hedge yet.
Our side will get the upper hand yet.

The surest promisers are aye the slackest payers.
– The Ettrick Shepherd.

The sweer corner.
An old phrase applied to the corner of the street in small towns where the work-shy loafers used to congregate.

The swine's gane through it.
Spoken in olden times when an intended marriage does not take place. It comes from an old superstition that 'if a swine come between a man and his mistress, they will never be married' – Kelly.

The tae hauf the warld thinks the tither hauf daft.

The teeth of the sheep shall lay the plough on the shelf.
Thomas the Rhymer – It might be argued that Thomas had foretold the Highland clearances.

The thatcher said unto his man, 'Let's raise this ladder if we can.' 'But first let's drink, maister.'
Said when we propose to do something and another proposes that we have a drink first.

The thiefer like the better sodger.

The thing that liesna in your gait breaksna your shins.

The thing that's deen the day, winna be adee the morn.
Used in Johnny Gibb of Gushetneuk, *by William Alexander.*

The thing that's dune's no to do.

The thing that's trusted is nae forgiven.

The things that wives hain cats eat.
'What is too niggardly spared is often as widely squandered' – Kelly.

The thrift o' you and the woo o' a dog wad make a braw wab.
A sarcastic way of telling someone that they are lazy.

The thrift o' you will be the death o' your gude dame.

The third time's lucky.

The time ye're pu'in runts ye're no setting kail.
Be aware that time spent doing one thing is at the expense of something else.

The tod keeps aye his ain hole clean.
In Kelly's time this phrase was 'apply'd to batchelors who keep women servant's, whom they ought not to meddle with'.

The tod ne'er fares better than when he's bann'd.
'Spoken when we are told that such people curse us, which we think is the effect of envy, the companion of felicity. The fox is cursed when he takes our poultry.' – Kelly.

The tod ne'er kills the lamb except at a distance frae his ain hole.
The cunning wrongdoer never does wrong on his own territory.

The tod ne'er sped better than when he gaed his ain errand.
Every man is most zealous when working for his own interest.

The tod's whalps are ill to tame.
Like parent, like offspring.

The todler tyke has a very gude byke,
And sae has the gairy bee;
But leese me on the little red-doup,
Wha bears awa' the gree.
A Forfarshire rhyme on bees collected by Chambers.

The tongue of a tale-bearer breaketh bones as well as a Jeddart staff.
A tribute to the power of propaganda.

The tree doesna fa' at the first strake.
It takes perseverance to bring down large objects/people.

The unsonsy fish gets aye the unlucky bait.

The vassal o' the kirk is seldom found with the basket bare.
The monks were proverbially celebrated as good landlords.

The virtuous number of thirty-eight.
'This phrase refers to the thirty-eight advocates who supported Henry Erskine for the office of Dean of Faculty, when he was opposed on account of his political action, in presiding at a meeting, held in Edinburgh, for the purpose of protesting and petitioning against the continuance of the war with France. The election took place on the 12th January, 1796 when 123 advocates supported Lord Advocate Dundas of Armiston, and thirty-eight voted for Mr Erskine. The phrase was introduced into a toast in honour of the thirty-eight given at a dinner held in Edinburgh, in 1820, for the purpose of welcoming Lord Erskine on his return to Scotland, after an absence of fifty years. Burns celebrates this election in his ballad "The Dean of Faculty".' – Cheviot.

The ware evening is long and tough,
The harvest evening runs soon o' the heugh.
In spring the days are lengthening, in autumn the reverse. This makes one seem long and the other short.

The warld is bound to nae man.

The warld's like the tod's whalp, aye the aulder the waur.
From Galt's The Entail *chap. 4.*

The warst be her ain.

The warst may be tholed when it's kenn'd.
Scott's Heart of Midlothian *chap. 20.*

The warst warld that ever was, some maun win.

The warst warld that ever was, the malt-man got his sack again.
'It is hard when people get no satisfaction for what they have sold, no, not so much as the bag that carried it' – Kelly.

The water o' Aven runs so clear,
'Twould beguile a man of a hundred years.
An Aberdeenshire rhyme about the clearness of one of its rivers.

The waters shall wax, the woods shall wane,
Moss, moor, and mountain will a' be ta'en in,
But the bannock will ne'er be the braider
– Ascribed to Thomas the Rhymer.
'This rhyme refers to the draining of swamps, the destruction of forests, and the reclamation of waste land, and predicts that when all this is done food will not be more abundant. It is a question if the necessaries of life are not, in many cases, more difficult of attainment in a highly civilised than in a ruder yet more natural age.' – Cheviot.

The water will ne'er warr the widdie.
Literally the water will never cheat the gallows. This is a Scottish version of the English proverb 'He that's born to be hanged will never be drowned'.

The waur luck now the better anither time.
A suggestion that the law of averages supplies to fortune.

The way of those you live with is that you must follow.
If you live in my house, you must follow my rules.

The way to catch a bird is no to fling your bannet at her.

The weakest gangs to the wa'.
The law of the jungle.

The weetin' o' the stoups.
The old term for a groom-to-be's stag night. According to Cheviot 'The water stoups were a portion of the marriage providing, invariably purchased by the bridegroom, and "the weetin' o' the stoups" was the popular name for the supper which he partook of in company with his old cronies.'

The weird is dreed.
The ill fortune is suffered – the destiny is fulfilled.

The wife's ae dochter an' the cottar's ae cow, the taen's ne'er weel and the tither's ne'er fu'.
A warning against spoiling children.

The wife's aye welcome that comes wi' a crookit oxter.
The person carrying a present is always welcome, hence the 'crookit oxter'.

The willing horse is aye wrought to death.
The willing worker is often abused/taken advantage of.

The wolf may lose his teeth, but never his nature.
Age will not change someone/thing's essential character.

The word o' an honest man's enough.

The words cam' rinnin' oot o' their mouth like a burn at Beltane.

The worth o' a thing is best kenned by the want o't.

The worth o' a thing is what it will bring.
Something is only worth what someone else is prepared to give for it.

The wrang side o' the bannock to a Monteith.
'So great was the horror in Scotland at the treachery of Sir John Monteith to his friend Wallace that for many centuries it was common in Scotland when presenting a bannock to a Monteith to give it with the wrong side uppermost' – Chambers.

The wrinkled skin easily conceals a scar.

The wun's in that airt.
Matters are heading in that direction.

They are all alive whom you slew.
A phrase applied to a foolish boaster to cut them down to size.

They are as wise as speir not.

They are eith hindered that are no furdersome.
Those who are not keen are easily distracted from doing something.

They are lifeless wha're fautless.

They are sad rents that come in wi' tears.
A play upon the words rent and tear. The phrase is given as an answer to those who, on seeing your ragged clothes, say your rents are coming in.

They are speaking o' you where there are ill-licked dishes.
It has long been a superstition that someone is speaking about you if you feel your ears burning. This proverb 'is an answer as if people were only saying, that if you were there you would lick them cleaner.' – Kelly.

They are very full in their ain house that'll no pick a bane in their neighbour's.
Spoken to guests who refuse refreshment, saying that they had already eaten at home.

They are wise folk that let wave and withy haud their ain.

They aye gang frae Auchterless to Auchtermair.
Spoken of mercenary people. This phrase was sometimes applied to ministers who searched for more profitable parishes.

They buy goods cheap that bring naething hame.

They can do ill that canna do gude.
Spoken when children break anything.

They can fin' fauts wha canna mend them.

They craw crouse that craw last.
He who laughs last laughs longest. Hislop says 'Because they who 'craw' last exult that a matter is definitely known to be in their own favour.'

They dinna 'gree best wha never cast oot.

They draw the cat harrow.
They thwart one another.

They fill corn sacks.
A phrase spoken to children when they say they are full.

They gae far aboot that dinna meet ae day.
The world is a small place.

They girn early that girn about their kale.

They got nothing o' the mare except the halter.

They 'gree like butter and mells.
Spoken when people do not agree.

They hae been as poor as you who came to a pouch fu' o' green peas e'er they died.
'Spoken to poor boys whom we think hopeful' – Kelly.

They hae need o' a canny cook that hae but ae egg to their dinner.

They had ne'er an ill day that had a gude even.

They hang the gither like bats in a steeple.

They'll break me oot o' house an' ha'.
They will ruin me.

They'll gree better when they gang in by different kirk doors.
Said about two people who have argued, meaning that it is best if they avoid each other.

They lo'e me for little that hate me for nought.

They maun be sune up that cheat the tod.

They maun hunger in frost that winna work in fresh.
A warning that one must work hard when one can to provide for times when it is not possible.

They may dunsh that gie the lunch.
This saying means that those upon whom we depend can do whatever they like with us. There is no accurate translation into English of the word 'dunsh', but it roughly means to jog or thrust in violent manner.

They may ken by your beard, what lay on your board.
The remains of your last meal are stuck to your face, or your face will give away what you have been up to.

They may lift the cattle that feed upon the grass of their enemy.
The Highlanders believed themselves to be justified in stealing cattle from those with whom their clan was feuding.

They mense little the mouth that bite off the nose.
'Mense' means honour. 'Spoken when those who profess friendship for us traduce our relatives and friends' – Kelly.

They need muckle that naething will content.

They ne'er baked a gude cake but may bake an ill ane.

They ne'er gie wi' the spit but they gat wi' the ladle.
Said of people who never confer a small favour without expecting a large one in return.

They ne'er saw great dainties that think haggis a feast.

They're a' ae sow's pick.
They are all of one kind.

'They're a bonny pair,' as the craw said o' his legs.

'They're a bonny pair,' as the deil said o' his cloots.

They're a' gude that gies.

They're a' gude that's far awa.
Distance can dim the memory and be illusory.

They're aye gude will'd o' their horse that hae nane *or*
They're free wi' their horse that hae nane.
People are always willing to help who are not in a position to do so.

'They're curly and crookit,' as the deil said o' his horns.

They're fremit friends that canna be fash'd.
If they cannot be bothered to help, they are a strange sort of friend.

They're gustin' their gabs.
They are eating heartily.

They're keen o' company that taks the dog on their back.

They're lightly harried that hae a' their ain.

They're like the grices, if ye kittle their wame they fa' on their backs.
Give them an inch and they will take a mile.

They're no a' saints that get the name o't.

They're no to be named in the same day.
The two things are totally different.

They're queer folk that has nae failings.

They're scarce o' horseflesh that ride on the dog.

They're tarred a' wi ae stick.
This phrase is applied to people who all share some common feature/behaviour. It originates from the custom of marking sheep with tar to distinguish ownership.

They're terrible grit thegither.

They're unco thick.
The above two sayings mean that those referred to are on very intimate terms.

They're warst when they're warst guided.

They're weel guided that God guides.

They rin fast that deils and lasses drive.
In Cheviot's collection the word 'rin' is supplanted by 'sin'.

They should hae light hands that strike ither folks' bairns.

They should kiss the gudewife that wad win the gudeman.

They speak o' my drinking, but ne'er think o' my drouth.
Said when people complain about the actions of an individual, without considering the causes of their behaviour.

They that are born on Halloween ken mair than ither folk.

They that bourd wi' cats count upon scarts.
If you play/stay with dangerous people you are bound to get hurt.

They that burn you for a witch will lose their coals.
According to Hislop this is a saying 'applied to stupid people who pretend to be very clever'.

They that come wi' a gift dinna need to stand lang at the door.

They that deal wi' the deil get a dear pennyworth.

They that drink langest live langest.
An old saying which will appeal to some and be objected to by others.

They that gang jumpin' awa aft come limpin' hame.

They that get the neist best are no ill aff.

They that gie you, hinder you to buy.

They that hae maist need o' credit seldom get muckle.

They that hae muckle butter, may lay it thick upon their breid.

They that hide ken where to find.
It takes inside knowledge to fully understand.

They that laugh in the morning will greet ere night.

They that lie down for love should rise up for hunger.

They that like the midden see nae motes in't.

They that live longest fetch wood farthest.

They that lose seek, they that find keep.
An older version of finders keepers, losers weepers.

They that love maist speak least.

They that marry in green, their sorrow is sune seen.
Green has long been held by superstitious folk as a sign of bad luck.

They that mourn for strangers or trifles may soon hae mair to grieve them.

They that ne'er filled a cradle shouldna sit in ane.
Kelly says 'Because such will not consider whether there may be a child in it, whereas they who have had children will be more cautious'.

They that play wi' cats may count upon scarts.

They that rise wi' the sun hae their wark weel begun.

They that see but your head dinna see your height.
Said to people who are not physically very tall, but who have high-spirited personalities.

They that see ye a'day, winna brak the house for ye at nicht.
Familiarity breeds contempt.

They that speak in the dark may miss their mark.

They that stay in the howe will ne'er mount the height.

They that wash on Mon(an)day,
Hae a' the week to dry,
They that wash on Tuesday
Are no far by,
They that wash on Wednesday
Are no sair to mean [are well enough off],
They that wash onThursday
May wash their claes clean,
They that wash on Friday
Hae gey muckle need,
They that wash on Saturday
Are dirty daws indeed.

They tint never a coo that grat for a needle.

They've ill will to ca' that lets the gad fa!
Those who throw aside their tools are obviously not very interested in working.

They wad be fonder o' cock birds than me who wad gie tippence for the stite o' a howlet.
'Reply of a woman who is chaffed about a sweetheart' – Cheviot.

They wad gar ye trow that a'e thing's twa, an' yer lug hauf a bannock.
They would have you believe anything, i.e. they are trying to fool you.

They walk fair that naebody finds faut wi'.

They were fain o' little, that thank'd you for a fart.
'A word of contempt to them that unreasonably think that we are obliged to them' – Kelly.

They were never fain that fidg'd, nor fu' that licket dishes.
'Spoken when people shrug their shoulders, as if it was a sign that they were not content' – Kelly.

They were never first at the work wha bade God speed the work.

They were scant o' bairns that brought you up.
A saying applied to a very rude and bad-mannered person as a rebuke.

They wha are early up and hae nae business hae either an ill wife, an ill bed, or an ill conscience.

They wha break a head are the best to find a plaster.
An example of learning by experience.

They wha hae a guid Scots tongue in their heid are fit to gang ower the warld.
Presumably because of the good reputation of the Scots throughout the world.

They wha live in glass houses should not throw stones.
During the reign of James VI, Buckingham and other courtiers indulged in the frolic of blowing pebbles through a glass tube, to break the windows of the king's Scottish followers. The enraged Scotsmen took revenge by attacking the windows of the favourite's house (in St Martin's field) which were unusually numerous. When Buckingham complained to the king the 'Scottish Solomon' warned him that 'They wha live in glass houses should not throw stones'.

They wha pay the piper hae a richt tae ca' the tune.

They wha put plough into new land must look to have it hank on a stone now and then.
No new enterprises go without an occasional hitch.

They wha use the gad like to see the plunge.

They wha will break rude jests maun put up wi' rude answers.

They will know by a half-penny if the priest will take an offering.
'A small experiment will discover a covetous inclination' – Kelly.

They will let little gang by them, that'll catch at a fart.
'Spoken to them that quarrel with you for breaking wind' – Kelly.

They wist as weel that didna speer.
A short answer given in reply to an impertinent question.

They wyte you an' you no wyteless.

They wyte you, and they wyte you wrang, and they gie you less wyte than you deserve.
'A jocose jargon when we make people believe we are condoling them, when we are really accusing them' – Kelly.

Think mair than ye say.
Thirteen o' you may gang to the dizzen.
Spoken of worthless people.

This and better may do, but this and waur will never do.
A suggestion that a thing has been badly done.

'This beats a' oot an' in,' as the wife said when she couldna find an end to the puddin'.

This is a gude meat house.
A phrase used when we wish to drink at dinner.

This is siller Saturday, the morn's a resting day,
Monanday up and till't again, and Tyesday push away.
Chambers – a working man's week.

This is the tree that never grew,
This is the bird that never flew,
This is the bell that never rang,
And this the fish that never swam.
An old rhyme used to describe the armorial bearings of the City of Glasgow.

This is the way to heaven.
This phrase is the motto of the old Burgh of Canongate, now a part of Edinburgh.

This warld's a widdle as weel as a riddle.
A 'widdle' is a wriggly motion; metaphorically a struggle.

This world will not last ay.

Tho' Thomas the Lyar thou call'st me,
A sooth tale I shall tell to thee;
By Aikyside
Thy horse shall ride,
He shall stumble, and thou shalt fa',
Thy neck bone shall break in twa,
And dogs shall thy bones gnaw,
And, maugre all thy kin and thee,
Thy own belt thy bier shall be.
– Ascribed to Thomas the Rhymer.
*'One of the Cummins, Earls of Buchan, who lived in the reign of Alexander III,
called Thomas the Rhymer by the name of Thomas the Lyar, upon which the seer
denounced him in the words of this rhyme' – Cheviot.*

Thole weel is gude for burning.

Though auld and wise still tak advice.
It is never too late to learn.

Though Cheviot's top be frosty, yet he's green below the knee.

Though the deil mars muckle he maks naething.

Though you say it, that should not say it, and must say it if it be
said.
'A ridicule upon them that commend themselves' – Kelly.

Though you tether time and tide,
Love and light ye canna hide.

Thought can kill and thought can cure.

Thoughts are free, and if I maunna say I may think.

Thoughts beguil'd the lady.
Kelly gives the following note of explanation – 'Taken from a lady that did something amiss, when she thought only to break wind backward; apply'd to them who foolishly say, I thought so.'

Thoughts beguile maidens.

Three can keep a secret when twa are awa.
You can only trust yourself.

Three failures and a fire make a Scotsman's fortune.

Thrift is a gude revenue.

Through storm and wind, sunshine and shower,
Still will ye find, groundsel in flower.
From Chambers' collection.

Till other tinklars, ill may you agree,
The one in a peat pot, and the other in the sea.
'A senseless, uncharitable saying! – when two, whom you do not affect, are at odds' – Kelly.

Time and thinking tame the strongest grief.

Time and tide for nae man bide.

Time tint is ne'er found.

Time tries a' as winter tries the kail.
Kail is said to be much improved once the first frosts have come, although this inevitably kills some of it off. Hence this proverb alludes to the idea that people who have suffered hardships in life can come through them much improved.

Time tries the truth.

Tine book, tine grace.
Addressed to school children when they have lost their school books.

Tine cat, tine game.
Comes from the game cat i' the hole. The phrase is spoken when lawyers have lost their principal evidence.

Tine heart, tine a'!

Tine thimble, tine thrift.

Tine needle, tine darg.
Literally this means that the person who loses their tools of the trade loses their day's work. A saying applied to lazy people who complain loudly when the first thing goes wrong with them.

Tip when ye like ye shall lamb wi' the lave.
'All in a company, must pay an equal share of the reckoning irrespective of the time of their arrival' – Kelly

Tit for tat, quo' the wife when she farted at the thunder.

Tit for tat's fair play.

To as mickle purpose as to wag your hand in the water.

To bite the bairns.
To behave badly by repaying a kindness with an unkindness.

To fazarts hard hazards are death ere they come nigh.
Comes from Montgomerie's 'The Cherrie and the Slae':

> *Then feir nocht nor heir nocht,*
> *Dreid, danger, or despair,*
> *To fazarts hard hazarts*
> *Is deid or tey cum their.*

To gar the key keep the castle and the rash bush keep the coo.
To maintain law and order.

To hain is to hae.
The motto of thrift.

To him that wills, ways are seldom wanting.

To keep elders' hours.
To go to bed at a reasonable hour. At one time the Kirk elders used to patrol the streets at 10 o'clock to supervise the behaviour of those leaving the local hostelries.

Toom pokes will strive.

Toom stalls mak biting horses.

To play Jock needle Jock Preen.
To play fast and loose.

To promise is ae thing, to keep it's anither.

Touch a gaw'd horse on the back an' he'll fling.
'Spoken when you have said something to a man that intrenches upon his reputation, and so have put him in a passion' – Kelly.

Touch me not on the sair heal.
Don't joke about things dear to my heart.

To work for naething maks folk dead-sweer.
When there is no personal gain to be made, people are extremely averse to exertion.

Traitor's words ne'er yet hurt honest cause.
Scott's Rob Roy *Chap. 35.*

Tramp on a snail an' she'll shoot oot her horns.

Tramp on a worm an' she'll turn her head.
The above two proverbs mean that even those who are put at the bottom of the social order will show their resentment when injured.

Traveller's words are no aye to be trusted.

Tread on my foot again, and a boll of meal on my back.
According to Kelly this was spoken when we trod on the foot of anything.

Trot faither, trot mither, how can the foal amble?
A warning not to expect too much from the offspring of bad parents.

True blue will never stain, but dirty red will dye again.

True enough, false liar.
'An ironical consent to them whom we hear telling lies' – Kelly.

True love is aye blate.
True love kythes in time o' need.
'Kythes' means shows itself.

True love's the waft o' life, but it whiles comes through a sorrowfu' shuttle.

Truth and honesty keep the crown o' the causey.
The crown o' the causey was the highest part of the street, which people kept to if they wanted to stay out of the mess in the gutter. Hence truth and honesty will keep one out of trouble.

Truth and oil come aye uppermost.
Truth cannot be concealed and like oil and water will rise to the surface.

Truth can neither be bought nor sold.

Truth will aye stand without a prop.

Try before you trust.

Try your friend ere you need him.

Tulying dogs come halting hame.
A warning not to get into fights.

Tush swims best that's bred in the sea.
'The best sailors are bred to the sea from infancy' – Kelly.

Twa blacks winna make ae white.
Two wrongs do not make a right.

Twa cats and ae mouse, twa mice in ae house, twa dogs and ae bone, ne'er will agree in ane.

Twa dogs were strivin' aboot a bane, an' the third ran awa wi't.

Twa gudes seldom meet,
What's gude for the plant is ill for the peat.

Twa fools in ae house are a pair ower mony.

Twa hands may do in ae dish, but ne'er in ae purse.

Twa hangings on ae widdy mak's twa pair o' shoon to the hangman, but only ae ploy to the people.
'A warning to an evil-doer that his punishment is certain, as it will ensure extra profit, without further trouble, expense or commotion' – Cheviot

'Twa heads are better than ane,' as the wife said when she and her dog gaed to the market.

Twa heads are better than ane, though they're but sheep's anes.
Said when someone offers advice on a matter which you are considering.

Twa heads may lie upon ae cod, and nane ken whaur the luck lies.
'Spoken when either husband or wife is dead, and the sorrowing party goes back in the world after' – Kelly.

Twa hungry meals mak the third a glutton.

Twa things ne'er be angry wi' – what ye can help and what ye canna.

Twa to flight and ane to redd.
According to Cheviot, 'There is said to be an ideal number of children in a family, two to fight, and one to settle the dispute.'

Twa wits are better than ane.

Twa wolves may worry ae sheep.

Twa words maun gang to that bargain.
Said to someone who is over-eager to conclude a transaction suggesting that the speaker has not satisfied him/herself of the goods/terms quite yet.

Tweed said to Till
'What gars ye rin sae still?'
Till said to Tweed,
'Though ye rin wi' speed,
And I rin slow,
Yet where ye droon ae man,
I droon twa.'

'Tween Martinmas and Yule, water's wine in every pool.
This phrase refers to the value of rain in the latter part of the year.

'Tween the Isle of May, and the links o' Tay,
Mony a ship's been cast away.

'Tween Wigton and the toun o' Ayr,
Portpatrick and the Cruives o' Cree,
No man need thin for to bide there,
Unless he court Saint Kennedie.
This saying attests to the one-time influence of the Kennedy family in Ayr and Galloway.

Twine tow, your mother was a gude spinner.
'Spoken to those who curse you or rail upon you, as if you would say, take what you say to yourself' – Kelly.

U

Under water dearth, under snaw bread.
A flooded field will yield a poor crop, but one which has been covered by the snow will flourish.

Unseen, unrued.
Out of sight, out of mind.

Untimeous spurring spoils the steed.

Upon my ain expense, as the man built the dyke.
A saying taken from the Kirkyard at Foot Dee or 'Fitty', in Aberdeen:

   I, John Moody, cives Aberdonensis,
   Builded this kerk-yerd of fitty upon my own expenses.

Use maks perfyteness.
Practice makes perfect.

Use of hand is faither of lear.
First use your hands – if opens the way to other knowledge.

Unco folk's no to mird wi'.
'Mird' is to jest.

Unsaid be your word, and your nose in a turd.
'Spoken when people predict ill things to us, we wish his word may be void, and the other as a reward of his ill will' – Kelly.

'Unsicker, unstable,' quo' the wave to the cable.
'Unsicker' means not secure, not safe, unsteady.

Up hill spare me, down hill bear me, plain way spare me not;
Let me not drink when I am hot.
As below, sayings on how to use a horse in a journey.

Up hill spare me, doun hill tak tent o' thee.

V

Vengeance! Vengeance! When? And Where?
Upon the house o' Cowdenknowes, now and evermair.
Attributed to Thomas the Rhymer. This is said to refer to some former proprietor of Cowdenknowes in Berwickshire who is variously represented as a persecutor, a cruel feudal baron, or a wicked laird.

Very weel; thanks to you that speers.
'An answer to the question, How do you do?' – Kelly.

Virtue is abune value.
There are certain things which cannot be bought.

Virtue ne'er grows auld.
Virtue is a quality which never ages.

W

Wad ye gar us trow that the mune's made o' green cheese, or that
spade shafts bear plooms?
Would you really have us believe such an absurd tale?

Wad ye let the bonnie May die i' your hand,
And the mugwort flowering i' the land?
*This was the advice given by a mermaid in Galloway to a young man as to how
he should cure his sweetheart, whom consumption had brought near death.*

Waes them that hae the cat's dish, and she aye mewting.
*'Spoken when people owe a thing to, or detain a thing from, needy people who are
always calling for it' – Kelly*

Wae's the wife that wants the tongue, but weel's the man that gets
her.
*The wife who is quiet will have many troubles, but lucky is the man who marries
her.*

Waes unite faes.
Shared troubles can bring together one-time adversaries.

Wae to him that lippens to ithers for tippence.
Woe betide the person who trusts to another for a small obligation.

Wae to the coward that ever he was born,
Who did not draw the sword before he blew the horn.
It is foolish to awaken danger before we are prepared to resist it.

Wae to the wame that has a wilfu' maister.

'Wae worth ill company,' quo' the daw o' Camnethan.
*Spoken when we have been drawn by bad company into a bad thing. A jackdaw
in Cambusnethan learned this from a guest in the house, when he was upon his
penitentials after hard drinking.*

Wage will get a page.
'That is servants can always be got for hire' – Kelly.

Wait till your betters are served, or else eat wi' your equals.
Scott's Redgauntlet, *Chap. 20.*

Wait's a wersh dish.

Wallace wight, upon a night, coost in a stack o' bere,
And ere the morn at fair day light, 'twas a' draff to his meer.

Waly, waly! bairns are bonny;
Ane's enough and twa's ower mony.
Potential parents beware!

Want is the warst o't.
'Spoken when we must take a mean thing or lose all' – Kelly.

Want o' cunning's nae shame.

Wanton kittlens mak douce cats.

Want o' warld's gear aft sunders fond hearts.

Want o' wit is waur than want o' gear.

Wark a God's name and sae does no witches.

Wark bears witness o' wha does weel.

War makes thieves and peace hangs them.

War's sweet to them that never tried it.
A warning to the young not to be taken in by the seeming glamour of war.

Watch harm, catch harm.

Water stoups haud nae ale.
'An excuse for not drinking, because we have not been accustomed to it' – Kelly.

Waur and mair o't.
Spoken when a fresh misfortune occurs.

We a' come to ae door at nicht.
A comment on the equality of mortality.

Wealth gars wit waver.
A warning of the power of money to make fools of us all.

Wealth has made mair men covetous than covetousness has made
men wealthy.

Wealth in the widow's house, kail, but salt.
*A humorous expression made when we have obtained something better than we
expected.*

Wealth, like want, ruins mony.

Wealth maks wit waver.
Scott's St.Ronan's Well, *Chap. 15.*

Weapons bode peace.

We are a' life-like and death-like.

We are as mony Johnstons, as you are Jerdans [Jardines].
According to Kelly this phrase is 'Taken from two families who were always on one side; though now the proverb signifies that we have as many to take our part, as you have to take yours, yet I am inclined to believe that at first it signified that we contribute as much to the common cause as you do.' See 'There's as mony Johnston's etc.' above for another alternative meaning.

We are aye to learn as lang as we live.

We are bound to be honest, and no to be rich.

We can live without our kin, but no without our neighbours.

We can be wise enough on our neighbour's weaknesses.

We can drink of the burn when we canna bite of the brae.

We canna baith sup and blaw.
We cannot do two opposing things at once.

We canna restrain our heart or our stomach.
Not unless we have extraordinary willpower, that is.

We can poind for debt, but no for unkindness.

We can shape their wylie coat, but no their weird.
We can influence somebody's appearance, but not their destiny.

Wedding and ill wintering tame baith man and beast.
A rather severe view of the 'hardship' of marriage.

Weel begun is half done.

Weel done, soon done.

Weel enough, but nothing too wanton.
An answer to the question, 'How do you do?'

Weel is that weel does.

Weel kens the moose that the cat's oot o' the house.

'Weel minded, Marion, to thy life's end.'
'Spoken to them that remember something opportunely' – Kelly.

'Weel,' quo' Willie, when his wife dang him,
She took up a rope, and she swore she wo'd hang him.
Kelly calls this 'a senseless rhyme'. Hislop says it is an expression of indifference on the part of the husband at the punishment being administered to him.

Weel saipet is half shaven.
This saying, ascribed to Dr Hill of St Andrews, was his humorous Scottish translation of the old Latin aphorism 'Qui bene cepit dimidium facti fecit'.

Weel's him and wae's him that has a bishop in his kin.

Weel-timed daffin'.
Dr Adam, the nineteenth-century Rector of the High School of Edinburgh, translated the Horation expression 'Desipere in loco' *by this Scottish phrase according to Ramsay's* Reminiscencies, *1867.*

Weel to breuke [enjoy], and many mo,
Weel to breuke, and me the old.
'A good wish to him who has got something new; the last from an inferior' – Kelly.

Weel won corn should be housed ere the morn.
'Weel won' corn meant that it had been dried by exposure to the air. This proverb urges people not to leave a job half done lest everything be lost.

Weel worth a' good tokens.
According to Kelly this is 'Spoken facetiously when we are told that such an one is easing nature, or some such thing that is not to be spoken', i.e. spending a penny!

Weel worth a' that gars the plough draw.
Good luck to everything by which we can earn money.

Weel worth aw, it maks the plough draw.
'Spoken when people are overawed to do a thing which otherwise they would not do' – Kelly.

Wee things fley cowards.

'We hounds slew the hare,' quo' the messan.
Said to insignificant people when they falsely claim to have made a major contribution to some achievement.

Welcome's the best dish in the kitchen.
A testimony to the power of good hospitality.

We'll bark oursel's ere we buy dogs sae dear.
A phrase addressed to people who are asking exorbitant prices for the goods they are selling.

We'll bear wi' the stink, when it brings in the clink.
So long as they are profitable, we will endure hardships.

We'll be as right and tight as thack and rope can mak' us.
In the particular circumstances we will be perfectly secure.

We'll meet ere hills meet.
That is to say – never!

We'll ne'er big sandy bowrocks thegither.
We will never build sandcastles together, i.e. we will never be on intimate terms.

We'll ne'er ken the worth o' water till the well gang dry.

'Well,' quoth Wallace, and then he leugh, 'the King of France has gold enough, and you'll get it all for the winning.'
'Intimating that he will get nothing without labouring for it' – Kelly.

We'll wet thoombs on that.
Shake hands on it. Swear solemnly to keep faith.

We maun a' dee when our day comes.

We maun a' gang ae gate.
(To achieve success) we must all be going in the same direction.

We maun big oor dykes wi' the fail we hae.
'Fail' means turf, i.e. We must make do with what we have.

We maun keep the banes green.
We must live as comfortably as our means will permit.

We maun live by the living, and no by the dead.

We maun mak a baik and a bow.
We must be courteous and conciliatory.

We maun tak the crap as it groes.

We maunna fa' that.
We must not hope to get that.

We may ae day play at change seats, the King's coming.
A Jacobite phrase. From Scott's Rob Roy, *Chap. 32.*

We may ken your age by the wrinkles on your horn.

We may ken your meaning by your mumping.
'To mump' is to hint at, or aim at.

Were it no for hope the heart wad break.

We're no sae far ahint but what we may follow.
Scott's Rob Roy, *Chap. 26.*

We're to learn while we live.

Wersh parritch, neither gude to fry, boil, nor sup cauld.
Scott's Old Mortality *Chap. 9.*

Wet your wizen or else it'll gizen.
Hislop says this is spoken to a person who is telling a story. It may be kindly meant, or a hint that the story is too long-winded.

Wha burns rags will want a winding sheet.

Wha can help misluck?

'Wha can help sickness?' quo' the wife when she lay in the gutter.
According to Kelly, 'Taken from a woman, who being drunk, pretended to be sick; apply'd when men make a false pretence for what they do.'

Wha can hold that will awa'.

Wha canna gie will little get.
You only get out what you put in.

Wha comes oftener, and brings you less?
A humorous remark made to a frequent visitor.

Wha daur bell the cat?
A question supposedly asked by an experienced mouse when another suggested that they put a bell round the cat's neck, to warn of its approach. This saying is well known to students of Scottish history. At the time of James III, the Scottish nobles proposed to meet at Stirling and take Spence, the King's favourite, and hang him. However the worldly wise Lord Gray is said to have asked the above question. The Earl of Angus undertook the task, accomplished it, and thereafter was known as Archibald Bell-the-Cat.

Wha invited you to the roast?
Spoken when uninvited people put their hand to what is not theirs.

Wha may woo without cost?

Wha never climbs never fa's.

What a' body says maun be true.
Another version of there's no smoke without fire.

What better is the house whaur the daw rises soon?
'Spoken often by mistresses to their maids, when they have been early up and done little work' – Kelly

What canna be cured maun be endured.

What carlins hain, cats eat.

What comes by wreck comes by death.
A reflection upon the infamous practice of wrecking.

What comes with the wind, will go by the water.

What fizzes in the mou' winna fill the wame.
Outward appearances can be deceptive.

What folk disna ken, disna anger them.

What makes you sae rumgunshach and me sae curcuddoch?
Why are you so rude and unpleasant to me when I am so friendly and anxious to please you?

What may be done at ony time will be done at nae time.
Said when people put off some chore saying they can do it any time.

What may be mayna be.

What puts that in your head that didna put the sturdy wi't?
'Spoken to them that speak foolishly, or tell a story that you thought they had not known' – Kelly.

What rake [signifies] the fead [enmity] where the friendship dow not.
'Signifying our contempt of mean persons, whose hatred we defy, and whose friendship we despise' – Kelly.

What's a tongue for if its never to wag?

What serves dirt for if it does not stink?
'Spoken when mean, bare born people, speak proudly or behave saucily' – Kelly.

What's fristed [put off] for a time is no forgiven.

What's gairly gathered is roundly spent.

What's gotten ower the deil's back is spent below his belly.

What's held in at the door gangs out at the window/lum.
One saving is offset by another expenditure.

What's in your wame's no in your testament.
Spoken to encourage someone to eat, i.e. if they eat all that is in front of them they cannot possibly leave it in their will.

What's like a dorty [saucy] maiden when she's auld?
A 'Dorty' is a female who is saucy to her suitors.

What's my case the day may be yours the morn.

What's nane o' my profit shall be nane o' my peril.
A refusal to run a risk if there is no share of the spoils.

'What's no i' the bag'll be i' the broo,' quo' the Hielandman when he dirked the haggis.

What's pleasure to you bodes ill to me.

What's waur than ill luck?

What's yours is mine, what's mine's my ain.
Motto adopted by selfish partners.

What the eye sees not, the heart rues not.

What we first learn we best ken.

What will ye get frae an oily pat but stink?

What will you say if this should come to hand,
Perth's Provost London's Mayor shall command.
When Earl of Gowrie, Provost of Perth, was killed in connection with the Gowrie Conspiracy, King James VI offered himself for the office in order to allay the irritation of the citizens, and was sworn in with much ceremony. As King of England he afterwards commanded the Lord Mayor of London, hence the allusion.

What winna do by might do by flight.

What winna mak a pot may mak a pot lid.

What ye do when ye're drunk, ye may pay for when ye're dry.

What ye gie shines aye, what ye get smells next day.

What ye want up and doun you hae hither-and yont.
Hither-and-yont means topsy turvy. A saying applied to someone who has all the necessary parts to complete a task, but not necessarily in the right place.

What ye win at that ye may lick aff a het girdle.
The prospect of success is exceedingly slim.

What your ee sees your heart greens for.
'To green' is to covet.

Whaur th' Tweed droons ane,
the Till droons twa.
A warning to any traveller on approaching the banks of the latter river.

Wha wats wha may keep sheep anither day.

Wha will pay the piper?
Who will bear the expense, or take the consequences.

When Adam carded, and Eve span, where was all our gentry then?
Up starts a carle and gather'd good, and thence came all our gentle blood.

When ae door steeks anither opens.

When a ewie's drowned she's dead.
Said when a thing is lost and past recovery.

When a fool finds a horseshoe he thinks aye the like to do.

When a' freets fail, fire's gude for the fiercy.
'Spoken after ordinary attempts, we betake ourselves to extraordinary' – Kelly.

When a' fruits fail, welcome haws *or*
When all fruit fa's, welcome ha's.
Said when we start eating the coarser food after we have finished the finer fruits.

When a hundred sheep rin, how mony cloots clatter?

When a' men speak, nae man hears.

When ane winna, twa canna cast oot.
It takes two to make a fight/quarrel.

When a's in, and the slap dit, rise herd and let the dog sit.
*'Slap dit' is a shut gate. Said as a humorous remark to herd boys after harvest,
as if there were no further use for them.*

When Cheviot ye see pit on his cap
O rain ye'll hae a wee bit drap;
When Ruberslaw draws on his coul
Wi' rain the burns will a' be full.
A Borders weather proverb. The lower the clouds the more rain.

When clouds appear like rocks and towers,
The earth's refreshed with frequent showers.

When cloudy Cairnsmuir hath a hat
Palmour and Skairs laugh at that.
*Cairnsmuir is a hill in Kirkcudbrightshire – Palmour and Skairs are two
mountain burns in its vicinity.*

When Craigowl puts on his cowl, and Coolie Law his hood,
The folk o' Lundie may look dool, for the day'll no be good.
A piece of Angus weather-lore, relating to the Sidlaw hills.

When death lifts the curtain it's time to be startin'.

When Dee and Don shall run in one,
And Tweed shall run, and Tay,
And the bonnie water o' Urie
Shall bear the Bass away.
*A rhyme ascribed to Thomas the Rhymer. The Bass is a green mound adjoining
the town of Inverurie. The mound was believed to contain the ruins of a castle,
which had been destroyed and covered with earth because the inhabitants were
infected with the plague. Hence the people of Inverurie believed that if the River
Urie flooded and took away the mound, the plague would be released, and to
guard against this, they raised barriers to resist the encroachments of the stream.*

When drink's in wit's out.

When Falkland Hill puts on his cap, the Howe o' Fife will get a drap,
And when the Bishop draws his cowl, look out for wind and
weather foul!
*Another piece of weather-lore similar to the one above, but this time originating
from Fife.*

When Finhaven Castle rins to sand,
The world's end is near at hand.
*A saying ascribed to Thomas the Rhymer. The rhyme refers to the original strength
of Finhaven Castle in Kincardineshire, the ancient seat of the Earls of Crawford.*

When folk canna get the gowden gown, they should be thankful when they get the sleeve.
From Galt's The Entail.

When folk's missed then they're moaned.
Scott's Guy Mannering, *Chap. 9.*

When folk's ready to buy, ye can want to sell.

When frae Leslie ye wad gae,
Ye maun cross a brig and doun a brae.
'The peculiar and high situation of this Fifeshire village with water on all sides is indicated in this rhyme' – Chambers.

When friends meet hearts warm.

When gude cheer is lacking friends go a-packing.

When heather bells grow cockle shells,
The miller and the priest will forget themsel's.
Only then will the miller and the priest forget their own interests.

When he dees of age ye may quake for fear.

When I am dead make me cawdle.

When I did weel I heard it never, when I did ill I heard it ever.
A reflection on the lack of positive reinforcement received. A saying applied to those who only give negative criticisms.

When ilka ane gets his ain the thief will get the widdie.
On the day of reckoning.

When lairds break carls get land.

When love cools fauts are seen.

When March comes in with an adder's head, it goes out with a peacock's tail;
When it comes in with a peacock's tail, it goes out with an adder's tail.

When my head's doun my house is theiked.
When I am busy I am free from debt.

When petticoats woo breeks come speed.

When poverty comes in at the door, love flies out at the window.

When pride's in the van beggin's in the rear.

When roond the moon there is a brugh
The weather will be cauld and reuch.

When Ruberslaw puts on his cowl, the Dunion on his hood,
Then a' the wives o' Teviot side ken there will be a flood.
Riberslaw and the Dunion are two hills in Roxburghshire, between Jedburgh and Hawick.

When she doesna scold she shores.
When she is not actively scolding she threatens to.

When the bag's fu' the drone gets up.
An analogy between bagpipes and drinking.

When the barn's fu' ye may thresh afore the door.

When the burn doesna babble it's either ower toom or owerfu'.

When the carry gaes west, gude weather is past,
When the carry gaes east, gude weather comes neist.
This rhyme originates from the east coast of Scotland. The 'carry' referred to is the current of the clouds.

When the Castle of Stirling gets a hat, the carse of Corntown pays for that.
When the clouds descend so low as to cover Stirling Castle, the surrounding environs may expect a deluge.

When the caup's fu' carry't even.

When the cow's in the clout, she soon runs out.
When the cow was sold and converted into money, it used to be wrapped in a piece of rag, it was easily lost or spent.

When the craw flees her tail follows.

When the deil gets in, the fire maun flee out.

What the deil gets in the joint o' his little finger, he will soon have in his whole hand.
Appears in The Ettrick Shepherd's 'The Brownie of the Black Haggs'.

When the gudeman drinks to the gudewife a' wad be weel; when the gudewife drinks to the gudeman a's weel.
This saying suggests that in times past, a husband only drank to the good health of his wife through fear rather than affection.

When the gudeman's awa' the board claith's tint, when the gude wife's awa' the keys are tint.

When the hand o' the chief ceases to bestow, the breath o' the bard is frozen in the utterance.

When the heart's fu' o' lust the mou's fu' o' leasing.

When the heart's fu' the tongue canna speak.

When the heart's fu' the tongue will speak.

When the heart's past hope the face is past shame.

When the hen gaes to the cock the birds may get a knock.
Spoken as a warning to the children of widows, i.e. when widows go looking for a second husband, the children may suffer as a consequence.

When the horse is at the gallop the bridle's ower late.

When the lady lets a fart, the messan gets a knap.
Spoken when someone is blamed for the wrongdoing of another.

When the man is fire and the wife is tow, the deil comes in and blaws't in lowe.

When the mind is free the body's delicate.

When the moon is on her back,
Gae mend yer shoon and sort yer thack.
A piece of weather forecasting based upon the visible shape of the moon in the night's sky.

When the pat's fu' it'll boil ower.

When the pea's in bloom, the mussel's toom.
The mussel is not in season during the summer.

When the saut gaes abune the meal,
Believe nae mair o' Tammie's tale.
Ascribed to Thomas the Rhymer. i.e. it is as impossible for the price of porridge to exceed that of meal as it is for his prophecies to fail.

When the tod preaches, look to the geese.
Kelly gives this amazing interpretation: 'When wicked men put on a cloak of religion, suspect some wicked design. Witness the solemn fasts and humiliations in time of the anarchy, when not only subtle foxes, but ravenous bears, treacherous crocodiles and devouring harpies actually preach'd.'

When the tod preaches, tak tent o' the lambs.

When the tod wins to the wood, he caresna how many keek at his tail.

When the wame's fu' the banes wad be at rest.

When the well's fu' it will run ower.

When the white ox comes to the corse,
Every man may take his horse.
Ascribed to Thomas the Rhymer. Expresses the gloomy fear of coming evil.

When the will's ready the feet's light.

When the wind is in the North, hail comes forth,
When the wind is in the West, look for a wat blast;
When the wind's in the Soud
The weather will be fresh and good,
When the wind is in the East, cauld and snaw comes neist.

When the wind's in the West, the weathers at the best,
When the wind's in the East,
It is neither good for man nor beast,
When the wind's in the South, rain will be fouth.
'Fouth' means in abundance.

When the wind's still the shower fa's soft.
Calm, equable natures endure trials best.

When the Yowes o' Gowrie come to land,
The Day o' Judgement's near at hand.
The village of Invergowrie is a very ancient village and it claims to have had the first Christian church on the north side of the Tay. According to folklore, the Devil was so outraged by this act of defiance that he began throwing stones across the water at the new church. Two stones fell short and became known as the 'Goors, or Yowes, of Invergowrie'. A third stone overshot by half a mile and is now called the Deil's Stane. Hence the above prophetic rhyme which was supposedly recorded by Thomas the Rhymer.

When thieves reckon leal fowk come to their gear.

When Traprain puts on his hat
The Lothian lads way look to that.

When Tweed and Pausayl meet at Merlin's grave.
Scotland and England will one monarch have.

When we go to the hills we like the deer that bears the horns.
When we undertake something we like to secure our object and to be rewarded for our pains.

When we want, friends are scant.

When wine sinks, words soom.

When ye are poor naebody kens ye, when ye are rich a'body kens ye.

When ye are weel haud yersel sae.

When ye can suit your shanks to my shoon, ye may speak.
Don't speak about me until you have been in a similar situation yourself.

When ye christen the bairn, ye should ken what to ca't.
Said to a vendor who is hesitant at giving the price of something.

When you're gaun and comin' the gate's no toom.
Said to those we suspect of going on a needless errand.

When you're ser'd a' the geese are watered.

When your neighbour's house is in danger tak tent o' yer ain.

When Yule comes, dule comes, cauld feet and legs;
When Pasch comes, grace comes, butter, milk and eggs.

Where drums beat laws are dumb.

Where it was, and not where it grew; and, where leal folk get gear.
The answer given to the request 'Where did you get such and such a thing?'

Where MacGregor sits is head of the table.
i.e. wherever the important person chooses to be is the centre of the action. This saying is sometimes attributed to Rob Roy MacGregor, the Highland outlaw, however the saying is used in many different lands where other names are substituted.

Where stands your great horse?

Where the buck's bound there he may bleat.
'Men must bear these hardships to which they are bound either by force or compact' – Kelly.

Where the deer's slain the blude will lie.

Where the dyke's laighest it's easiest loupit.

Where the head gaes the tail will follow.

Where the pig's broken let the sherds lie.

Where there are gentles there are aye aff-fa'ings.
A delicate allusion to the failings of the aristocracy. According to Kelly this phrase is said humorously to children when they have lost/forgotten something from where they were last.

Where there are no boys in arms there will be no armed men.

Where there are no bushes there can be no nuts.

Where there's ane better there's ten waur.
Scott's Heart of Midlothian, *Chap. 43.*

Where there's muckle courtesy there's little kindness.

Where there's naething, the king tines his right.

Where there's no fools there's no foxes.

Where there's stock there maun be broch [loss].

Where the scythe cuts, and the sock rives,
Hae done wi' fairies and bee bykes?
'Meaning that the ploughing or even mowing of the ground tends to extirpate alike the earth bee and the fairy' – Chambers.

Where they clip there needs nae kame.
Scott's The Antiquary, *Chap. 41.*

Where the deil shites, he shites in a heap.
According to Kelly this is 'enviously spoken when those we affect do not grow wealthy.'

Where vice is, vengeance follows.

Where will you get a park to put your yell kye in?
'Spoken to those who without any reason boast of their good management' – Kelly.

While ae gab's teething, anither's growing teethless.
The proverbial cycle of life.

Whiles you and whiles me, sae gaes the bailierie.
A saying used when people get positions of authority in turns.

While there is a green leaf in the forest, there will be guile in a Comyne.
This saying refers to the proverbial treachery of the Comyne or Cummin family, once a power in the land, but whose family was completely destroyed by Robert the Bruce.

Whistle on your thoom.
Please yourself. Scott's Heart of Midlothian, *Chap. 18.*

Whistling amang the tenantry.
This was applied when one tenant gave such information to the laird or estate factor about a neighbour, that the rent of the latter was raised.

White legs wad aye be rused.
Spoken when people fish for compliments.

Whitely things are aye tender.
'Taken from common observation, but spoken to people of all complexions when they pretend tenderness' – Kelly.

Whom God will help, none can hinder.

Whoredom and grace will not bide in one place.

Whose barn hast thou broken?
What tricks have you been up to?

Wi' an empty hand nae man can hawks lure.
You cannot expect to attract workers unless you offer them something.

Wide lugs and a short tongue are best.
People who hear everything but repeat none of it are safest.

Wide will wear but tight will tear.
Addressed to someone if they complain that an article of clothing is on the large side.

Wild geese, wild geese, ganging to the sea,
Good weather it will be,
Wild geese, wild geese, ganging to the hill,
The weather it will spill.
'Morayshire weather rhyme' – Chambers.

Wiles help weak folk.

Wilfu' waste maks woefu' want.

Wilful will do it.

Will and wit strive wi' you.

Will God's blessing mak my pot boil or my spit gae?
'A landlord, when people offered him all they could get, and bid him take it with God's blessing, replied sneeringly, Will God's blessing, etc....' – Kelly.

Will is a word for a man, must is no word for a lady.
Scott's The Abbot, *Chap. 3.*

Willie, my buck, shoot out your horn,
And you'll get milk and bread the morn.
A Forfarshire greeting to the snail.

Wink at sma' fauts, ye hae great anes yoursel.

Win it an' wear it.
Said when we are offering a reward in return for some action.

Winter thunder bodes summer hunger.

Wipe wi' the water and wash wi' the towel.
Spoken to children when they don't wash their hands properly.

Wise folk buy and sell, and fools are bought and sold.
Scott's Rob Roy, *Chap. 4.*

Wiser men than you are caught by wiles.

Wishers and woulders are poor house hauders.

Wish in ane hand and drite in anither, and see which will be first full.

Wit bought is worth two for nought.

Wit bought maks wise folk.

Wite yoursel' if your wife be wi' bairn.

Wit is better than wealth.
Scott's Rob Roy, *Chap. 23.*

Wit is worth a weel turned leg.

Without crack or flaw.
Taken from the description of sound timber and applied to honest upright men.

Wives and wind are necessary evils.

Wives maun be had whether gude or bad.

Wives maun hae their wills while they live for they mak nane when they dee.
This proverb is an example of the state of things before the introduction of the Married Women's Property Act in the nineteenth century.

Women and bairns layne what they ken not.
i.e. they conceal what they don't know.

Women and horned nowte are muckle the same a' the warld ower.

Women and wine, dice and deceit, mak wealth sma' and want great.

Women are kittle cattle, and the mair ye rin after them the mair they flee awa.

Women are wilfu', and downa bide a slight.

Women laugh when they can, and greet when they will.

Women's wark is never done.

Wonder at your auld shoon when you hae gotten your new.
An answer given to those who say they wonder at you or what you do.

Wonder lasts but nine nichts in a toun.

Wood in a wilderness, moss in a moutain and wit in a poor man's pow are little thought o'.

Woo sellers ken aye woo buyers.
It takes one to know one.

Words are but wind but dunts are the deil.
Assault is worse than abuse (compare with 'sticks and stones . . .').

Words are but wind, but seeing's believing.

Words go with the wind, but dunts are the devil.

Words go with the wind, but strokes are out of play.

Work for nought maks fowk dead sweer.

Work legs and win legs, hain legs and tine legs.

Worth may be blamed, but ne'er be shamed.

Wrang count is nae payment.

Wrang has nae warrant.
Noone can pretend they have authority to do a bad thing.

Wuddie haud thine ain.

Wyte your teeth, if your tail be sma'.
'Spoken to them who have good meat at their will' – Kelly.

Y

Ye and he pishes in ane nutshell.
You are in accord.

Years bring fears.
Fear can come with old age.

Ye aye mak boggles o' windlestraes.
Mountains out of molehills. You are easily frightened.

Ye breed o' auld maids, ye look high.
'To breed' is to resemble or to take after. The phrase is applied to those who overlook what is before them. Supposedly the only reason 'auld maids' remained unmarried was because they refused to consider the available suitors before them.

Ye breed o' foul weather, ye come unsent for.

Ye breed o' gude maut, ye're lang o' comin.

Ye breed o' leddy Mary, when ye're gude ye're ower gude.
According to Kelly, 'A drunken man begged Lady Mary to help him on his horse and having made many attempts, to no purpose, he always reiterated the same petition; at length he jumped right over. "O Lady Mary," said he, "when thou art good, thou art ower gude."'

Ye breed o' nettle-kail and cock-lairds, ye need muckle service.
A phrase used by servants whose employers were mean and troublesome.

Ye breed o' our laird, ye'll no do right and ye'll tak nae wrang.
Used in the past by people who had suffered at the hands of the local master.

Ye breed o' Saughton swine, yer nebs ne'er out o' an ill turn.
Said of a troublemaker.

Ye breed o' the baxters, ye loe yer neighbour's browst better than yer ain batch.

Ye breed o' the butcher, ye seek the knife, and it is in yer teeth.

Ye breed o' the chapman, ye're ay to handsel.
'Spoken to those who ask us hansel (that is, the first bit in the morning, the first money for their parcels of wares, or the like). Taken from pedlars who, coming into a house, will say, "Give us hansel".' – Kelly.

Ye breed o' the chapman, ye're never oot o' yer gate.
A saying applied to those who do business wherever they go.

Ye breed o' the craw's tail, ye grow backwards.
Spoken to children who do not improve at their school work.

Ye breed o' the gowk, ye hae ne'er a rhyme but ane.
Used when someone always talks on the same subject.

Ye breed o' the gudeman's mither, ye're aye in the way.

Ye breed o' the herd's wife, ye busk at e'en.

Ye breed o' the leek ye hae a white heid and a green tail.
A rebuke to old men full of bawdy talk.

Ye breed o' the miller's dochter, that speir'd what tree groats grew on.
Said when people claim not to know what their family background is.

Ye breed o' the miller's dog, ye lick your lips e'er the pock be open.
Said of covetous people.

Ye breed o' the tod's bairns, if ane be gude, they're a' gude.

Ye breed o' the tod, ye grow grey before ye grow gude.

Ye breed o' the witches, ye can do nae gude to yoursel.

Ye burn day light.
You waste your time.

Ye ca' hardest at the nail that drives fastest.
'Meaning that a person pretends to work much harder than is really required'
– Hislop

Ye cangle about uncost kids.
i.e. quarrel about unbought goods. Said when people quarrel over things which have not even occurred.

Ye canna do but ye ower-do.

Ye canna fare weel but ye cry roast-beef.

Ye canna gather berries aff a whinbush.
Don't expect favours from ill-humoured people.

Ye canna get leave to thrive for thrang.
Literally, you are so busy you don't have time to get rich.

Ye canna hae mair o' a soo than a grumph.

Ye canna mak a silk purse oot o' a sow's lug.

Ye canna preach oot o' yer ain pu'pit.
A saying applied to people who are not very adept at describing things which do not usually occur in their everyday lives.

Ye canna put an auld head upon young shouthers.

Ye canna see the wood for the trees.

Ye canna tak clean water oot o' a foul well.

Ye can neither mak tap, tail, nor mane o't.
You cannot understand it/make sense of it.

Ye come o' the M'Taks, but no o' the M'Gies.
Spoken of those more eager to receive than to give.

Ye come to the gait's house to thig woo'.
'Gaits' are goats, i.e. you seek a loan from someone who has nothing to give.

Ye could tie the toun wi' a strae.
A phrase used to indicate extreme surprise.

Ye crack crousely wi' yer bannet on.
A not-so-subtle hint that a person is being over familiar.

Ye cut lang whangs aff ither folk's leather.
Said to cheeky people who are a little too free in their use of others' property.

Ye daur weel but ye downa.
You try to do well, but cannot.

Ye daurna for yer arse.
'A contemptuous answer to them that threaten us' – Kelly.

Ye didna draw sae weel when my mear was in the mire.
You were not as helpful to me as I am being to you.

Ye didna lick yer lips since ye leed last.

Ye dream'd that ye dret under you, and when ye rose it was true.
A phrase said in reply when someone asks 'Guess what I dreamt last night'.

Ye drive the plough before the owsen.

Ye fand it where the Hielandman fand the tangs.
You found it in its proper place. Used as a way of suggesting that someone has stolen something, when they say that they have just 'found' an object.

Ye fike it awa, like auld wives baking.
To 'fike' is to waste time in carrying out some business; to lose time by procrastination while appearing to be busy.

Ye gang round by Lanark for fear Linton dogs bite ye.

Ye gie gude counsel, but he's a fool that taks't.

Ye glower like a cat oot o' a whin bush.

Ye got ower muckle o' your ain will, and ye're the waur o't.

Ye got yer will in yer first wife's time, and ye shanna want it now.
Said as a humorous aside to a self-willed man.

Ye green to pish in uncouth lays.
Spoken of those who are fond of seeking new places/things.

Ye had aye a gude whittle at yer belt.
You always had a ready answer.

Ye hae a constant hunger and perpetual drouth.
Spoken to people with huge appetites.

Ye hae a crap for a' corn.
To further strengthen this proverb the phrase 'and a baggie for rye' is sometimes appended.

Ye hae a head, and so has a nail.

Ye hae a ready mou' for a ripe cherry.
Spoken to those who are ready to take what we have to offer.

Ye hae a saw for a' sairs.

Ye hae a sleek tongue tae lick a sair arse.
A reproof to those who try to flatter us falsely.

Ye hae a streak o' carl hemp in ye.
You possess a strong will and mind. The carl hemp was the toughest fibre.

Ye hae a tongue, and sae has a bell.

Ye hae as mony dogs as ye hae banes to pike.

Ye hae as muckle chance o' that as ye can see through a whinstane.
You have no chance whatsoever.

Ye hae aye a fit oot o' the langel.
A 'langel' was a chain or rope used to tie a horse's hind foot to its fore foot. Hence this saying was applied to people who oppose everything.

Ye hae bedirten yoursel', and wad hae me to dight you.
Spoken to people who expect us to help them out of bad situations they have got themselves into.

Ye hae been smelling the bung.
You've been drinking.

Ye hae been gotten gathering nits, ye speak in clusters.

Ye hae been lang on little eird.
Taken from ploughing this phrase means that you have little to show for all your work.

Ye hae brought the pack to the pins.
'You have dwindled away your stock' – Kelly.

Ye hae ca'd your pigs to an ill market.

Ye hae come aff at the loupin-on-stane.

Ye hae come in time to tine a darg.
You have come in time to lose a day's work, i.e. you're too late.

Ye hae come to a peeled egg.
You have attained a ready-made, excellent position.

Ye hae done a darg and dirten a worm.
A very 'down to earth' expression suggesting you have really worked very hard and got your hands dirty.

Ye hae fasted lang, and worried on a midge.

Ye hae found a mear's nest, and laugh at the eggs.
Said when someone laughs without cause.

Ye hae gien baith the sound thump an' the loud skirl.

Ye hae gien the sair knock and the loud cry.
'Spoken to those who do the greatest injury, and yet make the loudest complaints' – Kelly.

Ye hae gien the wolf the wedders to keep.
You have entrusted a thing to someone who will either lose, spoil, or use it himself.

Ye hae got an office an' arse to kiss.
'Spoken to children when they delight in some silly thing' – Kelly.

Ye hae got a piece o' Kitty Sleitchock's bannock.
Spoken when young ones flatter us for something.

Ye hae got a stipend; get a kirk when ye like.

Ye hae got baith the skaith and the scorn.

Ye hae got butter in a burd.
'Spoken to one who sings, speaks, or calls with a loud voice. In olden times farmers' wives used to give butter to those chickens they wanted to rear as house cocks, so that they might crow clearer' – Kelly.

Ye hae gotten a ravelled hemp to redd.
You have got a very complicated situation to sort out.

Ye hae gotten the chapman's drouth.
You have an insatiable thirst.

Ye hae gotten to your English.
A taunting reply given at one time to a fluent and insolent adversary. It appears in Scott's Rob Roy, *Chap. 35.*

Ye hae got the bitch in the wheel band.
'A thing you can't keep long' – Kelly.

Ye hae got the first seat on the midden today.
You have got out of the wrong side of bed today, i.e. you are in a bad mood.

Ye hae grown proud since ye quatted the begging.
A cheeky remark to someone who passes by without acknowledging acquaintances.

Ye hae gude manners but ye dinna bear them about wi' you.
Said as a witty response when someone is rude.

Ye hae gude skill o' roasted woo', it stinks when it's eneuch.
Said to those who pretend to have a skill which they do not possess.

Ye hae hit it, if ye had a stick.
You have hit the nail on the head. You are spot on.

Ye hae hurt yer hand wi't.
Spoken ironically when people give little.

Ye hae little need o' the Campsie wife's prayer, 'That she might aye be able to think enough o' hersel.'
Applied to conceited or selfish individuals.

Ye hae made a hand like a foot.
Said to those who are disappointed in their expectations.

Ye hae mind o' your meat though ye hae little o't.
'A return of wanton girls to young fellows, when they talk smutty' – Kelly.

Ye hae miss'd that, as ye did yer mither's blessing.

Ye hae muckle to speak o' a chapin o' ale among four folk, and my share the least o't.
A phrase used when people make much fuss about nothing.

Ye hae nae been longsome and foul farren baith.
'Foul Farren' means dirty, rough. 'Applied to them that have done a thing in great haste' – Kelly.

Ye hae nae mair heart than a cat.
Scott's Guy Mannering, *Chap. 48.*

Ye hae nae mair need for't than a cart has for a third wheel.

Ye hae nae mair sense than a sooking turkey.

Ye hae nae the pith o' a cat.
Scott's Guy Mannering, *Ch26.*

Ye hae nae the stamach o' a cat.
A phrase applied to someone who is a poor eater.

Ye hae naething to do but suck, an' wag your tail.
'Spoken to them who have a plentiful condition' – Kelly.

Ye hae ower foul feet to come sae far ben.
Hislop says 'Spoken jocularly to persons who, when they go to visit a friend, ask "Will they come in?"' Murison however gives the following meaning – 'i.e. you are getting above your station.'

Ye hae ower muckle loose leather about your chafts.
Said to those who speak too freely of things they should not.

Ye hae pish'd on nettles I trow.
'Spoken to a woman who is angry without a cause; as if she only vented her passion on us, but that the real cause of her anger was, that she had piss'd upon nettles and they had stung her' – Kelly.

Ye hae put a toom spune in my mouth.
'A country farmer complained of having been fed with a "toom spune" when he had listened to the exhortations of a very poor preacher' – Hislop.

Ye hae run lang on little ground.

Ye hae seen nine houses.
'An invitation to eat with us, for you have gone so far as to pass nine houses since you ate last' – Kelly.

Ye hae sew'd that seam wi' a het needle and a burning thread.
Said facetiously when a hasty repair gives way.

Ye hae sitten your time, as mony a gude hen has done.
Spoken to someone who has sat patiently waiting. Alternatively the phrase is sometimes applied to those who have lazily sat watching whilst an opportunity passes them by.

Ye hae skill o' man and beast, and dogs that tak the sturdy.
A joke made against those who have pretensions to be skilled at something they are not.

Ye hae skill o' man and beast, ye was born between the Beltanes.
i.e. between 1 and 8 May.

Ye hae stayed lang, and brought little wi' ye.
Spoken to an unwanted guest.

Ye hae tae'n the measure o' his foot.
You have got the measure of him.

Ye hae tae'n't upon you, as the wife did the dancin'.

Ye hae the best end o' the string.
You have the best of the argument.

Ye hae the wrang sow by the lug.
You have got hold of the wrong end of the stick, i.e. you have misunderstood.

Ye hae tied a knot wi' yer tongue ye winna loose wi' yer teeth.

Ye hae tint the tongue o' the trump.
You have lost the main thing. A 'trump' is a Jew's Harp, and to lose the tongue of it is to lose what is essential to its sound.

Ye hae tint yer ain stamach an' found a tyke's.
A humorous saying applied to those who eat a great deal when they are hungry.

Ye hae wraught a yoke and loused in time.
You have worked to little purpose.

Ye hae yer nose in every man's turd.
Spoken to people who are always meddling in others' affairs.

Ye ken naething but milk and bread when it's mool'd into ye.
You know or care about nothing but your meat.

Ye kenna what may cool your kail yet.

Ye ken what drinkers drees.
You know by experience what others suffer.

Ye ken yer groats in ither folk's kale.
You can identify your work even amongst that of others.

Ye let little gae by you, unless it be the swallow.

Ye live beside ill neebors.
'Spoken when people commend themselves, for if they deserved commendation their neighbours would commend them' – Kelly.

Ye live on love as laverocks do on leeks.
Said as a joke to people who eat little.

Ye'll be a man afore yer mither yet.

Ye'll beguile nane but them that lippens till ye.

Ye'll be hang'd and I'll be harried.
Spoken to naughty boys who play tricks on us.

Ye'll be like the singed cat then, better than you are likely.
Said in reply when someone threatens you with a beating, suggesting you do not think them capable of it.

Ye'll be made up at the sign o' the wind.
The promise made will not be performed.

Ye'll be the better o' findin' the grund o' yer stamach.
An answer given to an inopportune request for food.

Ye'll break your neck as sune as your fast in this house.

Ye'll cool and come to yoursel, like MacGibbon's crowdy when he set it out at the window-bole.

Ye'll dance yet by the crook frae a widdie.
You will assuredly be hanged at some time.

Ye'll dee like a trooper's horse – wi' your shoon on.
You will be hanged.

Ye'll dee without amends o't.
You will get no satisfaction on that point.

Ye'll do onything but work and rin errands.

Ye'll drink afore me.
You have said exactly what I was about to, which is a token that you'll get the first drink.

Ye'll follow him lang or he'll let five shillings fa'.

Ye'll gang a gray gate; *and*
Ye'll gang up the car gate yet.
You will come to a sticky end.

Ye'll gang the gate MacEwan's cauf gaed, an' it worried in the band.
'Worried in the band' means choked in the binding. The phrase was applied to people as a warning that they would be hanged.

Ye'll gang up the Lawnmarket yet.
You will end up being hanged. In Edinburgh the procession of criminals to the gallows passed through the Lawnmarket.

Ye'll gar him claw a sair haffit.
'Haffit' or 'Haffet' means the side of the head. The phrase means metaphorically you will do something to injure or annoy him.

Ye'll gar me seek the needle where I didna stick it.
You will send me begging. The phrase used to be spoken to thriftless wives and spending children according to Kelly.

Ye'll gather nae gowd aff windle-straes.

Ye'll get as muckle for ae wish this year as for twa fern year.
'Fern' signifies the previous year. Hence the proverb means that wishing begets nothing.

Ye'll get him waur ye left him.
A phrase applied to even-tempered persons.

Ye'll get nae mair o' the cat but the skin.

Ye'll get the cat wi' the twa tails.
'A jest upon persons of large expectations' – Kelly.

Ye'll get waur bodes ere Beltane.
Applied to someone who refuses the price offered for an object, suggesting that worse offers will be made before May.

Ye'll get yer gear again, and they'll get the widdie that stole't; *and* Ye'll get yer gear again, and they'll get the widdie that should hae kept it.
The first spoken with resentment, the second in good humour.

Ye'll get yer heid in yer hands and yer lugs to play wi'.
A phrase used as a threat/warning/reprimand.

Ye'll hae anither Lord Soulis mistake.
When some complaints were made to King Robert the Bruce about Lord Soulis, he thoughtlessly told the aggrieved parties they should boil the offender if they pleased. Taking him at his word, they seized Soulis and boiled him in a sheet of lead. Hence the phrase is used when rash advice is given to those who will probably overreact and carry out commands to the letter.

Ye'll hae baith your meat and your mense.
You will be well provided for and respected.

Ye'll hae the half o' the gate and a' the glaur.
You'll have half of the road and all of the mud. Said in jest when we make someone walk on the outside of a footpath.

Ye'll hang a' but the head yet.

Ye'll hear it on the deafest side o' yer lug.

Ye'll learn yer faither to get bairns.

Ye'll let little gae by ye, but speedy lads, ye canna get gripped.
Said to those who grasp at everything.

Ye'll let naething tine for want o' seeking.

Ye'll mak claw a sary man's haffet.
'By your squandering and ill management you will undo me' – Kelly.

Ye'll mend when ye're grown better.

Ye'll nae believe that a bannock is hardened unless ye knock on't wi' yer nail.
'Spoken to them that will believe nothing but upon plain demonstration' – Kelly.

Ye'll ne'er be auld wi' sae muckle honesty.
Spoken to people who are a little too blunt in what they say to others.

Ye'll ne'er cast saut on his tail.
You will never catch up with him. He has got clean away.

Ye'll ne'er craw in my cavie.
You will never be welcomed into my house.

Ye'll ne'er get twa breads of ae cake.
'You will not be so obliging as to be twice served out of the same parcel' – Kelly.

Ye'll ne'er grow bowbackit bearing your friends.
You do not seem to trouble yourself unduly on account of your friends.

Ye'll ne'er harry yoursel' wi' yer ain hands.

Ye'll ne'er learn younger.

Ye'll ne'er rowte in my tether.
To 'rowte' is to low.

Ye'll neither dee for your wit nor be drown'd for a warlock.
A saying applied to those we consider to be lacking in both wisdom and intelligence.

Ye'll neither dance nor haud the candle.
You are unwilling to either participate or to help.

Ye'll never mak a mark in yer Testament by that bargain.
You will probably lose money by that deal.

Ye'll no crow tread.
'Spoken when people fall in, or near, the fire; we alledge that rooks will not tread those hens that smell of the fire' – Kelly.

Ye'll no let it be for want o' craving.

Ye'll no mak made wood.
Spoken of someone who is considered too old to reform.

Ye'll no mend a broken nest by dabbin' at it.
Galt's Sir Andrew Wylie, *Chap. 38.*

Ye'll no sell your hen on a wet day.

Ye'll no sleep and the beetle without.
'Spoken to those who are importunate to get back their loan' – Kelly.

Ye'll play a sma' game before you stand out.

Ye'll sit till ye sweat, and work till ye freeze.

Ye'll spin and wind yersel' a bonny pirn.
Scott's Rob Roy, *Chap. 23.*

Ye'll tak mair in your mou' than yer cheeks will haud.
You will bite off more than you can chew. You will take on more responsibility/ work than you have time to cope with.

Ye'll win ower this trouble, and be better aff.

Ye'll worry in the band like McEwen's cauf.
'In plain English – you'll be hang'd' – Kelly.

Ye loe a' ye see, like Rab Roole when he's ree.
Spoken as a rebuke to greedy persons. When Rab Roole was 'ree' he was crazy with drink.

Ye look as bauld as a blackfaced wedder.

Ye look as if butter wadna melt in your mou', but cheese will no choke ye.
From Scott's St Ronans Well.

Ye look as if ye had fa'en frae the gleds.
You look shaken or ruffled.

Ye look like a Lochaber axe.
You have sharp features. Sometimes used to describe someone who looks highly aggressive.

'Ye look like a rinner,' quo' the deil to the lobster.
'Spoken to those who are very unlikely to do what they pretend to' – Kelly.

Ye look like Let-me-be.
You look very quiet and inoffensive, or possibly spoken to those who appear to be in a sullen mood.

Ye look liker a thief than a horse.

Ye look liker a deil than a bishop.

Ye look like the deil in daylight.

Yelping curs will raise mastiffs.
'Spoken when mean and unworthy people, by their private contentions, cause difference among greater persons' – Kelly.

Ye mak mony errands to the ha', to bid the laird gude day.
Spoken to those who pretend errands where they have a mind to go.

Ye maun be auld ere ye pay sic a gude wad.
'Literally, you will be very old ere you can perform such a promise; proverbially, of course, that you look upon such a promise as of no value' – Hislop.

Ye maun hae't baith simmered and wintered.
To 'simmer and winter' is to take a long time in thinking or formulating a plan.

Ye maun redd yer ain ravelled clue.
You must sort out your own difficulties for yourself.

Ye maun spoil ere ye spin.

Ye maun tak the will for the deed.

Ye maun thole or flit mony a hole.

Ye may as weel try to lift the milkin' stane o' Dumbarton.
'The milkin stane' is the name given to an enormous rock, which, according to local tradition, fell from the castle rock of Dumbarton into the park beneath so killing a number of women who were milking cows in the park. The saying is applied to indicate an impossibility.

Ye may be godly, but ye'll ne'er be cleanly.

Ye may be greedy but ye're no greening.
To 'green' is to covet, or to long for. 'An excuse for denying what one asks of us, because the want of it will not make them miscarry' – Kelly.

Ye may be heard where you are nae seen.

Ye may bite on your bridle.

Ye may dight your neb and flee up.
An expression of indifference addressed to someone whose opinion we consider of no value. The saying is taken from pullets who always wipe their bills on the ground before they go to roost.

Ye may be heard whaur ye're no seen.

Ye may dance at the end o' a raip yet without teaching.

Ye may ding the deil into a wife, but ye'll ne'er ding him out o' her.
'That is, a wife is seldom mended by being beaten' according to Kelly. Sadly it would appear that wife-beating was common practice in those days.

Ye may end him but ye'll ne'er mend him.

Ye may gae through a' Egypt without a pass.
Spoken to people of a dark complexion in olden times, according to Kelly.

Ye may gang far and fare waur.
You may go far and fare worse. An invitation to stop and partake of local hospitality. This phrase has been displayed above the Stracathro service station for many years.

Ye may gape lang enough ere a bird flee into your mou'.

Ye may hae a gude memory, but ye hae a confounded/puir judgement.
Spoken to the tactless when they suddenly call something to mind at an inappropriate moment.

Ye may hew doun the tree but ye canna change its bend.
Scott's Heart of Midlothian, *Chap. 20.*

Ye may live and no pree the tangs.

Ye may tak a drink oot o' the burn, when ye canna tak a bit oot o' the brae.
'Spoken when people are in want of food; cold water is usually available' – Kelly.

Ye may thank God that yer friends were born afore ye.

Ye may tine the faither looking for the son.

Ye may wash aff dirt, but never dun hide.
You cannot hide your true origins/background.

Ye measure my corn by yer bushel.

Ye mete my peas wi' yer ain peck.

Ye missed that as ye did yer mither's blessing.
Said when someone has thrown something at you and missed.

Ye needna bite a mark in my arse then.
'A spiteful answer to them that say, surlishly, they know you' – Kelly.

Ye needna lay wi'out for want o' a nest egg.
According to Kelly this was 'spoken to him that has a handsome lusty young wife'.

Ye needna wyte God if the deil ding ye ower.
Spoken to people with great big legs.

Ye needna file the house for want o' legs to carry ye tae the midden.
The meaning is as above.

Ye ne'er bought salt to the cat.
'You do not know what it is to provide for a family' – Kelly.

Ye ne'er heard a fisher cry stinking fish.

Ye ne'er see green cheese but your een reel.
'Meaning that the person thus addressed is very covetous of everything he sees' – Hislop.

Ye putt at the cart that's aye ganging.
The more we help, the more help is expected from us.

Ye rave unrocked, I wish yer head was knocked.
Spoken to those who speak unreasonable things, as if they are raving.

Yer breid's baket, ye may hing up your girdle.
You've achieved what you set out to.

Yer conscience is like a grey friar's sleeve.
Your conscience is very accommodating.

Ye're a' blawin' like a burstin' haggis.
You are full of hot air.

Ye're a corbie messenger.
As with the raven sent out from Noah's ark, this saying is applied to those who are sent on an errand but who do not return.

Ye're a day after the fair.
You are late/too late.

Ye're a deil, and nae cow, like the man's bull.

'Ye're a fine sword,' quo' the fool to the wheat braird.

Ye're a foot behint the foremost.
You are too late.

Ye're a' grease, but I'm only grushie.
'Grushie' is thick, or flabby.

Ye're a gude seeker but an ill finder.

Ye're a' honest enough, but Lilly's awa'.
'Spoken when things are stolen in a house, and the servants deny it. It took its rise from a lady who privately dressed her lap dog (Lilly), which the servants stole and ate' – Kelly.

'Ye're a liar,' said the dummy.

Ye're a' made o' butter and sew'd wi' soor milk.

Ye're a maiden marrowless.
A saying satirically applied to conceited girls who hold high opinions of themselves, that they are matchless.

Ye're a man among geese when the gander's awa.

Ye're ane o' Cow Meek's breed, ye'll stand without a bonoch.
'Bonoch' is a binding used to tie a cow's legs during milking. Hence the phrase is applied to meek people.

Ye're ane o' snaw-ba's bairn time.
'That is, such as health and prosperity make worse, or who insensibly go behind in the world' – Kelly.

Ye're ane o' the house o' Harletillum.
Spoken to those who are catching at and taking away what they can get. The joke is based upon a play on the word harletillum – (Harle-to-him) draw to himself.

Ye're ane o' the tender Gordons – ye daurna be hang'd for gaw on your neck.
Said to those who readily complain of hurts/hardships.

Ye're an honest man, and I'm yer brither/uncle – that's twa big lees.
Said to compulsive liars.

Ye're a' out o't, and into strae.
You are quite mistaken.

Ye're as bad as Willie Ha', wha forgot his weddin' day.
A Berwickshire saying applied to forgetful persons. The person who supposedly forgot his wedding was William Hall of Whitehall in Chirnside.

Ye're as braw as Bink's wife when she beckit to the minister wi' the dishclout on her head.

Ye're as daft as ye're days auld.

Ye're as fu' o' mischief as an egg's fu' o' meat.

Ye're as lang in tuning yer pipes as anither wad play a spring.
You take as long in preparing to do something as another would do in performing it.

Ye're as learnt as a scholar o' Buckhaven College.

Ye're as mim as a May puddock.

Ye're as muckle as hauf a witch.

Ye're as sma' as the twitter o' a twined rusky.
A 'twitter' is that part of a thread that is spun too small. 'Rusky', a sort of vessel made of straw to hold meal in. Kelly says 'a taunt to a maid that would gladly be esteemed neat and small'.

Ye're as souple sark alane as some are mither naked.
A joke upon those who boast of their activity.

Ye're as stiff as a stappit faster.
You are full. A 'stappit faster' is a crammed pudding.

Ye're as weel on yer purchase as some are on their set rent.
According to Kelly it is 'often applied to them who have as many bastards as others have lawful children'.

Ye're a sweet nut, if ye were well crack'd.
Ironically spoken to bad boys.

Ye're as white as a loan soup.
'Loan soup' is the name given to milk given to strangers who come at milking time. 'A phrase spoken to flatterers whom the Scots call "white folk"' – Kelly.

Ye're a widdiefu' gin hanging time.

Ye're aye unco gude, and ye'll grow fair.
Used to flatter people.

Ye're aye in anger's room.
'Said to children when they are in the way, and likely to get hurt' – Kelly.

Ye're aye ready to blaw in his lug.
You are always prepared to flatter him.

Ye're best when ye're sleeping.

Ye're black about the mou' for want o' kissing.
'A jest upon a young maid when she has a spot about her mouth as if it was for want of being kissed' – Kelly.

Ye're bonny eneugh to them that loe ya, and ower bonny to them that loe ye and canna get ye.
'Spoken as a comfort to people of an ordinary beauty!' – Kelly.

Ye're busy seekin' the thing that's no lost.

Ye're busy to clear yoursel when naebody files ye.

Ye're buttoned up the back like Achmahoy's dogs.
Spoken to thin people on whom the backbone stands out.

Ye're but young cocks, your craw's roupy [hoarse].

Ye're cawking the claith ere the wab be in the loom.
You are chalking the cloth before the yarn is in the loom, i.e. another version of counting your chickens before they've hatched.

Ye're come o' blude, and sae's a pudding.
Said to deflate someone who is boasting of their noble lineage.

Ye're come to fetch fire.
Spoken to people who make short visits, or to borrow something.

Ye're Davy-do-a'-thing.
You think nothing can be done without you.

Ye're Davy-do-little, and gude for naething.
You are bone idle.

Ye're done wi't if ye had a drink.
Said of something which is past recovery.

Yer een's greedier than your guts.
Said when someone fills their plate with more than they can eat.

Yer een's no marrows.
'Spoken when people mistake what they look at' – Kelly. 'No marrows' means do not match.

Yer een's your merchant.

Yer eggs hae twa yolks.
Said to those who think highly of what they give.

Ye're either ower het or ower cauld, like the miller o' Marshach Mill.
You are never satisfied.

Ye're fash'd holding naething thegither.
You make a great deal of fuss and accomplish nothing.

Ye're feared for snaw, an' there's nane fa' in'.

Ye're feared for the day ye never saw.
You are worrying over nothing.

Ye're feared for the death ye'll never dee.

Ye're fit for coorse country, ye're rather strong than handsome.

Ye're gude eneuch, but ye're no bra-new.
'Spoken to them that commend themselves, intimating that they want not their faults' – Kelly.

Ye're gude to be sent for sorrow.

Ye're gude to carry a present, ye can mak muckle o' little.
'Spoken when people overvalue a small service, or complain too much of a slight trouble' – Kelly.

Ye're gude to fetch the deil a priest.
Applied to persons who take a long time to carry out an errand.

Ye're like a hen on a het girdle.
Spoken to someone who cannot keep still.

Ye're like an ill shilling – ye'll come back again.
A humorous saying applied to those who are about to depart.

Ye're like a rotten nit – no worth cracking for the kernel.

Ye're like a singed cat – better than ye're bonny.

Ye're like a sow, ye'll neither lead nor drive.

Ye're like Brackley's tup, ye follow the lave.

Ye're like the Ed's whalp, aye a day aulder a day waur.

Ye're like Gutty Shaw in Edencrew,
There's nae filling ye.
A phrase applied to anyone with a hearty appetite. James Shaw (henceforth known as Gutty) a poor man for concern is recorded as having been a great eater.

Ye're like laird Moodie's greyhounds, unco hungry like aboot the pouch lids.

Ye're like Mawly's mear, ye broke fairly aff.
Spoken to those who begin well, and afterwards fall behind.

Ye're like me, and I'm like sma' drink.
You are little worth.

Ye're like me, and I'm nae sma' drink.
The converse of the above.

Ye're like Piper Bennett's bitch – ye lick till ye burst.

Ye're like the cat, ye love fish but not to wet your feet.

Ye're like the cooper o' Fogo, ye drive aff better girds then ye ca'
on.
Spoken of those who try to reform things but simply make them worse.

Ye're like the cow couper o' Swinton, your drouth's unquenchable.
*A Berwickshire saying applied to hard drinkers. John Henderson, a Cow Couper
in Swinton towards the end of eighteenth century, was very fond of a drink. He
said this taste was due to the fact that on the day of his birth the midwife had
given him such a dose of salt and water that nothing ever after could quench his
thirst. At that time salt-water was given to new born infants, some say for
superstitious reasons, and others simply to clear the phlegm from their throats.*

Ye're like the dogs o' Dodha, baith trouble and twa-faced.
Spoken of someone whose behaviour towards one is unpredictable.

Ye're like the dogs o' Dunraggit – ye winna bark unless ye hae your
hinder end to the wa'.
*Spoken to those who never complain or stand up for something unless they are
assured of winning. In his collection Kelly uses the less polite phrase 'arse at
char'd' to denote back to the wall.*

Ye're like the dreigh drinker o' Sisterpath Mill,
Ye'll no flit as lang's a stoup ye can fill.
Applied to drinkers who will drink as long as they can get it by any means.

Ye're like the hens, ye gang aye to the heap.
*Said when people pick from the main pile rather than using up what is lying
around first.*

Ye're like the Kilbarchan calves – like best to drink wi' the wisp in
yer mou'.

Ye're like the lady o' Bemerside, ye'll no sell your hen in a rainy
day.

Ye're like the lady o' Luss's kain eggs, everyone of which fell
through the ring into the tub and didn't count.
*'Kain eggs' were part of the rent paid in kind, and only eggs of a certain size were
received, those which were so small as to fall through a ring of a standard size
being rejected. The saying is applied as meaning that the person indicated is not
up to the mark.*

Ye're like the Laird o' Blaverne – feared for a taed.
Applied to a very timid person.

Ye're like the lambs, ye do naething but sook and wag your tail.

Ye're like the man as lept o'er the mare, ye cannot do but ye o'er-do.

Ye're like the man that sought his horse, and him on its back.
Spoken of people who do not have the wit to see what is staring them in the face.

Ye're like the miller's dog – ye lick your lips ere the pock be opened.
Said to greedy people who are ready to receive before they have even been offered something.

Ye're like the minister o' Bellie, aye preachin' for sellie.
A Moray proverb applied to selfish persons.

Ye're like the swine's bairns, the aulder ye grow ye're aye the thiefer like.

Ye're like the towy's hawks, ye eat ane anither.

Ye're looking ower the nest, like the young craws.

Ye're mair flay'd than hurt.
Said to timid people who start shouting as soon as any danger approaches.

Ye're mista'en o' the stuff; its half silk.
Spoken jokingly to those who undervalue a person or thing which we think is better than they do.

Ye're muckle unmanly, like Tam Taylor's tyke.

Ye're nae blate.
You are forward, cheeky, impudent. Scott's Fortunes of Nigel *Chap. 32.*

Ye're nae chicken for a' ye're cheepin.
Applied to an older woman who puts on youthful airs.

Ye're nae fey yet.
You are not near your death.

Ye're nae flea-bitten about the gab.
You are evidently not kissed much.

Ye're never aff my tap.

Ye're never pleased, fu' nor fasting.

Ye're new come ower – your heart's nipping.

Ye're no fed on deaf nuts.
You are plump and evidently well-fed. Deaf nuts are nuts without a kernel.

Ye're no light where you lean a'.
Spoken to those who tread on us.

Ye're no sae poor as ye peep.

Ye're no worth ca'ing out o' a kail-yaird.

Ye're o' sae mony minds ye'll never be married.

Ye're obliged to yer goodam [grandmother], she left you the tune o' her tail.
Said in jest to people who sing badly.

Ye're out and in, like a dog at a fair.

Ye're ower auld farrant to be fley'd wi' bogles.

Ye're ower burd mou'd.
Too modest.

Ye're ower early thanking.
Said when someone says thank you before they have received anything.

Ye're ower het and ower fu', sib to some o' the laird's tenants.

Ye're queer folk no to be Falkland folk.
A Fife saying. According to Murison it is spoken 'about people who are ostentatiously polite or elegant'.

Ye're sae keen o' clockin', ye'll dee on the eggs.
Spoken to those who are fond of any new situation.

Ye're sae weel o' yer wooing, ye watna whaur to wed.
'You have so much choice' – Kelly.

Ye're sair fashed hauding naething thegither.
Said to those who make the loudest noise and fuss but do least.

Ye're seeking the thing that's no tint.
'Spoken to them that are taking up the thing they should not' – Kelly.

Ye're sib to ill may ye hear.
'Spoken to them that do not distinctly hear you' – Kelly

Ye're sick but no sair handled.
Said to those who pretend to be ill.

Ye're sorrowfu' strait shod.
'You are too nice and scrupulous' – Kelly.

Ye're sturted [troubled] – I wish I had your tail to draw.
'Spoken ironically when people have done little and think much of it' – Kelly.

Ye're thankfu' for sma' mercies.

Ye're the greatest liar o' yer kin, except yer chief that wan his meat by it.

Ye're there yet, and your belt hale.
Said when people tell us they will go to such a place and thrive and we doubt them.

Ye're the weight o' Jock's cog, brose and a'.

Ye're the wit o' the town head, that called the haddock's head a thing.
A taunt to those who say foolish things.

Ye're thrifty and thro' thriving, when your head gangs doun your bottom's rising.
'Spoken ironically to thriftless people' – Kelly.

Ye're too previous.
Spoken in jest when someone arrives early.

Ye're trying like the millers o' Dryden's mills which o' ye is best at twisting hemp.
You are behaving in a stupid manner as if you want to see who can ruin themselves soonest.

Ye're up to the buckle, like John Barr's cat.

Ye're very foresighted, like Forsyth's cat.

Ye're very short to be sae lang.
Your power is not equal to your pretensions. Scott's Heart of Midlothian, *Chap. 50.*

Ye're weel awa' if ye bide, an' we're weel quat.
Spoken about people whose company we do not like.

Ye're welcome, but ye'll no win ben.
'A civil denial of what we ask' – Kelly.

Ye're welcome to go, and ye're welcome to stay; *and*
Ye're welcome though ye never come again.

Ye're worn frae an armful to a horse car full.
'Applied to those who are become very big and fat' – Kelly.

Yer fortune's comin' wi' the blin' carrier.

Yer gear will ne'er ower gang ye.
'Spoken to thriftless persons' – Kelly.

Yer hand/head canna get up but yer stomach follows.
'Refers to those who are purse proud' – Kelly.

Yer head will ne'er fill yer faither's bonnet.
You will never live up to the reputation of your father.

Yer hindmaist gounie has nae pouches.
You cannot take your possessions with you when you die. 'Gounie' means nightdress.

Ye ride a bootless errand.

Ye ride sae near the rump, ye'll let nane loup on ahint you.

Ye rin for the spurtle when the pat's boiling ower.
You are too late in taking precautions.

Yer meat will mak ye bonny, and when ye are bonny ye'll be well lo'ed; when ye are well lo'ed ye'll be licht hearted, and when ye're licht hearted ye'll loup far.
A saying used to induce children to eat.

Yer mind's aye chasing mice.
You are a daydreamer.

Yer Minnie's milk is no out o' yer neb yet.

Yer mou's beguiled yer hands.

Yer neb is o'er near yer arse.
'Spoken to those that complain of a stink, as if it proceeded from themselves' – Kelly.

Yer purse opened not when it was paid for.
Used against those who abuse what is not even theirs. A manner of suggesting that the article in question has not already been paid for.

Yer purse was steekit when that was paid for.
See above.

Yer thrift gaes by the profit o' a yeld hen.
'A taunt upon them who boast of what they have wrought' – Kelly.

Yer tongue gangs like a lamb's tail.
Never stops.

Yer tongue gangs like the clatter bane o' a goose's arse.
You talk too much.

Yer tongue is nae slander.

Yer tongue rins afore yer wit.

Yer wind shakes nae corn.
Spoken to boasters to deflate them.

Yer winning is not in my tinsel [loss].

Yer wit will ne'er worry ye.

Ye seek grace wi' a graceless face.

Ye'se get yer brose oot o' the lee side o' the pat.
You will get the best the pot contains.

Ye ser'd me, as the wife did the cat – coost me into the kirn, and
syne harl'd me out again.
You have placed me in a good position merely to take me from it again.

Ye shanna be niffered but for a better.

Ye shanna want as lang as I lae, but look weel to yer ain.

Ye shape shune by yer ain shauchled feet.
You judge others by your own poor standards.

Ye shine like a white gir about a shairney cog.

Ye shine like the sunny side o' a shairney wecht.
*'A ridicule upon people when they appear fine' says Kelly. A shairnie/sharnie
weight was the fan used to winnow corn with, daubed with cow-dung.*

Ye sleep like a dog in a mill.
. . . with one eye open.

Ye sleep like a dog when the wife's baking.
As above.

Ye soon weary o' doin' weel.

Ye strive about uncost gait.
*'Uncost gait' means unbought goats. The general meaning is much ado about
nothing. According to Kelly 'A man told his neighbour that he was going to buy
goats, he ask'd him, Which way he would drive them home? He answered, that
way: the other said, he should not, and so they fell out and beat one another; but
in the struggle the buyer lost his money, and so the goats were never bought.'*

Ye tak a bite out o' yer ain buttock.
What you say reflects upon your self/your family.

Ye tak but a foal's share o' the harrow.
You don't pull your own weight.

Ye tak mair in yer mou' than yer cheeks can hold.
You take on more than you can accomplish.

Ye tak the first word o' flyting.

Ye tine the ladle for the licking of the arse of it.
You lose something expensive for the want of spending a little to begin with.

Ye tine the tuppeny belt for the twapeny whang.
Twapeny is one sixth of a penny.

Ye've a lang nose, and yet ye're cut lugget.
'In appearance you have an advantage in one way, but not in another' – Hislop.

Ye've been eating sourocks instead of lang kail.
Spoken to someone in a bad mood, who is out of sorts. Used in Galt's The Entail, *chap. 34.*

Ye've got yer health into the barnyard again.
Your health is restored.

Ye've grown proud since ye quatted the begging.
Said satirically to people who walk by without acknowledging one's acquaintance.

Ye've wared yer siller, no spent it.
You have made a good bargain.

Ye wad be a gude Borrowstone sow – ye smell weel.
'Spoken when people pretend to find the smell of something that we would conceal' – Kelly.

Ye would be a gude piper's bitch; ye smell oot the weddins.
A cheeky remark made to gossips who made matches between certain couples.

Ye wad be a sweet nut if ye were well cracked.

Ye wad clatter a cat to death.
To 'clatter' is to prattle. Hence this phrase is applied to someone who is a gossip.

Ye wad dae little for God an' the deil was dead.
A sarcastic way of expressing one's doubt that a person would be well-behaved were it not for fear, rather than because of the principle involved.

Ye wad ferlie mair if the craws bigg'd in your cleaving an' flew awa wi' the nest.
'Implying that one is surprised at a very trifling matter' – Hislop.

Ye wad gar men trow that spade shafts bore honey pears.

Ye wad gar me trow my head's cowed, though there's no a hair o't wanting yet.
You would have me believe something I know to be false.

Ye wad kiss ony man's dirty shune for leave to bake in his oven.

Ye wad mak a gude wife, ye haud the grip ye get.

Ye wad mak muckle o' me if I was yours.
Spoken to those who make a great deal out of what they have done/suffered.

Ye wad marry a midden for the muck.

Ye wad say that aback o' the Hirsel Law.

Ye wad think ye had been brocht up in a cart shed.
Spoken to those who leave doors open.

Ye wad wheedle a laverock frae the lift.
You would charm the birds from the sky, i.e. you are smooth-tongued.

Ye wad wonder mair if the craws should big on yer cliff and rin awa' wi' the nest.
'A senseless return to them that say they wonder at you' – Kelly.

Ye was bred about the mill, ye hae mooped a' yer manners.
'Spoken to inferiors when they show themselves rude in their speech or behaviour'
– Kelly.

Ye was ne'er born at that time o' year.
Said to people who expect a certain place or condition which is considered above their birth/station in life.

Ye was ne'er far frae yer mither's hip.
'Spoken to those who are harsh to strangers' – Kelly.

Ye was put oot o' the oven for nippin the pies.
You cannot keep your hands off others' belongings.

Ye was sae hungry ye couldna stay the grace.
Said when someone inadvertently starts eating before grace has been said.

Ye watna what's behint your hand.

Ye watna what wife's ladle may cog your kail.

Ye watna where a blessing may light.

Ye winna craw trade.
You will never admit that trade is good.

Ye winna put out the fire wi' tow.

Ye wist not sae weel when day break.
Said when something comes suddenly, or takes us by surprise.

Ye yirr and yowl – ye bark, but daurna bite.

Young bairns should learn at auld men's schools.

Young ducks may be auld geese.

Young folk may dee, auld folk maun dee.

Young men's knocks, auld men feel.

Young wives seldom like auld gudemithers.

Youth and age will ne'er agree.

Youth and eild never sowder well.

Youth ne'er casts for perils.
Youth is always headstrong and unaware of danger.

Yule is young on Yule even, and auld on Saint Steven.
According to Kelly this is 'spoken when people are much taken with novelties, and as soon weary of them'.

Z

Zeal catches fire at a slight spark as fast as a bruntstane match.
Scott's Heart of Midlothian, *chap. 18.*

BIBLIOGRAPHY

OF PROVERB COLLECTIONS AND REFERENCE WORKS

Anderson, M. L., (ed.), *James Carmichaell Collection of Proverbs in Scots* (Edinburgh, 1957).

Anon, *National Proverbs: Scotland* (London, Frank & Cecil Palmer, 1913).

Beveridge, E., *Fergusson's Scottish Proverbs from the Original Print of 1641 together with a larger Manuscript Collection of about the same period hitherto unpublished* (Edinburgh, Scottish Text Society, 1924).

Bohn, H. G. (ed.), *Ray's Collection of English Proverbs* (London, George Bell & Sons, 1893).

Carmichaell, James, *Collection of Proverbs in Scots* (see Anderson above).

Chambers, R., *Popular Rhymes of Scotland* (3rd ed.) (Edinburgh, W.& R. Chambers, 1841).

Cheviot, A. (Rev. J. H. Watson), *Proverbs, Proverbial Expressions, and Popular Rhymes of Scotland* (Paisley, Alexander Gardner, 1896).

Fergusson, D., *Scottish Proverbs* (gathered together before 1598, published 1641, 1785, Scottish Texts Society 1924). See Beveridge above.

Henderson, A., *Scottish Proverbs* (Edinburgh, Oliver & Boyd, 1832) (contains introductory essay by William Motherwell).

Henderson, G., *The Popular Rhymes, Sayings, and Proverbs of the County of Berwick* (Newcastle-on-Tyne, 1856).

Hislop, A., *The Proverbs of Scotland. Collected and arranged, with notes, explanatory and illustrative and a glossary* (Glasgow: Porteous & Hislop, 1862)

Jamieson, J., *An Etymological Dictionary of the Scottish Language* (Edinburgh, Edinburgh University Press, 1808 and 1825).

Kelly, J., *A Complete Collection of Scottish Proverbs Explained and made Intelligible to the English Reader* (new ed., orig. 1721) (London, Rodwell & Martin, 1818).

Macgregor, F., *Scots Proverbs and Rhymes* (Edinburgh, The Moray Press, 1948)

Murison, D., *Scots Saws: From the Folk-Wisdom of Scotland* (Edinburgh, The Mercat Press, 1981).

Paterson, T. W., *Auld Saws in New Scots Sangs* (Paisley, Alexander Gardner, 1915).

People's Journal Competition Editor (ed.), *Proverbs and Sayings Maistly Scotch* (Cupar, A. Westwood & Sons, 1889).

Ramsay, A., *A Collection of Scots Proverbs dedicated to the Tenantry of Scotland* (Edinburgh, 1818) (found in three volumes of poetical works – orig. 1737).

Scottish Notes and Queries. Various dates and issues. Aberdeen.

Stevenson, B., *Stevenson's Book of Proverbs, maxims and familiar phrases* (1949).

Stirling, W., *The Proverbial Philosophy of Scotland: An address to the School of Arts* (Stirling and Edinburgh, 1855).

Trench, R. C., *On the Lessons in Proverbs: Being the substance of Lectures delivered to Young Men's Societies at Portsmouth and elsewhere* (3rd rev. ed) (London, 1854).

GLOSSARY

a'   all
abune   above
adreich   askant, or at a distance
ae/ane   one
aff   off
afore   before
aft   often
ahint   behind
aiblins   perhaps/possibly
aik   oak
ain   own
airt   a direction, way or manner
aith   oath, promise
aiver   a cart horse
amaist   almost
ance   once
ane   one
anither   another
aucht   eight
aught   own
auld   old
aumrie   cupboard
auncient   ancient
ava   at all
awa   away
awmous   alms
aye   always

baik   to curtsey or bow
bairn(s)   child(ren)
baith   both
bane   bone
bannet   bonnet
bannocks   home-made flour cakes
barefit   barefoot
bauchle   an old shoe
bauld   bold
bawbee   halfpenny
bawty   a dog
beild   shelter
bein   in good condition, comfortable
beit   to renew, to kindle
Beltane   the first of May
belyve   immediately, bye and bye
besom   broom
bicker   small wooden dish
bide   to stay
bien   *see* bein
big   to build
biggin   a building, small house
bink   bench, seat
birk   birch
bit   piece

bladry   foolishness
blate   bashful
blaw   to blow
bleer-e'ed   bleary-eyed, or weak-sighted
blin   blind
blirt   cry, weep
bluid   blood
bocht   bought
bode   a portent, or to earnestly wish for
bodle   small copper coin
bore   hole
bouk   bulk
bourd   a jest, to fool with
bourtree   elder tree
bowrock   a heap, a clump
brae   hillside, steep road
brak   to break
brat   a coarse apron
brattle   a loud clatter (of hooves)
braw   fine
breed   to resemble, to take after
breeks   trousers
brither   brother
brocht   brought
brose   a dish of oatmeal and water
browst   a brewing
browster   a brewer
brugh   the halo effect around the sun or moon
bubbly-jock   turkey cock
buirdly   strongly made, stout
bum   to buzz like a bee
burd   bird
buskit   dressed, decorated
but-and-ben   two adjoining rooms

ca'   to call, to name, to drive
cadger   beggar
callant   an associate, a fellow
canty   lively, cheerful, pleasant
carl   a man, a fellow
carlin   old woman
cauf   calf
cauff   chaff
cauld   cold
caumstane   limestone
causey   paved area, roadway, street
causey saint   a person who is well-behaved when away from home

cawk	to chalk	dint	chance
chafts	chops	dit	to close
chancy	lucky, fortunate	dizzen	dozen
chanter	double-reeded pipe on which a bagpipe melody is played	dochter	daughter
		doesna	does not
		dominie	school master
chapman	a pedlar	donnart	dull, stupid, witless
chiel	a young man, or a fellow	donsy	unlucky, unfortunate
		doo	dove, pigeon
chokit	choked	dool	sorrow, misfortune
claes	clothes	dosen	to settle/cool down
claith	cloth	douce	respectable
clarty	dirty	doun	down
cleck	to hatch, to give birth to	doup	the bottom of an eggshell
cled	clothed	draff	brewer's grain
clink	money	drap	a drop, a small drink
clishmaclaver	gossip, idle talk	draunt	to drawl
clout	cloth	dree	to endure, to suffer
clung	empty	drite	to defecate
cog	wooden dish, milk pail	drouth(y)	thirst(y)
collop	a (thin) slice of meat	drucken	drunken
coo	cow	drumly	(of water) clouded, troubled, muddy
corbie	a raven		
cottar	peasant labourer	dub	puddle
counts	sums or accounts	dune	done, exhausted
cowp	to tip	dunt	a knock, a blow
cowte	colt	ee(n)	eye, eyes
crab	to be angry	e'ening	evening
crack	to chat, a chat	eident	diligent
craig	the neck	eider	more prominently
craik	to complain	eild	age, old age
crap	crop	eird	earth
craw(ing)	to crow, crow(ing)	eith	easy
creep	to crawl	eldin	fuel
creeshy	oily, greasy	elshin	an awl
crooning	singing	eme	uncle
crouse	bold, courageous	eneuch	enough
culye	to gain, to draw forth	ettle	to endeavour, to aim, an intention
curcuddoch	friendly, warm with affection		
cutty	short-handled spoon	fa'	fall
		fain	eager, keen, anxious
dae	to do	fair fa'	good luck
daffin'	playing	faither	father
darg	a day's work	fand	found
daur	to dare	farden	a farthing
daurna	dare not	fash	trouble
daw	drab, lazy person, slut	fashious	troublesome
dawly	untidy, slovenly	fause	false
dawt	to dote on, to pet	faut	fault
deave	to deafen	fecht	fight
dee	to die	feckless	silly or weak (mentally or physically)
deem	to judge		
deil	devil	ferlie	to wonder at, a wonder
dicht	see dight	fit	foot, or to count up
dight	to wipe/rub clean/dry	fleech	to flatter
ding	to knock over, to surpass	flesh-flee	bluebottle
		fley	to frighten
dink	neat, trim, dainty	flichter	flutter
dinna	do not	fling	to kick, to jilt

flisket	fretful, easily annoyed or upset	grat	cried
flit	to move house	gree	to agree
flyting	scolding, quarrelling	green	to long for
foisonless	insipid, without substance	greet	to cry
		grice	*see* gryce
forefoughten	fatigued	grip	to catch
forgie	forgive	grosset	gooseberry
forejeskit	jaded, worn out	grund	ground
forejidged	prejudged	gryce	young pig
forpit	the fourth part of a peck	gude	good
frae	from	ha'	hall
freits	superstitious beliefs	hae	to have
fremit	strange	hail	whole
fu'	full	hain	to save, to economise, to use sparingly
furdersome	industrious		
fyle	to make dirty, to soil	hairst	harvest
		hame	home
		handfu'	handful
gab	to speak, the mouth	hansel	a gratuity, a present
gae	go	hantle	a number, a quantity
gaislin	gosling	hap	chance
gait	*see* gate	harns	brains
gang	to go	haud	to hold
gar	to force, to cause	hauf	half
gate	road, way	hause	the throat
gaunt	to yawn	haver	to speak nonsense, to gossip
gawsie	jolly, plump, handsome		
gaylie	middling	hawse	*see* hause
gear	wealth, possessions	heid	head
ghaist	ghost	het	hot
gie	to give	heuk	hook
giff-gaff	give and take	Hielandman	Highlander
gin	if or by	himsel	himself
girdle	a circular iron plate used for baking	hirsel	flock
		hoch	hind leg of an animal
girnin'	fretful, grinning	hoolie	*see* hooly
glaiket	wanton, playful, trifling	hooly	moderate, slow, cautious, careful
glaur	mud, mire		
gled	a kite (bird)	hurlbarrow	wheelbarrow, handcart
gleg	keen, quick, sharp	hutch	poor cottage
gley	to squint, to cast a sideways glance		
glib	quick, ready in speech	i'	in
gloom	frown	ilka	each, every
glunsh	to scowl	ingan	onion
gowan	name for various yellow wild flowers especially daisy, dandelion, buttercups	ither	other
		jaup	(of water/mud) to splash
gowd	gold		
gowdspink	goldfinch	jouk	to avoid a blow, to yield to circumstances
gowk	a simpleton		
gowpen	two hands joined together to contain something, or the quantity so contained	jundie	a passing blow or thrust
		kail yard	kitchen garden
		kame	to comb, a comb
graip	dung fork	kamester	a wool comber
graith	harness	kebbuck	a cheese
gramashes	gaiters	keckle	to cackle

keltie	to give/force a large drink upon someone who doesn't want it, or to give someone a double punishment	mavis	a thrush
		mayna	may not
		mear	mare
		mease	to appease
		mends	amends
kelty	*see* keltie	mennan	minnow
ken	to know	mense	manners, discretion
kep	to catch	mensefu'	discreet, well-mannered
kirn	churn		
kittle	ticklish, or difficult	menseless	unmannerly, rude, ill-bred, forward
knowe	hilltop		
kyte	the belly	merle	blackbird
kythe	to appear	messan	a mongrel dog
		midden	dung heap
		mim	prim, demure
lack	to depreciate, to slight	mint	endeavour, to intend to, to plan or attempt
laigh	low		
laith	slow	mislear'd	mischievous, wild
lang	long	misterfu'	needy, begging
langsyne	long ago, old times	mither	mother
lave	the rest, the remainder	moistify	to moisten, to drink
laverock	a lark	mony	many
lawin'	reckoning in a public bar	mool	to crumble; the earth of a grave
leal	loyal, true, honest	mou'	mouth
leddy	lady	moudiewort	mole
lee	to lie, a lie	mouthfu'	mouthful
leear	a liar	mow	a heap e.g. hay or wood
len'	lend, a loan		
lichtit	alighted	moyen	interest, influence
licht	light	muckle	great, much
lickt	*see* licht	muggins	mugwort
lift	sky	mune	moon
lintie	a linnet		
lippen	to trust, to depend upon	nae	no
		naething	nothing
loan	lane	naig	a nag, a small horse
lo'e	love	nane	none
loof	palm of the hand, or paw of an animal	neb	nose, point
		neebor	neighbour
loon	boy, young fellow	ne'er	never
loup	to leap, to jump	neist	next
lout	to submit to, to stoop to	nicker	(of a horse) to neigh
		nieve	fist, hand
lowe	a flame	niffer	to barter, to trade
lug(s)	ear(s)	nitty-now	a lousy head
luif	*see* loof	nocht	nothing
lum	chimney	nowte	nought or nothing
lurden	a worthless fellow	nurish	wet nurse
madge-howlet	an owl	o'	of
mailin'	farm	olite	active, nimble
mair	more	ony	any
maister	master	oo	wool
mak	to make	oot	out
malison	a curse	orts	that which is rejected or set aside
marrow	an equal, a match		
maukin	a hare	ower	over
maun	must	owercome	a common or overused expression
maunna	must not		

owsen	oxen
oxter	armpit
Paik	to beat, punish
parritch	porridge
partan	crab
Pasch	Easter
pat	pot
paut	to stamp the foot
peesweep	lapwing
perfyteness	perfection
pickle	small amount
pike	to pick
plack	two bodles, or one third of an old English penny
plew	plough
ploom	plum
pock	a bag, sack
poortith	poverty
pouther	powder
pow	head
pownie	pony
pree	to taste, to sample
preen	a pin
prent	print
puddock	frog, toad
pyat	magpie
pyot	*see* pyat
quire	choir
quo	said
quoth	*see* quo
raggit	ragged
raip	rope
rattan	rat
rax	to stretch
ream	*see* reem
redd	to put in order, to sort out
ree	tipsy, drunk
reek	smoke
reem	cream
reid	red
reive	to rob, to steel
remede	remedy
richt	right
riggin'	the ridge of a house
rin	to run
rippling-kame	a flax comb
rive	to tear, to rent asunder
rizle	to beat violently
rodden tree	rowan tree
routh	many, an abundance
row	to roll up
rumgunshach	rude, unkind
ruse	to praise

sae	so
saft	soft
sair	sore
sairy	poor
sang	song
sap	sop
sark	shirt
sauch	willow
saucht	peace, ease
saunt	saint
saut	salt
saw	a proverb, wise words
scabbit	scabby
sca'd	scabbed, scared
scart	scratch
sclater	slate
scrimpit	scanty
sea-maw(s)	seagull(s)
seil	to pass liquid through a sieve
shank(s)	leg(s)
shanna	shall not
shauchle	to shuffle, to walk lazily
shaup	husk
shool	shovel
shoon	shoes
shore	to threaten
shouther	shoulder
shune	*see* shoon
sib	akin, related
sic	such
sicker	sure, certain
siller	silver, money
simmer	summer
sindle	seldom
skaith	injury, harm
sliddry	slippery
slocken	to put out a fire
sma'	small
smit	infect
smoor	to smother
snaw	snow
snite	to blow one's nose
sonsy	healthy, thriving, prosperous
soom	swim
soop	sweep
sooth	true
sour(r)ock	sorrel
soutar	shoemaker
sowans	*see* sowens
sowens	a dish made from oat husks and fine meal steeped in water
spail	a chip of wood
speir	to enquire/ask
spring	a tune
spurtle	short stick for stirring porridge
stamack	stomach
stane	stone

stark	strong	vreet	N.E. verb past tense – to write
steek	a stitch, or to close		
stey	steep		
stirk	a young cow or bull	wab	web
stoor	dust	wabster	webster, weaver
stot	young bull or ox	wad	would
stoup	a jug with a handle	wae	woe, sadness
strae	straw	wame	stomach
straucht	straight	wark	work
stravaig	to stroll about idly	warld	world
sturt	rage	warling	a worldling
sune	soon	warr	outrun
sweerd	unwilling, slow, lazy indolent	warst	worst
		wast	west
sweird	see sweerd	wat	wet
syne	since, after then	watna	know not
		waukrife	wakeful
		waur	worse
tae	toe	wecht	weight
taiken	token	weel	well
tak	to take	weet	to wet
tangs	tongs	weird	destiny
tansie	ragwort	weise	to guide
tappit	crested/tufted	wersh	tasteless, insipid
tarrow	to linger, to delay, to hesitate	wha	who
		whang	a large slice, a thong
tauld	told	whase	whose
taupie	a foolish or idle woman	whaup	a curlew
		whaur	where
taury	tarry	whilk	which
tawpie	see taupie	wi'	with
tent	care	wick	a corner of the mouth or eye
theek	to hatch		
thegither	together	widdie	a rope, gallows
thig	beg, cadge	wight	courageous
thoom	thumb	windlin	a bottle of straw or hay
thow	thaw	winna	will not
thrang	throng, busy	wispit	cleaned, swept
thrapple	throat/windpipe	wizen	throat
thraw	to form	woo'	wool
tine	to lose	woodie	diminutive of wood
tinkler	tinker	wot	to know
tint	lost	wrang	wrong
tocher	dowry	wud	mad
tod	a fox	wun	wind
toom	empty	wyte	to blame, to find fault with
toun	town		
tout	to blow a horn		
tow	rope, cord		
trewed	trusted, believed	Yeld	an animal unable to have young because of age or accident
trogger	dealer, small trader, pedlar		
trow	to believe		
tulzie	a quarrel		
twa	two		
twal	twelve		
tyke	a clumsy person, a dog		
unca'd	uncalled		
unco	very, extremely, or strange and unknown		